DATE DUE

DEMCO 38-296

Levels of
Socio-economic
Development Theory

Levels of Socio-economic Development Theory

SECOND EDITION

David Jaffee

PRAEGER

Westport, Connecticut
London

Library of Congress Cataloging-in-Publication Data

Jaffee, David.
    Levels of socio-economic development theory / David Jaffee.—2nd
ed.
        p. cm.
    Includes bibliographical references and index.
    ISBN 0–275–95658–X (alk. paper).—ISBN 0–275–95659–8 (pbk. :
alk. paper)
        1. Economic development.   2. Economic development—Social aspects.
    3. Organizational change.   4. Dependency.   5. Developing countries—
    Economic policy.   I. Title.
    HD75.J33   1998
    338.9—dc21   97–50048

British Library Cataloguing in Publication Data is available.

Library of Congress Catalog Card Number: 97–50048
ISBN: 0–275–95658–X
        0–275–95659–8 (pbk.)

First published in 1998

Praeger Publishers, 88 Post Road West, Westport, CT 06881
An imprint of Greenwood Publishing Group, Inc.

Printed in the United States of America

The paper used in this book complies with the
Permanent Paper Standard issued by the National
Information Standards Organization (Z39.48–1984).

10 9 8 7 6 5 4 3 2 1

Again,
For
Marianne,
Katy,
and Anna

Contents

Preface to the First Edition

The aim of this book is to acquaint readers with contemporary theories of development. Most theories of development attempt to explain international disparities in income, wealth, standard of living, and economic growth. The complexity of this task has given rise to a vast assortment of competing explanations. A basic challenge for students sifting through the literature is to organize the theories in a way that illuminates the differences and similarities among the various theories. With this purpose in mind, the theories of development in this book are organized by "levels of analysis—individual, organizational, societal, and international. Some theories focus on the characteristics of individuals within a nation; others on the structure of work organization; others on the existing social, economic, and political institutions; and still others on a nation's position in the international system. These levels of theory identify a particular set of factors as the cause of development or underdevelopment. Organizing theories of development in this way serves to emphasize the important role of theory and of the levels of theory in shaping one's description, explanation, and interpretation of the development process. It also points to one of the leading sources of debate and controversy among development theorists: What is the appropriate level of analysis for understanding socio-economic change?

The material presented in this book is geared for advanced undergraduate and graduate courses in development, social change, and comparative sociology, as well as those dealing with topics in political economy and socio-economics. The scope is inevitably interdisciplinary. The study of development touches the subject matter of sociology, economics, political science, and psychology. The book discusses theories associated with each of these fields. Further, the focus of theoretical concern extends beyond the problems of less-developed nations to the advanced industrial societies. No nation is immune to the continuous struggle for economic growth and accumulation. Recent and chronic economic crises plaguing advanced capitalist economies indicate the precarious nature of each and every development strategy.

I wish to express my sincere thanks to the following friends and colleagues who read sections of the manuscript and offered many valuable suggestions: Alan Neustadt, Harland Prechel, Sally Simpson, Randall Stokes, and Rhys Williams.

Special thanks are due Marilyn Glass, who typed the manuscript with skill, patience, and a good measure of tolerance.

Preface to the Second Edition

Since the publication of the first edition in 1990, the global economic scene, and accordingly the field of social and economic development, has changed dramatically. The most notable developments have been the rise of the Pacific Rim and East Asian economies that were once relegated to the "periphery" of the global system, the demise of East and Central European socialism, and the expansion of global economic activity prompting the development of a new globalization thesis. All of these events have had an impact on theories of development and yet, as in 1990, there remains a great deal of uncertainty and flux and it is difficult to incorporate all these developments into a definitive theoretical framework. In this book I attempt to address these three major developments and incorporate them into discussions at the various and appropriate levels of analysis.

As a way to point the reader to what has remained the same and what new sections and topics have been added to the text, I should note the following:

1. Chapters 1 and 2 have undergone the least number of revisions. The introductory chapter retains a discussion of the meaning of social change and development as well as the outline of the levels of analysis framework that serves as the organizing scheme for the material and chapters. The chapter on individual-level theories has been revised and reorganized but little has been added, since this is not where most of the action in development studies has occurred. I will confess, however, that I am more open today than when I wrote the first edition to appreciating some of the individual-level and cultural forces that can interact with the development process.

2. The chapter on organizational-level theories (Chapter 3), an area which I viewed as relatively neglected back in the late 1980s, has taken off over the past five years. Organizational analysis now plays a critical role in some of the

most innovative theorizing on development. The chapter is expanded to consider the new organizational strategies that revolve around the concepts of flexibility and networks.

3. The societal-level chapters (Chapters 4 and 5) have both been expanded to include (a) a further discussion of alternative measures of development, another area of significant activity throughout the 1990s; (b) an elaboration of variations in capitalist development strategies and the blend of market and government forces; and (c) the demise and recent developments in the former European socialist states and the effort to build market-based economies.

4. The international-level chapter (Chapter 6) retains an extended discussion of dependency and world-economy theory with some of the more recent critical assessments included, and also concludes with a discussion of the key elements of the globalization phenomenon and an assessment of this thesis.

If things had just remained the same, my task would have been much simpler. Nonetheless, I have tried to address the key issues while also keeping the length of the book to its original dimensions. There is much more that could have been said and much more that could have been added, but that would be another book.

I again owe a debt of gratitude to Marilyn Glass, who patiently received the endless stream of drafts, additions, and corrections to the manuscript while at the same retaining her sense of humor about the obsessive habits of academicians.

Finally, in spite of spending countless hours hibernating in what has come to be known as my "cave," I still have a wonderful family to thank for their patience and indulgence—my wife, Marianne, and my daughters, Katy and Anna.

1

Introduction:
The Meaning of Development
and the Levels of Theory

In any area of scholarly inquiry, there are always several ways in which the phenomena under study may be sorted and arranged . . . the observer may choose to focus upon the parts or upon the whole, upon the components or upon the system. . . . Whether he selects the micro- or macro-level of analysis is ostensibly a mere matter of methodological conceptual convenience. Yet the choice often turns out to be quite difficult, and may well become a central issue within the discipline concerned. . . . The responsible scholar must be prepared to evaluate the relative utility—conceptual and methodological—of the various alternatives open to him, and to appraise the manifold implications of the level of analysis finally selected. (Singer 1961:77)

The study of socio-economic development is a truly interdisciplinary venture. Analyzing the causes and consequences of social change requires crossing the conventional boundaries of academic social science. Each field of social science—anthropology, economics, history, political science, psychology, geography, sociology—has some insight to contribute. Socio-economic change shapes, and is shaped by, individual perceptions and beliefs, cultural patterns, economic organizations, methods of production and distribution, socio-political arrangements, and the international economy. The process of development is broad and all-encompassing. It is difficult to discount the importance of any social pattern or institution.

Explaining development is further complicated by the fact that each discipline is composed of subdisciplines, subareas, and subfields that tend to emphasize one particular slice of social reality. Social scientists tend to focus upon one or a small number of factors as the key to understanding socio-economic development. The purpose of this book is to review some of the most prominent contemporary theories of development.

It is important to understand the way theory shapes our interpretation of all social events, including socio-economic development. Theories provide a framework for making sense of the world. Most things we observe, experience, and study are extremely complex and are caused by a variety of factors. Each and every factor responsible for some event or process cannot be taken into account. We therefore, often unconsciously, rely on a theoretical framework that directs our attention to a very small part of the larger reality. In this way theories serve to simplify complex processes by offering a set of concepts that allows us to select, categorize, and label various forms of action and change, and to make inferences about cause and effect.

The process of socio-economic development, which is complex and wide-ranging, has given rise to a multitude of theories, explanations, arguments, and assertions. Students of development are often perplexed by the vast assortment of explanatory models. There are so many theories, perspectives, and approaches, all claiming to explain development; yet they conflict with and contradict one another. How is one to choose among competing explanations? Are there correct and incorrect theories? What evidence can be used to determine the empirical validity of the various models of development?

These questions hound all areas of scientific inquiry, but they are especially problematic for the social sciences. Explanatory precision is a difficult task, given the subject matter of social science. Humans and their social organizations defy the regularity and predictability of the natural and physical sciences. There are no iron laws of social behavior and social change. Therefore, the field of social science is open to a variety of equally compelling explanations and interpretations.

The political content of the subject matter in the social sciences is an equally important reason for divergent and contradictory theoretical claims. All social theories contain certain political assumptions and policy implications. There are conservative, mainstream, orthodox, liberal, radical, and Marxist social theories. The development and selection of a theoretical model is, therefore, heavily influenced by one's political predilection rather than by an objective assessment of the available data and evidence. Even when social scientists consult the available evidence, questions can be raised about the validity of data or the methods of analysis employed, or empirical results can simply be ignored. A theoretical conversion is an unlikely outcome.[1]

This book makes no claim or attempt to rise above this theoretical and methodological fray. I do not subject the theories of development reviewed in this book to any rigorous systematic empirical assessment. Rather, the fundamental purpose here is twofold. First, the book seeks to illuminate the diversity of theoretical perspectives, the assumptions and logic underlying them, and their political implications. Second, it is important to recognize that a large part of the debate among development theorists hinges on the level of analysis at which the various theories operate. The "level-of-analysis" question is particularly critical and serves as the organizing theme for the chapters in this book. We turn to that question after a discussion of the meaning of development and social change.

THE MEANING OF SOCIO-ECONOMIC DEVELOPMENT

There is considerable disagreement over the meaning and measurement of socio-economic development and what actually constitutes "true development" (see Baster 1972). Some of the different approaches will be discussed in Chapter 4. Most of the theories reviewed in this book attempt to explain international disparities in economic wealth and social welfare. *Socio-economic development*, in this sense, refers to the ability to produce an adequate and growing supply of goods and services productively and efficiently, to accumulate capital, and to distribute the fruits of production in a relatively equitable manner. The gap between rich and poor, developed and underdeveloped, or First and Third World nations reflects variations in these socio-economic capacities. While there is widespread agreement that socio-economic development involves production, accumulation, and distribution processes, the study of development has been heavily influenced by particular sociological concepts and economic measures. Sociological studies have emphasized the traditional-to-modern transition as part of the larger process of social change. Economists, on the other hand, tend to view development in terms of economic growth. Each of these perspectives has shaped the contemporary definition of socio-economic development.

The Concept of Social Change

In sociology, the terms *social change* and *development* are frequently used interchangeably. A closer examination of the development literature, however, indicates that the two terms differ in their level of generality. Social change is usually regarded as a constant, ongoing process affecting many areas of life, whereas development is used to denote more specific, empirically measurable, forms of change.

According to Kornblum (1988:566), social change refers to "variations over time in the ecological ordering of populations and communities, in patterns of roles and social interactions, in the structure and functioning of institutions, and in the cultures of societies." Social change, as this definition implies, is a broad, multidimensional process affecting numerous aspects of social life. It operates at a variety of socio-economic levels. At the individual level there are the changes in cultural beliefs and attitudes; at the organizational level there are changes in roles and patterns of interaction; at the societal level there are changes in the functioning of major institutions and the demographic processes of rural-to-urban migration.

The classical study of social change has been dominated by the assumption that each of these patterns of change—ecological, cultural, interactional, and institutional—is an inevitable subcomponent of a broader logic moving societies from the traditional to the modern form. This *modernization perspective*, along with the associated *traditional-modern dichotomy*, has a long legacy in classical sociological thought, and it is deeply entrenched as the leading conceptual apparatus employed for the purpose of understanding the most significant features of social change and development.

The traditional-modern dichotomy owes a great debt to the classical sociological thought of Emile Durkheim (1858–1917) and Ferdinand Tonnies (1855–1936). Durkheim's (1966) primary concern was with the mechanisms holding societies together and promoting social order. He believed that the bases of social order differ in traditional rural and modern industrial societies. Durkheim used the term *mechanical solidarity* to describe the form of cohesion and solidarity in traditional society. Under mechanical solidarity, social order is derived from the similar experiences and shared sentiments of members of the rural preindustrial community. Common values serve to promote order and harmony, and to regulate social behavior.

Mechanical solidarity is undermined in the transition to the modern industrial society. In place of similar sentiments and experiences, the increasingly complex division of labor in modern society subjects members to different roles and experiences. There is a shift from a "collective conscience" to an emphasis on individualism. Members of the society assume specialized roles and occupations. Differentiation, rather than similarity, is the defining characteristic of the modern society.

In Durkheim's scheme the changing organization of society is problematic because members no longer share common experiences and sentiments—there is no value consensus. Durkheim used the term *anomie* to describe the destabilizing effect of the breakdown of mechanical solidarity on individuals and the larger society. Anomic society is characterized by normlessness. Norms regulating and controlling behavior are absent or poorly defined, and the society is threatened with conflict and collapse.

In Durkheim's model, however, a new form of solidarity emerges that stems from the division of labor in the modern society. This is called *organic solidarity*. Cohesion in modern systems is based on the functional interdependence of members of society. With the complex division of labor each and every member of society depends on other members for the provision of goods, services, and needs. Like the biological organism, the parts are interdependent and complement one another. This results in a different but equally effective form of social unity and a new normative system that regulates the occupational responsibilities and forms of exchange and interaction among members.

Ferdinand Tonnies (1963) presented a similar scheme that described the most significant features of the traditional-to-modern transition. Tonnies used the term *gemeinschaft* to refer to the rural traditional society, in which personal relationships are close and informal and there is a general sense of community among members. This is contrasted with the *gesellschaft*, the modern urban society characterized by formal organizational and impersonal relationships among members. In the transition from *gemeinschaft* to *gesellschaft*, close-knit communal bonds are severed and replaced by relationships in the modern urban milieu that are transient, short-term, and shallow. Under *gesellschaft* individuals are said to be isolated, atomized, and poorly integrated components of a larger mass.

The theories of Tonnies and Durkheim are precursors of contemporary models of social change that use the traditional-modern distinction. These contemporary models assume that the labels ''traditional'' and ''modern'' are empirically applicable and that the transition from the traditional to the modern is inevitable and desirable. Tonnies and Durkheim emphasized the roles and interaction patterns in traditional and modern societies. Contemporary modernization theorists, following this model, believe that the role and interaction patterns of the modern society—differentiated, specialized, and impersonal—are requirements for development.

Another element of the traditional-modern scheme that has been accepted by certain contemporary development theorists is the assumption that the traditional-to-modern transition creates social-psychological strains on the population. Durkheim's concept of anomie and Tonnies' argument about the negative consequences of broken communal ties raise the specter of potential instability in the modern urban milieu. These reservations have been incorporated in the theory of the *mass society*. This theory assumes that rapid social change will have negative psychological effects, increasing the likelihood of unconventional, radical, and violent political behavior. Such instability is regarded as a negative by-product of the traditional-to-modern transition and has resulted in development theories that prescribe institutional mechanisms aimed at preventing potential insurrection.[2]

The classical sociological theory of Max Weber also plays a prominent role in the traditional-modern image of social change. The most notable feature of modern society for Weber was the emergence of bureaucratic organization. Bureaucratic operating principles, applied to organizations and institutions, were regarded by Weber as the superior and most efficient means for the accomplishment of goals. Because the characteristics of bureaucratic organization—clearly defined goals and duties, universal rules and regulations, specialization, meritocracy, accountability, rational legal authority—are associated with modern society and its central institutions, many theories of development prescribe these institutional characteristics and operating procedures as requirements for socioeconomic development.

The Meaning of Development

While the concept of social change tends to be used as a catchall term for any and all forms of change over time within a society, the concept of development usually refers to some measurable form of progress. The most common measure of development, by far, is gross national product (GNP). GNP measures the total value of goods and services produced by a nation during a single year. For purposes of comparability, GNP is expressed in a common currency, usually dollars, and reported in per capita terms to take into account the size of a nation. Thus, GNP per capita is interpreted as the value of output per person in a given year.

Using this measure, development is said to take place when GNP per capita increases over time. The change in GNP per capita between two points in time is referred to as the *economic growth rate*. The growth rate is calculated as the percentage change in GNP per capita. GNP and growth rate data are reported on an annual basis for most nations in the world.

A 1977 study by David Morawetz (1977) examined post–World War II changes in GNP for "rich" and "poor" nations from 1950 to 1975, a period of rapid global economic growth. The rich nations included all members of the Organization for Economic Cooperation and Development (OECD).[3] The poor nations included non-OECD nations that make up the regions of South Asia, East Asia, Africa, Latin America, and the Middle East. Morawetz was interested in whether the gap between rich and poor countries, as measured by GNP, grew, shrunk, or remained stable during the post–World War II period.

Morawetz calculated two different measures of the gap between rich and poor nations—the absolute and the relative gaps. The *absolute gap* is the difference between the average GNP per capita of the rich and poor countries. In 1950 the gap was $2,218; in 1975 it had grown to $4,863. Thus, the absolute gap between rich and poor nations more than doubled over the 25-year period.

The *relative gap* is measured as the GNP per capita of poor nations as a percent of the GNP per capita of rich nations. Such a measure is often used to indicate that even though the average GNP per capita of the poor nations (or a single nation) increases, it may still make up a smaller percent of the average GNP per capita of the rich nations. This is because the rich nations may have experienced even higher rates of growth. Thus, the relative position of nations remains unchanged.

The relative gap decreased from 1950 to 1975. In 1950 the average GNP per capita of poor nations amounted to 6.7% of the average GNP per capita of the rich nations. In 1975 it increased to 7.2% of the average GNP per capita of rich nations. However, it should be pointed out that the closing of the relative gap indicated by these figures was primarily the result of the inclusion of Middle East oil-exporting nations. Extreme disparity still exists. If we examine the change in the relative gap for different regions, the data indicate that the average GNP per capita of South Asia, Africa, and Latin America was a smaller percentage of the average GNP per capita of the rich nations in 1975 than in 1950.

A replication of Morawetz's analysis (Passé-Smith 1993), using more recent data from 1962 to 1990, indicates a continuing and persistent gap between the rich and nonrich nations. Passé-Smith's analysis groups countries into rich, middle-income, and poor categories based on their GNP/per capita in constant 1980 U.S. dollars. The absolute and relative gaps between the rich and poor, and rich and middle-income nations, are calculated using the same methodology employed by Morawetz. The absolute gap between rich and poor countries grew from $6,549 to $10,671 for the 1962–1990 period; the absolute gap between rich and middle-income countries increased from $5,540 to $9,428 over the same period. The relative gap, which Morawetz reported had decreased during the 1950–1975 period, increased from 1962 to 1990. The GNP per capita of the middle-income countries was 19% of the rich countries in 1962 and 14% in 1990. The poor nations dropped from 4.2% to 2.6% of the GNP per capita of the rich countries. Much of this book is devoted to examining explanations for why these gaps are so large and why they continue to grow.

The data analyzed by Morawetz and Passé-Smith paint a rather pessimistic picture about the future prospects for less-developed nations. At least collectively they seem to be falling farther and farther behind advanced industrialized nations on the GNP measure. On the other hand, there is some, albeit limited, upward mobility. Passé-Smith (1993) reports that from 1962 to 1990 fourteen nations moved from the middle-income to rich nation category. There were also eleven nations moving from the poor to middle-income group. The general pattern, however, is one of stability in terms of national income category with 91 of the 118 nations remaining in the same income category in 1990 that they occupied in 1962.

A more general issue concerns the adequacy of GNP as a measure of development. Suppose the data indicated—which they do for certain nations—a rapidly growing GNP and a closing gap. Would this economic performance signal development, modernization, and progress? There is considerable debate over this question. It was once believed that a growing and expanding GNP was the ultimate goal of development because a growing economy brought an improvement in all spheres of life. The economy would be richer, jobs would be created, people would have more money, the quality of life would improve, poverty would disappear, industry would expand, and life as we know it in the advanced industrial economies would be reproduced in the less-developed nations.

This optimistic scenario has not come to pass. More important, even for nations that have been lucky enough to experience rapid rates of economic growth, many of the assumed positive by-products have not materialized. This fact calls into question the validity of GNP as an adequate indicator of development. Rapid growth has not necessarily resulted in higher incomes for workers, better health care, more housing, a reduction in poverty, or a more democratic or egalitarian society. On the contrary, there are numerous examples of rapid growth accompanied by a decline in the standard of living, increasing poverty, rising inequality, and political repression. In fact, these are frequently regarded as necessary, though hopefully temporary, conditions for growth.

These problems with GNP measures have led to an increasing emphasis on alternative measures of development. Development is more than a purely quantitative economic process; it should also involve a qualitative improvement in the life of a nation's population. Much of the contemporary theoretical and empirical literature is concerned with the provision of basic needs and the physical quality of life as alternative means of assessing the developmental performance of nations (Chapter 4). This typically involves focusing upon the poverty rate, infant mortality, literacy, educational enrollment, caloric intake, access to medical care, and the availability of housing and sanitation facilities. While the provision of these basic needs is related to a nation's level of economic development, economic growth is an insufficient condition for ensuring the availability of these services. These components of the quality of life are potential, but not inevitable, products of an expanding economy. An important question for development researchers is the conditions under which economic growth translates into an improvement in the quality of human life or, conversely, is achieved at the expense of the population.

The overemphasis on GNP also tends to obscure the structural obstacles to development that pervade many less-developed economies. The concept of *underdevelopment*, also widely used in the contemporary development literature, denotes a socio-economic structure characterized by a reliance on the export of raw materials and primary products, regional disparities in economic growth, poorly integrated economic sectors, domination by external forces, a poorly developed class structure, and a chronic balance-of-payments crisis fueling the accumulation of debt. The historical and contemporary forces responsible for these structural impediments are a major focus of the international-level models of dependency and world-system theory (Chapter 6).

LEVELS OF ANALYSIS AND SOCIAL SCIENTIFIC EXPLANATION

Levels of Analysis and Socio-economic Development

This chapter began by noting the vast number of theories designed to explain socio-economic development. In this book theories of development are distinguished by their level of analysis. In the scheme proposed here, a theory's *level of analysis* is based on the "units of analysis" selected to explain socio-economic development.[4] Different theories draw attention to particular sets of causal factors. In the study of development these might be the attitudes and values of individuals, or the system of industrial relations, or the rules and logic governing the economic system, or the policies of the state, or a nation's position in the international division of labor. These independent variables, or predictors of development, are observed at different levels of analysis. Attitudes and values operate at the *individual level*, industrial relations at the *organizational level*, the logic of the economic system and policies of the state at the *societal* (or national) *level*, and position in the international division of labor at the *international level*.

This book examines these four distinct levels of theory guiding the explana-

Table 1.1
Levels of Analysis in the Study of Socio-economic Development

Level of Analysis	Causal Mechanism	Example of Theoretical Proposition
International	World Economic Institutions, Forces, and Interactions	The greater the dependence on direct foreign investment, the slower the rate of socio-economic development.
Societal	National Political, Economic, and Social Institutions and Policies	The greater the reliance on free market principles, the greater the rate of socio-economic development.
Organizational	Intra- and Interorganizational Structure and Management of Business Enterprises	The greater the use of Japanese-style management principles, the higher the rate of productivity and socio-economic development
Individual	Individual Values, Attitudes, Motives, and Characteristics	The greater the "need for achievement" among the population, the greater the rate of socio-economic development.

tion of socio-economic development. The general framework is summarized in Table 1.1.

At the level closest to individuals and their beliefs and actions are individual-level theories. These theories of development focus on the values, motives, attributes, and characteristics of individuals as the source of socio-economic development. Theories of this type emphasize individual traits such as the level of achievement motivation, the degree of entrepreneurial talent, the attachment to modern ideas, or the possession of human capital. These perspectives share the assumption that individual-level characteristics are the primary causal factor in explaining national social development.

Theories at the organizational level of analysis examine the structures and practices of work organizations and enterprises in order to determine how they influence human behavior and contribute to social, economic, and political development. Organizations are structures with characteristics distinct from those at the individual level. The structural properties of organizations cannot be reduced to the individual attributes of their members.

An organizational level theory might argue, for example, that successful agricultural development requires a particular land tenure arrangement, or that economic growth depends on the use of certain industrial organizational techniques, such as a Japanese management system. In both cases the organizational arrangement used for producing goods is assumed to be a (or the) leading causal factor in explaining socio-economic development.

The societal level of analysis directs attention to the causal role of broader social institutions in the process of development—how social institutions are organized, the economic system used to produce and distribute goods, the type of political system, and the role of government policies. This level of analysis links societal characteristics—institutional, political, and economic—to the level and rate of socio-economic development. The societal level is distinct from, and often determines, organizational- and individual-level attributes, and its properties cannot be reduced to the organizational or individual components. One might argue, from the societal perspective, that rational bureaucratic principles must govern a society's institutions if the society is to develop in a smooth and efficient manner, or that free-market capitalism is the most effective economic system of production and distribution.

Furthest from individuals, the international level of analysis focuses on political and economic forces that operate at the global level. In the international system nations interact with one another, commodities are traded and exchanged, capital investment flows across national borders, and nations are subjected to interdependence, domination, and exploitation. These global dynamics are seen as significant factors for socio-economic development. Existing at the highest level of analysis, the international system subsumes all those levels below it, and is not reducible to the properties of the lower levels of analysis. International-level theories of development, such as dependency and world-systems theory, are powerful models that have gained considerable prominence since the mid-1970s. These theories focus on the role of colonialism, imperialism, foreign capital investment, trade patterns, and the process of globalization as central factors shaping the course of social change in less-developed nations.

Organizing development theories by levels of analysis serves four important purposes. First, this organizing framework introduces readers, in a sequential and systematic way, to a subject matter that grows increasingly complex as broader levels of analysis are considered. Second, the presentation of topics follows a logical hierarchy of analytic schemes that are fundamental to social scientific theory and explanation. Third, this organizing framework reveals one of the major sources of debate and controversy in the field of development— the appropriate level of analysis. And fourth, this method provides an analytic framework for the study of national and international development that cannot be gained from a strict case study approach.

Two final points about the levels of analysis framework deserve mention. First, many theories of development cannot be pigeonholed into a single level of analysis. While most theories tend to focus on a particular level as the site of the primary causal factor, the best theories integrate and account for different levels of analysis in an interconnected causal chain. Second, while we distinguish among explanatory levels of analysis, all the theories of development discussed in this book seek to explain social change and development at the national level. For this reason theories of socio-economic development can be regarded as systematic or macro because they are concerned with change in whole societies or social systems over time. The primary theoretical variation, therefore, lies in the accounts and causal factors used to explain societal-level changes.

Levels of Analysis and Social Theory

The level-of-analysis issue extends far beyond the field of socio-economic development. The debate among development theorists over the appropriate level of analysis is just one component of a more fundamental theoretical debate in social science (see Edel 1979). One of these theoretical divisions involves the distinction between *individualistic* and *structural/holistic* explanations of human behavior. Individualistic explanations view human behavior as largely the product of individual characteristics and personality traits. Structural/holistic explanations, in contrast, interpret human behavior in a broader social context, as the result of external social forces, structures, and institutional arrangements.

In the study of development these two positions are often counter-posed when we seek to explain human behavior in the economic sphere. Agricultural producers or peasants, for example, have often been described as behaving in traditional and irrational ways because they do not attempt to maximize agricultural output or invest in methods that would enhance agricultural productivity. This behavior, in turn, is said to hamper the development of the agricultural sector. This individualistic explanation locates the problem in the attitudes and values of peasants and, therefore, suggests the need for modern rational values to be internalized by these agricultural producers. The structural/holistic approach, on the other hand, examines peasant behavior in the context of the incentive systems of broader institutional structures. From this perspective peasant and tenant systems of agricultural organization, and the associated lack of control over the agricultural surplus by producers, serve as disincentives for extra investment of labor and capital.

These divergent theoretical interpretations have different policy implications. For the individualistic approach the solution is to change the mind-set of the peasants; for the structural/holistic model the solution is to change the organizational system under which goods are being produced. Many of the major theoretical and policy disputes in social science stem from the individualistic versus structural/holistic theoretical cleavage (see Campbell 1981 for some other dividing lines).

Some additional examples from the contemporary social science literature illustrate the broad scope of this level-of-analysis debate. One question is whether it is appropriate to use individual level attributes to explain structural and societal-level phenomena. Unlike the study of peasant behavior, this question involves explaining a nonindividual-level outcome using individual-level variables. One might argue, for example, that national development depends upon a certain set of individual beliefs about the value of work. This is an individual-level explanation of development. The use of individual characteristics as explanatory variables is a hotly contested issue. A common position on this question argues that:

individual interests, motivation, and perceptions, can never adequately explain individual behavior. Both organizational and societal factors must be taken into account in explaining variations in rates of individual behavior occurring in different types of situations. *But the reverse is not possible—one cannot explain organizational or societal processes by theories of individual behavior or social interaction.* (Alford and Friedland 1985:15) [emphasis added]

When the level of analysis of the dependent variable is nonindividual, the individual-level factors lose their explanatory utility. Organizational and structural factors take precedence. This is a significant issue for the study of development, given the propositions advanced by theorists employing the individual level of analysis.

A second, related problem emerges when connecting the individual and nonindividual levels of analysis. A common tendency is to infer, from organizational and societal characteristics, the psychological attributes of the individuals within these organizations and societies. Individual attributes are then used as the explanation for organizational and societal characteristics. A recent study of working-class consciousness directly addresses the logic of this argument, and views it as:

an example of the fallacy of *psychological reductionism*—the assumption that the structure of any society can be reduced to the wishes and motivations of its members. Society is much more than a straightforward embodiment of the wills of the people within that society. . . . The attempt to explain structural phenomena solely in terms of psychological attributes has been justifiably derided in social science as psychological reductionism. (Vanneman and Cannon 1987:15, 19)

Examining the causal role of different levels of analysis also raises the distinction between ''voluntarism'' and ''determinism.'' The *voluntarist* perspective assumes that social actors—individuals, organizations, and nation—can easily convert desires into actions; that actors exercise free will to do as they please and shape their own destiny. The *determinist* view tends to emphasize the obstacles, structural impediments, institutional arrangements, and power relations that prevent actors from freely realizing their subjective desires. There is considerable overlap between the individualistic and voluntaristic, as well as the structural/holistic and deterministic, modes of social explanation.

Finally, the levels-of-analysis framework is closely tied to recent theoretical efforts in sociology to integrate the *micro* and *macro* levels of theorizing (Ritzer 1990) and reconcile the relationship between *agency* and *structure* (Archer 1988; Giddens 1984). These two theoretical issues overlap in important ways. Micro-level theories tend to focus upon objective patterns of behavior and interaction and/or the subjective thought processes of individuals as the most critical sociological phenomena. Macro-level theories focus upon the larger, objective institutional structures within which individuals operate and/or the cultural value systems of the larger society (Ritzer 1992).

The issue is not simply whether it is the micro or macro level that represents the most important focus for sociological analysis but the causal connection or interrelationship between the two levels. This is even more explicitly the case if we consider the agency–structure debate. Sociological theories that emphasize agency tend to argue for the determinant and purposive role of human action in shaping larger organizational arrangements and social institutions.

The concept of agency is often associated with the micro level since it stems from the action of individuals or collectivities. Structure, on the other hand, is viewed as both a constraint on the action of individuals as well as a determinant of micro-level objective and subjective processes. It is regarded as something that operates above and often beyond the control of individuals and is therefore often associated with the macro level of theorizing. As applied to the levels-of-analysis framework advanced above, agency would involve individual-level processes shaping and impacting upon the higher levels of analysis. Structure would place the greatest emphasis on the nonindividual levels of analysis of organizations, societal institutions, and the global political economy.

The most interesting theoretical work today is aimed at integrating micro- and macro-, and agency and structure, phenomena (see Collins 1981; Ritzer 1990; Alexander and Giesen 1987; Wiley 1988; Coleman 1986). For example, in Coleman's integrative model individual values are shaped by a macro-level cultural system; the individual values then translate into particular kinds of economic behavior; this individual behavior then impacts on the larger macro-level economic system. In reviewing the various levels of analysis and associated theories of development we will emphasize the importance of integrating the different levels rather than viewing one level as determining all other levels of analysis.

The competing levels of analysis and associated theories of development reviewed in this book reflect these general theoretical debates. The levels-of-analysis scheme can be viewed as a ''nested hierarchy'' of progressively broader levels of analysis where behavior and change at each level is shaped by actions at lower levels and constrained by forces operating at higher level(s) of analysis. While individual values and actions may shape broader levels of analysis, the freedom of individuals to act upon their values, beliefs, and convictions is often constrained by the organizational context in which they work, the distribution of power in the society, and even the forces of the international system. As we move to higher reaches of the hierarchy, away from the individual level, inter-national factors may seem remote and distant, yet they affect individuals through their impact on the intermediate societal and organizational levels. In a similar fashion, productive enterprises (organizations) may both shape, and be con-strained by, societal-level arrangements and international forces. Last, the action of nations may influence the international level but the freedom of nations to act as they please and pursue particular policies is also constrained by a global system of inequality and world-market forces. Situating the relationship between levels of analysis in this way points to the agency from below as well as the structural constraints from above on social action and socio-economic processes.

THE PLAN OF THE BOOK

The chapters in this book are organized around the levels-of-analysis scheme outlined above. Chapter 2 reviews some of the leading individual-level theories of development. These include theories that focus upon psychological attributes and cultural practices as well as those which emphasize the human capital char-acteristics of the population. In addition, this chapter elaborates the philosophical and sociological sources of the individual-level theses. The claims and logic of the individual-level model of development are subjected to a critical assessment. The purpose of this chapter is to introduce students to individual-level expla-nations for development and point to the significant shortcomings of such mod-els.

Chapter 3 is devoted to the organizational level of analysis. The organization of work and production at the enterprise level has been, until recently, a largely overlooked area of development theory, yet there are many models and case studies that point to the importance of organizational arrangements and struc-tures. The chapter begins by pointing out the role of organizations in shaping the motives and behavior of individuals. The purpose is to provide a corrective to the purely individual-level formulations. Both agricultural and industrial or-ganizational arrangements influence the pace of development, political dynam-ics, and the geographic distribution of populations. These features of the development process are discussed for both developed and less-developed nations. The last section of the chapter reviews some of the contemporary ar-guments of organizational theorists regarding the most appropriate organiza-tional form for dynamic economic production.

Chapters 4 and 5 address theories of development that operate at the societal level. These are the national forms of social, political, and economic organiza-tion that are said to influence development. In Chapter 4 some of the classic arguments of structural functionalism and the modernization school are critically examined. Included as well are economic theories of development, GNP models, and alternative approaches to the measurement of development. Chapter 5 takes up issues of comparative socio-economics and the claims about the relative efficacy of capitalism and socialism. Much of this literature is now devoted to an analysis of comparative capitalist economic strategies. The chapter concludes with a discussion of the current transition from state socialist to market-based economies.

Chapter 6 moves the analysis of development to the highest plane—the international system. In this chapter the highly popular dependency/world-economy approach is presented. This includes an outline of the basic propositions of this perspective and some of the modern theorists associated with this framework. The international mechanisms affecting development—the capitalist world system, the exchange of commodities, the flows of capital and investment, and the interaction among nations are examined. The last section of the chapter is devoted to a discussion of recent literature on globalization.

Chapter 7, the conclusion, summarizes the main points and arguments advanced throughout the book and encourages efforts to integrate the different levels of analysis.

NOTES

1. On the subjective and political nature of theory construction and selection, see Gouldner (1970:chs. 1 and 2). The problems of "imperfect empiricism" in the social sciences are neatly reviewed in Spencer (1987).

2. See Wright (1976) and Hamilton and Wright (1986) for valuable critiques of the mass society perspective.

3. Members of the OECD are Australia, Austria, Belgium, Canada, Denmark, Finland, France, Federal Republic of Germany, Greece, Iceland, Ireland, Italy, Japan, Luxembourg, the Netherlands, New Zealand, Norway, Portugal, Spain, Sweden, Switzerland, Turkey, the United Kingdom, and the United States.

4. The term "level of analysis" is widely used in discussions of social theory and explanation and in the analysis of different social scientific topics. The definition tends to vary depending on the context. Perrow (1986:142) uses the term to denote the "levels of environment" that progress upward toward the world level and regress downward toward individuals and their biological makeup. Scott (1981), in sharp contrast with the usage here, determines the theoretical level of analysis by the nature of the dependent variable. Alford and Friedland (1985) use levels of analysis to construct a metatheoretical model, and attempt to link each level of analysis to major theoretical perspectives on the state.

2

Individual-Level Theories of Socio-economic Development

At the most basic level, all forms of economic accumulation involve human energy and effort. For this reason a great deal of development theory is aimed at the micro level and considers psychological and cultural attitudes, dispositions, values, and needs related to human motivation and effort. Without the expenditure of human energy, there is no production, no surplus, no growth. Where individual differences correlate with variations in the size or growth of output, it is common for these individual differences to be held accountable for the developmental performance. Such a logic has produced myriad explanations directed toward discovering the key motivating psychology conducive to high rates of output. This chapter explores the origins of the link between individual characteristics and socio-economic development, and reviews the literature isolating the individual characteristics required for development.

INDIVIDUALISM AND DEVELOPMENT

It is not surprising that individual-level explanations for development look to ideologies and values that prevailed alongside the rise of industrial capitalism. The Industrial Revolution brought forth the most rapid development of the productive forces and accumulation of wealth. It is logical, therefore, to examine not only the material but also the subjective forces that may have been responsible for this monumental economic expansion. This question—the causal role of subjective versus objective factors as explanations of social change—has generated an intense and ongoing debate among social scientists. It has been taken up as part of the broader conflict between Weberian and Marxist social theory.

Max Weber and the Protestant Ethic

A major theoretical impetus for individual-level models is provided by the classical sociological theory of Max Weber, most notably in *The Protestant Ethic and the Spirit of Capitalism* (1930). Weber is closely associated with the argument that ideas foster the emergence of socio-economic systems. This *primacy of ideas* position—that individual and collective beliefs are causally prior to the development of social structures, institutions, and systems—was presumably motivated by Weber's desire to challenge the Marxian contention that the dominant beliefs and ideas of a society are merely a reflection of the material interests of the ruling class. In the Marxist model, the ruling ideas of any period are seen as ideological beliefs that legitimate and justify the existing socio-economic system. Thus, in contrast with the "primacy of ideas" logic, socio-economic systems emerge first and are followed by the development of an ideological belief system that supports the existing institutional arrangements and the interests of the dominant class. Weber's response to this position should be seen, more precisely, as an attempt to demonstrate the mutually reinforcing nature of, or "elective affinity" between, the socio-economic organization and prevailing value system of a society (see Lowy 1989).

For our purposes, however, the key question is what kinds of ideas are said to have an elective affinity with capitalist forms of social organization or those that contribute to rapid economic growth. For Weber, Protestantism contained certain beliefs that supported and promoted the rise of capitalism. There are two basic elements of Protestantism that tend to be linked to capitalism in Weber's work. The first, associated with Lutheranism and the Reformation, is the break from the Catholic tradition of the church as the sole intermediary between God and the believer, and the establishment of a more individualized system of belief. Under Protestantism, believers have a direct relationship with God that goes beyond the church. The Protestant concept of the "calling" implies that one's duty to God extends to all spheres of life, including work. This represents a departure from the traditional, collective, and institutional forms of social control of the Catholic Church, a rejection of the distinction between monastic and worldly pursuits, and the promotion of greater individualism and autonomy. These developments are viewed as consistent with the demands of a capitalist market economy.

The second and more important component of Protestantism said to support the institutions of capitalism is derived from the Calvinist sect. Calvinism associated hard work and job commitment with godly duty and virtue, and ultimate salvation. The association of work, and the worldly pursuit of material gain, with religious sanctity represented a sharp break from traditional Roman Catholic ethics and provided religious justification for forms of economic behavior and motivation demanded by an emerging capitalist economy. This Calvinist version of Protestantism, emphasizing individual effort devoted to hard work and worldly success, is the foundation of the Protestant ethic. A crude and vulgarized version of the Weberian perspective might, therefore, argue that attachment to the ideals of the Protestant ethic is a necessary condition for dynamic capitalist expansion.[1]

In fact, Weber's analysis did not posit such a causal ordering. Prior to the emergence of a Protestant belief system, capitalist socio-economic forces were already operating. Weber's point was to show how the material interests and behaviors of the emerging bourgeoisie were supported by a particular religious ideology. The "elective affinity" between material interests and beliefs suggests that each facilitates the advancement of the other. The mutually reinforcing nature of ideas and interests has largely been obscured in the more recent individual-level models of development that instead assert the causal priority of ideas and culture.

Eisenstadt's (1968b) treatment of the Protestant ethic thesis represents a more balanced approach in its elaboration of the institutional and structural factors facilitating and reinforcing Protestant religious beliefs. This distinguishes Eisenstadt from some of the modernization theorists to be considered shortly. As he points out, many of the new social roles, such as entrepreneur, existed prior to the rise of Protestantism. Protestantism was absorbed and institutionalized, and eventually flourished, because it complemented many preexisting forms of social and political organization. For example, the individualism and autonomy often associated with Protestant doctrine were, in Western Europe, already established to some degree in social and political organizations. The regional and political autonomy of urban areas, and the politically decentralized structure of Western towns, are often cited as major explanations for the rise of the West (Chirot 1986:ch. 2). More generally, the strength of Eisenstadt's analysis is its recognition of the contingent nature of religious beliefs. The extent to which Protestantism, or any other belief system, will generate modernization or economic expansion hinges on the presence or absence of a variety of other economic, social, and political structures.

Liberalism and Individualism

The philosophy of classical liberalism has also had a major influence on individual-level theories of development in two important ways. First, the philosophy of liberalism has contributed to the Western bias for explanations that emphasize the causal role of individual beliefs and actions. Second, liberalism advances a number of assumptions about essential human motives and behavior that are assumed to promote development.

Methodological individualism is a mode of inquiry that tends to focus on individual beliefs and actions as the primary explanation for social phenomena. This perspective can be linked to classical liberal theory and its development alongside the emergence of capitalism. The rise of institutions unique to capitalism—free and mobile labor and free markets—shaped the basic assumptions of classical liberal theory regarding the latitude of human freedom and the role of human action. The deterioration of feudal bonds of servitude and lifelong ties to the land led to the development of a free labor force that had a greater ability to move voluntarily to employment opportunities and determine the conditions of its employment. Likewise, free markets involve the voluntary association of buyers and sellers of goods and services, and free choice over what to buy and what to sell. In the classical liberal worldview, individual freedom is embodied in the free choices available in labor and commodity markets. Since market exchange requires no heavy-handed institutional intervention or coercion, and is based on free and voluntary choice and association, individuals are viewed as sovereign and autonomous agents able to shape their lives and futures.[2] It is a short, logical step to then argue that human agents, through their beliefs and actions, shape the organization and development of societies.

With the emergence of market institutional arrangements, liberal philosophy apportions significant weight to the actions of individuals in the explanation of social phenomena. No longer do caste, craft, and feudal distinctions determine one's life chances and the shape of society. The individual freedom and choice characteristic of a liberal capitalist society elevate the causal role of human action. Liberal philosophy's individualist bias permeates Western social science and is evident in the widespread tendency to explain human action with psychological models, social problems as the product of individual deficiencies, and development as the result of individual beliefs. Often overlooked are the institutional, structural, and environmental forces shaping human behavior, generating social problems, and influencing development.

A second key element of classical liberalism is the assumption that human action is motivated by selfish, greedy, or material desires. In this view, human choices are driven by utilitarian principles of self-interest. Macpherson (1973) uses the term *possessive individualism* to describe this strand of liberal thought. According to Macpherson, liberal philosophy defines human freedom as the ability of humans to use their individual capacities to maximize satisfaction. One's level of satisfaction, in turn, is based on dominance over things and objects—the ownership, consumption, and possession of material goods. It is assumed that individuals have an inherent and insatiable desire for material goods, and therefore the liberal notion of freedom involves the right of individuals to pursue these strivings.

This assumption about the human essence has worked its way into theories of development at two different levels. At the individual level, self-interest and the desire to maximize material gain are regarded as rational sentiments that promote aggregate socio-economic development. At the societal level, the argument for the superiority of capitalism as a development strategy is based on the assumptions that humans are by their very nature selfish and greedy and, thus, development requires adopting socio-economic institutions that are consistent with these inherent human motivations.[3]

The Work Ethic

Elements of the Protestant ethic and classical liberal theory have been combined to produce the contemporary notion of the "work ethic."[4] The work ethic refers to "beliefs about the moral superiority of hard work over leisure or idleness, craft pride over carelessness, sacrifice over profligacy, earned over unearned income, and positive over negative attitudes toward work" (Andrisani and Parnes 1983:104). This overworked concept has been incorporated into countless theoretical explanations at a variety of levels of analysis. The typical argument runs something like this: Individual adherence to the work ethic is the key to successful collective performance. Therefore, economically effective organizations and societies contain members with a strong attachment to the work ethic; less successful enterprises possess members who have not internalized or developed the work ethic. According to this logic, the lack of growth can be attributed to the decline or absence of the work ethic.

A more limited application of the work ethic thesis, but one that illustrates an important point about the potential pitfalls of individual-level explanations, concerns the relationship between the work ethic and individual outcomes. A more specific research question might ask whether one's attachment to the work ethic can predict one's labor market status and/or economic success. The standard logic posits that those with a well-developed work ethic will be more successful economically than those who lack this trait. This view of economic success reinforces the belief that individuals are ultimately responsible for their status and position in society. The empirical literature attempting to determine the effects of the work ethic on labor market success is full of contradictory findings and "nonfindings." The evidence is mixed. One can show a broad set of results that conform to the expected association between the work ethic (measured empirically in about as many ways as it is used stylistically) and labor market outcomes, such as occupational status and income.

However, concurrent association does not establish causality. One can argue that the causal direction of the hypothesis should be reversed, with the work ethic malleable and subject to modification based on one's labor market status and experience. There is strong evidence suggesting this pattern. Longitudinal studies, for example, indicate that those with the highest rates of unemployment and fewest weeks worked experience the greatest weakening of the work ethic; low-paying jobs with little room for career advancement are related to increasing anti-work attitudes; youths in low-status jobs at the start of a period, and those who move into low-status jobs, are more likely than comparable youths in high-status jobs to lower their labor market ambitions and decrease their commitment to the work ethic (see Andrisani and Parnes 1983). In short, the studies suggest that initial labor market status has a greater influence on the work ethic than vice versa.

Given this ordering of the relevant variables, and the fact that labor market status is to a large extent determined by social class background, there will be a substantial portion of the population who, due to their lower position in the stratification system, have a loose attachment to the work ethic as measured attitudinally. Behaviorally, on the other hand, this same population generally chooses work over nonwork and is realistically aware that economic success requires more than positive attitudes about the goodness of hard work.

Finally, even if everyone were to start out with a solid work ethic, it is difficult to imagine how this state of affairs could be maintained in stratified societies and organizations that base their ability to accumulate wealth on the very inequalities that seem to undermine the work ethic. Capitalist market economies, for example, are based on and maintain an unequal distribution of income and productive resources. In fact, work organizations in most societies are built upon hierarchical structures of unequal authority and power. In this sense, the structural reality of economy and work organization mediates the attitudinal disposition of individual workers. Thus, even when we are examining individual-level (rather than national-level) outcomes, individual-level explanations can be problematic. The lesson one learns from consulting the literature on the work ethic is that the relationships between individual attitudes and objective outcomes is highly complex. We will return to this point shortly.

MODERN INDIVIDUALS AND NATIONAL DEVELOPMENT

We can now turn to a more direct examination of theoretical models and arguments that link individual characteristics to national-level outcomes. The theoretical logic that leads theorists to examine the values and attitudes prevalent during the rise of industrial capitalism informs the *individual modernization approach* to development. This perspective argues that development depends upon the diffusion and adoption of modern Western values. It is based on the comparative logic that turns the *association* between modern values and wealthy societies into a proposition about the *causal prerequisites* for socio-economic development. The causal logic assumes that values and attitudes *precede* forms of social organization and economic growth; that values and attitudes prevalent in the industrial societies are responsible for the aggregate level of social wealth. Conversely, the aggregate poverty of less-developed nations is the result of the inappropriate values held by people living in these nations. The individual modernization arguments represent only one component of the broad modernization paradigm. Broadly, the process of modernization involves the proliferation of modern ideas and institutions to "traditional," "backward," or "stagnant" regions and nations. The *diffusion* of modern culture and social structure is said to facilitate development, growth, and industrial progress. In this optimistic scenario all nations are seen as potential recipients of the modern ingredients for development. As modern ideas, behaviors, and organizational systems are inevitably adopted, nations will follow the path and eventually achieve the status of the advanced industrial nations of the West. Development, in this model, is viewed as an evolutionary and unilinear process whereby all nations evolve from traditional to modern forms and follow a single trajectory of socio-economic progress.

Modernization theorists have tended to emphasize the modernizing impact of ideas and/or institutions. In this chapter we focus on the arguments at the individual level that identify the necessary cultural beliefs and behavior patterns required for development. What follows is a sampling of some of the leading works in this area.

The literature emphasizing the dynamic role of the individual entrepreneur fits squarely into this tradition. The social economist Joseph Schumpeter (1949) considered the entrepreneur to be the harbinger of economic growth. Schumpeter defined entrepreneurs as innovators who take the factors of production, combine them in new ways, and apply these novel amalgamations to the production process. The introduction of innovative techniques by entrepreneurs restructures the production process and moves it to a qualitatively higher level. This is the essence of innovation and the key to socio-economic development.

Less clear, in this formulation, is the motivation for entrepreneurial activity. Schumpeter suggests that the profit motive is an insignificant factor, and this is echoed in subsequent theories emphasizing the individual agent. For Schumpeter, the profit motive is incidental because the entrepreneur is not the bearer of risk and, therefore, is less concerned with the extent to which expenses are compensated by returns in profit. It is venture capitalists and shareholders who put up the capital and who, ultimately, are seen as the beneficiaries of entrepreneurial innovation.

Other writers have attempted to specify the conditions generating the entrepreneurial spirit and the factors facilitating the translation of this spirit into dynamic economic activity. This effort involves, inevitably, a consideration of other levels of analysis. Rostow (1956), for example, suggests that the emergence of an entrepreneurial elite requires more than simply an appropriate value system. The nascent elite must be denied access to the conventional sources of power and prestige—an oppositional elite. Additionally, the society in which this entrepreneur class emerges must be relatively flexible enough to allow this incipient elite opportunities for economic advancement, even if these may be unconventional. Finally, Rostow suggests that, despite all the emphasis placed on the "entrepreneurial precondition," there are a number of broader structural changes that precede or accompany most economic "take-offs" (see Chapter 4). Among those he cites are changes in agricultural techniques and the development of a market system of exchange.

Hoselitz (1957) also places entrepreneurship at the center of his explanation of development and, like Rostow, believes that there are a number of broader structural conditions that contribute to the institutionalization of this belief and behavioral system. Hoselitz maintains that many forms of social and cultural change begin with behaviorally deviant actions among certain members of the population; the actions of certain groups violate the norms of appropriate behavior. Merchants and businessmen, for instance, are deviants in the context of Western feudal society. Logically, deviant behavior is likely to be pursued by those culturally and socially marginal segments of society who, given their marginal status, must locate a niche in the social structure from which income can be derived. Jewish and foreign money lenders in medieval Europe are examples. A final condition for the institutionalization of entrepreneurialism is the redefinition of societal objectives by existing elites. However, "as long as an elite is interested primarily in maintaining its own position of power and privilege, this may mean that the masses are degraded, that economic progress is slow, and that general poverty prevails" (Hoselitz 1957:40). This is a rather common scenario in many less-developed nations today.

In spite of these theoretical attempts by Rostow and Hoselitz to broaden the framework for analyzing the emergence of value-cultural systems and associated forms of economic behavior, the fundamental question remains: If the entrepreneur is required for dynamic socio-economic development, what prevents their emergence in the less-developed societies? This question is troubling since, in the individual-level models, backward and less-developed nations by definition lack the particular personalities and individuals necessary for economic growth. The basic concern of individual-level modernization theorists is to identify the cultural variations between traditional and modern societies that are responsible for their divergent economic statuses.

One of the strongest and most influential statements on this issue is offered by Everett Hagen in his *On the Theory of Social Change* (1962). For Hagen, personality types and their behavioral manifestations are the source of social change. "The interrelationships between personality and social structure are such as to make it clear that social change will not occur without changes in personalities" (p. 86). As it happens, modern societies are possessed with *innovational personalities*, a psychological complex that should breed some version of the Schumpeterian entrepreneur. Traditional societies, on the other hand, are the recipients of a less flattering portraiture—the *authoritarian personality*.

The "innovative personality," according to Hagen, is the mirror image of the "authoritarian" type. Innovative individuals respond to new experiences and stimuli not with frustration but with a sense of understanding and imagination; they do not evade problems but are attracted to the challenge of dealing with new situations; they do not rely on fantasy or magic solutions because for them the world is orderly and understandable. If any anxiety exists among this personality type it is the "gnawing feeling that they are not doing enough, or not well enough" (p. 99). Anxiety is reduced through creative achievement. Members of traditional society, on the other hand, are uncreative.

He perceives the world as an arbitrary place rather than an orderly one amenable to analysis and responsive to his initiative. His unconscious processes are both inaccessible and uncreative. He resolves his relationships with his fellows primarily on the basis of ascriptive authority. He avoids the anxiety caused by facing unresolved situations in the physical world by reliance on the judgment of authority. (1962:98)

The psychology of development, expressed in Hagen's personality types, is also found in the work of Daniel Lerner (1958), whose study of Middle Eastern societies had an enormous impact on modernization theory. Lerner also identifies an ideal personality type, one he claims emerges from the experience of physical mobility in Western industrial society:

People in the Western culture have become habituated to the sense of change and attuned to its various rhythms. . . . We are interested in empathy as the inner mechanism which enables newly mobile persons to operate efficiently in a changing world. Empathy, to simplify the matter, is the capacity to see oneself in the other fellow's situation. This is an indispensable skill for people moving out of traditional settings. . . . It is a major hypothesis of this study that high empathetic capacity is the predominant personal style only in modern society, which is distinctively industrial, urban, literate, and participant. . . . To wit: social change operates through persons and places. . . . If new institutions of political, economic, cultural behavior are to change in compatible ways, then inner co-herence must be provided by the personality matrix which governs individual behavior. We conceive modernity as a participant style of life; we identify its distinctive personality mechanisms as empathy. (1958:47, 49–50, 78)

This empathetic style of life can be contrasted with Lerner's description of traditional society and people. Traditional societies, in his account, are nonpar-ticipant and characterized by a poorly developed division of labor. Traditional people are constrained by kinship ties and lack bonds of interdependence, their horizons are limited and parochial, their decisions involve only "known quan-tities" and familiar situations (Lerner 1958:50).

It should be noted here that Lerner's comparative descriptive analysis is also a well-known and familiar quantity as it conforms directly to the earlier obser-vations of Durkheim (1966) on the bases of social solidarity in traditional and modern societies, and Tonnies' (1963) *gemeinschaft* (traditional community) and *gesellschaft* (modern society) typology (see Chapter 1). The only difference is that Lerner employs these heuristic typologies as explanatory variables. Tradi-tional patterns of life, interaction, and decision-making are responsible for the traditional and backward state of the society. As with many of these kinds of models, cause and effect are muddled and it is difficult to establish whether beliefs and personalities are the cause or the consequence of traditionalism and modernity. Finally, in further differentiating the "participant" from "nonpar-ticipant" society, Lerner argues that in the modern participant society people are educated, highly informed, able to change jobs freely, and expected to hold opinions on important public matters. Traditional societies are characterized by just the opposite.

The influential work of David McClelland (1961) represents a further variant of the individual modernization approach. Instead of a work ethic, an innovative personality, or an empathetic participant orientation, McClelland argues that the central ingredient for economic progress is the presence in the population of a "need for achievement." According to McClelland, the motivational drive to overcome challenges, take risks, advance one's interests, and succeed for the sake of an inner feeling of accomplishment is derived from a national cultural context. His analysis indicates that this need for achievement is statistically associated with the socio-economic development level of nations. McClelland believes the need to achieve must be instilled in Third World populations if these nations are to develop economically.

This theory is not without systematic efforts at empirical verification, though methods and conclusions have been the subject of a great deal of debate. McClelland examined the content of popular documents, such as folk tales, children's stories, and textbooks from preliterate as well as modern societies, in an effort to gauge the cultural message disseminated and the extent to which it reflected the need for achievement. He then investigated the relationship between the level of the need for achievement displayed in the documents and socio-economic development. He found that the high need-for-achievement nations had higher levels of economic development. In spite of this innovative and interesting theory-testing strategy, little additional cross-national support has been garnered for the need-for-achievement formulation.

Inkeles and Smith (1974) provide yet another version of the individual modernization perspective. The classic sociological dichotomy differentiating traditional and modern societies is applied to individuals such that we find two kinds of people, those who are traditional in character and personality structure and those who are modern. Like McClelland, the authors construct an elaborate research methodology involving cross-national interviews and an overall modernization (OM) scale. The methodological sophistication and rigor of the research is impressive indeed, and the authors place a great deal of confidence in their findings. They define the "modern man" as follows:

> He is an informed participant citizen; he has a marked sense of personal efficacy; he is highly independent and autonomous in his relations to traditional sources of influence, especially when he is making basic decisions about how to conduct his personal affairs; and he is ready for new experiences and ideas, that is, he is relatively open-minded and cognitively flexible. (1974:290)

Inkeles and Smith believe that these basic attitudes and values support modern institutions and thus facilitate the modernization of society. They go on to note that modern institutions require people who can "discharge responsibility without constant close supervision"; who operate with trust, confidence, and sympathy toward co-workers and subordinates; who are "flexible and imaginative in the interpretation of roles" (1974:314–315). In sum, there is an identifiable modern personality type possessing a special set of traits which facilitate, and are compatible with, the process of modernization and economic development. A modern social structure requires modern individuals.

A third rendition of the modern individual model is found in the work of Clark Kerr and associates (1964). In their theory of industrialism they emphasize the particular value structure of industrial society:

In the industrial society science and technical knowledge have high values, and scientists and technologists enjoy high prestige and rewards. . . . Education also has a high value. . . . The industrial society is an open community encouraging occupational and geographic mobility and social mobility. Industrialization calls for flexibility and competition; it is against tradition based upon family, class, religion, race or caste . . . the work force is dedicated to hard work, a high pace of work, and a keen sense of individual responsibility for performance of assigned norms and tasks . . . industrialization requires an ideology and an ethic which motivate individual workers. (1964:25–26)

Unlike the previous formulations, there is greater ambiguity over whether these highly valued traits are the cause or the consequence of the industrialization process. In some sections of the work the standard causal order is reversed in dramatic fashion. Industrialism is viewed as an almost teleological force, having a purpose and logic all its own largely independent of social forces or forms of economic organization. Once industrialization takes hold other aspects of the society and polity conform to its imperatives. It is a package deal that includes only positive features. These are typically characteristics derived from advanced Western capitalist societies and seen as the inevitable by-product of the industrialization process.

This aspect of the theory of industrialism has given rise to *convergence theory*, the view that all industrial societies, regardless of political-economic philosophy, require certain values and modes of social organization. The ideologies that motivate and legitimate forms of authority and control, as well as the structure of control itself, are seen as imperatives of industrialism rather than the product of particular forms of social organization such as capitalism, socialism, or fascism. As societies industrialize they become more and more alike, and eventually converge, in their essential social, political, and economic features.

Many of the issues related to the industrialism theory are addressed in subsequent chapters on work organization and larger, societal-wide political economic arrangements. One component of the industrialism theory relevant to the individual level emphasizes the role of labor training, skills, and education. This "human capital" approach will be considered shortly.

A more contemporary version of the individual modernization approach is found in the work of Lawrence E. Harrison (1985). In his book with the revealing title *Underdevelopment Is a State of Mind*, Harrison (1985:xvi) argues that

more than any other of the numerous factors that influence the development of countries, it is culture that principally explains, in most cases, why some countries develop more rapidly and equitably than others. By "culture" I mean the values and attitudes a society inculcates in its people through various socializing mechanisms, e.g., the home, the school, the church.

Among the cultural traits most conducive for development, Harrison (1985: 6–7) cites a future (rather than present or past) time orientation, a rational orientation toward progress and change, and a belief in equality rather than hierarchical authority structures.

In order to provide supporting evidence for his thesis, Harrison conducts a comparative case study that includes an analysis of the development experiences and cultural traditions of Latin American nations, Australia, Spain, and the United States. After reviewing the historical, cultural, and economic patterns for the various nations, Harrison (1985:164–165) asks the central question:

> Is culture the principal determinant of the course and pace of development in the cases we have considered? . . . In each of the cases I have discussed, the world view of the society has expressed itself in ways that have affected the society's cohesion, its proneness to justice and progress, and the extent to which it taps human creative potential. And, I believe, those are factors that importantly explain why some societies are more successful than others.

More specifically, in explaining the socio-economic performance of Latin American nations, Harrison (1985:165) concludes that "In the case of Latin America, we see a cultural pattern, derivative of traditional Hispanic culture, that is anti-democratic, anti-social, anti-progress, anti-entrepreneurial, and at least among the elite, anti-work."

While this blanket indictment of Latin American culture may lead one to conclude that there is little hope for economic progress among the Hispanic-influenced nations of the world, Harrison provides a list of potential interventions that can change the values and attitudes of the population. He cites the role of exceptional leadership, religious reform, education and training, the media, development projects, management practices, and child-rearing practices as factors that can reshape cultural values in what he would view as a more positive direction.

Finally, the individual modernization perspective has been recently applied to the difficult transition currently underway in Eastern Europe and the former Soviet Union (see Chapter 5). This is best represented by the work of Piotr Sztompka (1997) who argues that in "investigating the dilemmas of the post-communism transition the most fruitful approach is cultural: the search for underlying *patterns for thinking and doing*, commonly shared among the members of society, and therefore, external and constraining with respect to each individual member." The indispensable cultural resource for a developed democratic market society to operate is labeled *civilizational competence*. This resource is a "complete set of rules, norms and values, habits and reflexes" that operate in and apply to four areas of modern society. *Enterprise culture* is required for participation in a market economy; *civic culture* for participation in a democratic polity; *discoursive culture* for participation in intellectual activities, and *everyday culture* for daily existence in "advanced, urbanized, technologically saturated and consumer-oriented society." According to Sztompka, the socialist legacy in Eastern and Central Europe "not only blocked the appearance of civilizational competency, but in many ways shaped a contrary cultural syndrome *civilizational incompetence.*" The further elaboration of this thesis entails the delineation of familiar polar opposites, or dichotomies, found in much of the modernization literature: private versus public spirit, past versus present orientation, fate versus human agency explanations, negative versus positive notions of freedom, mythology versus realism, East versus West, usefulness versus truth. As with the modernization formulations presented above, the post-communist nations fall on what is viewed as the negative side of each dichotomy. The "core cultural oppositions and biases typical of socialist societies, together with most of their psychological and behavioral expressions, have outlived the Communist system, and stand in the way of post-community reforms." In order to transcend this cultural dead end, Sztompka cites the role that will be played by education, globalization, exposure to Western culture, alternative cosmopolitan orientations, pressures emanating from technological progress, economic privatization, and gradual political democratization.

A CRITICAL ASSESSMENT OF INDIVIDUAL-LEVEL FORMULATIONS

There have been many criticisms of and problems raised with the individual-level modernization theories presented above. Some of these are aimed at the theoretical logic and assumptions made by the theorists, others point to the clear limits of these models as explanations for socio-economic growth. Portes (1976) presents a general critique that addresses several of the central problems with these theories. It is worth summarizing and elaborating some of his arguments.

Portes links the excessive emphasis on beliefs and values in modernization theory to the influence of *structural functionalism*. Structural functionalist theory dominated sociology in the 1950s and 1960s and viewed the cultural system—the value-normative features of society—as a leading source of social order, social structure, and social change. In this theory values and beliefs assumed a major explanatory role in understanding macro social phenomena. Subjective beliefs, operating at the individual level but shared by members of society, took precedence over objective structural forces in the explanation of social change. In turn, this led to a relative neglect of other factors, such as the organization of the economy, the material interests of different social classes, and the role of ideology.

A second difficulty identified by Portes concerns the "additive" nature of this model of social development, in which the transition to a modern industrial society is seen as a function of the number of people imbued with a particular set of Western values. Portes attributes this logic to the voluntarist position. In this formulation, individuals exercise free will and are therefore able to translate their subjective sentiments and desires into purposive action, unencumbered by structural obstacles and impediments. Thus, the greater the number of people who possess modern values, the greater the likelihood that the nation will experience socio-economic development.

Portes goes on to list three often neglected factors that must be considered in a sociological model of development. The first—*structural constraints*—is probably the most important, serving as a fundamental corrective to individual-level formulations. In contrast to the view of voluntarism, one must recognize the existence of structural constraints in the form of social organization and the distribution of material resources. These constraints place limits and obstacles not only on the emergence of certain value orientations and forms of behavior but also on the development of the larger society. Economic and political structures must be considered, and possibly transformed, in order for particular values and beliefs to have an impact on the developmental trajectory of a nation. For example, the set of values found in Inkeles' modern man—participant, independent, and autonomous—could only emerge and find expression in a society that possesses institutions that encourage and reinforce these traits. If societies lack these institutions, efforts to act on these beliefs are likely to produce violent struggle with entrenched interests and elites. Further, if we were to assume that all members of society could suddenly raise their "need for achievement," or some other praiseworthy level of consciousness, it is difficult to imagine that this would create a necessary and sufficient condition for the modernization or industrialization of society. More likely, we would then begin listing all the other societal features that would have to be adjusted for such a transformation to take place. This, in itself, is testimony to the limits of such a model and the need to consider these structural obstacles.

A second problematic aspect of the individual modernization approach to sociology of development, according to Portes, concerns those Western values whose impact might retard rather than promote economic development. Specifically, Portes cites "consumption-oriented" values. While these are an integral part of Western industrial culture, they may serve to stimulate excessive material demands that cannot be satisfied, or that place a strain upon existing resources more wisely directed toward other forms of investment. If we consider the behavior of those individuals in less-developed nations who have had the greatest exposure to Western values of entrepreneurship and consumption, we often find a legacy of elite behavior bordering on fraud, corruption, co-optation, and conspicuous consumption. The historical record is replete with documentation of the "comprador elite" who served, first and foremost, foreign multinational interests, or the wealthy landowning elite who squandered valuable foreign exchange in order to import Western luxury products. The larger point is that the internalization of Western values in non-Western, less-developed nations may prove as much an obstacle, as harbinger, to economic development.

This point is given further support in many recent writings on Western cultures that link individualism, consumerism, and economism to socio-economic crisis, stagnation, and decline. The very values which, in the individual modernization scheme, are elevated to the level of cultural prerequisites for growth are today deemed socially and economically destructive. The argument that this liberal tradition is now ''dysfunctional'' for the further expansion of advanced capitalism can be found in the work of Samuel Bowles and Herbert Gintis (1982) and James O'Connor (1984). The argument, exemplified in these theoretical accounts, contends that the most recent phases of economic crisis in the United States have stemmed from the unintended consequence of self-interested ''economism'' and the associated demands for higher wages, salaries, and profits as well as the expansion of welfare state programs. These can be regarded as political manifestations of ''possessive individualism'' that associates human freedom with the possession and accumulation of material goods.

The tension between the culture of individualism and the institutions of modern capitalism is further noted in the work of Abercrombie et al. (1986). Given that the contemporary corporate organization places the greatest emphasis on ''conformity to rules, deference and obedience to superiors, custodianship of other people's property, and collective organization instead of individual autonomy . . . individualistic traits bear no obvious functional relationship to the organizational forms typical of more recent capitalism'' (1986:138). More generally, the authors argue that the functional relationship between individualism and capitalism has been overstated and that the former is not a necessary prerequisite for the latter.

Again, contemporary developments would seem to support this assertion. The widespread fixation with corporate culture and a collective orientation among employees, as the most appropriate arrangement for corporate success, suggests the limited efficacy of the standard Western-based cultural traits. The contemporary case of Japan represents the most obvious challenge to this assertion, and there is no shortage of literature on the subject (Abercrombie et al. 1986:ch 5; Morishima 1983; Lehmann 1982; Cochran 1985; Dore 1973). The values of nationalism, paternalism, and anti-individualism are said to characterize modern Japan (Morishima 1983), and stand in significant contrast with Western value systems. Rather than obstacles to growth, these sentiments have been garnered in service to the most dynamic of contemporary capitalisms. Much of the success has been contingent on the interplay between the paternalistic and collectivist sentiments and the broader organizational structures that define Japanese industry. It is important to emphasize for the Japanese case the point which has been made for the Western experience—the culture values that are linked to economic success are not independent or autonomous but are reinforced and channeled in the context of objective organizational and societal structures and practices.

The main point of these various reassessments of the role of individualism and economic self-interest is *not* that these Western cultural traits played no role in the expansion of capitalism, but that in certain phases of capitalist development they may be impediments. One of the basic arguments of this chapter is that the "functionality" of individual attitudes, beliefs, behaviors, and cultural traits can only be assessed in relation to other structural features of society (or levels of analysis). Because these structural features have been transformed and altered, what was once regarded as a cultural necessity might now be viewed as problematic.

The *evolutionary character* of the individual modernization model represents the final point raised by Portes. This common criticism of the modernization model notes the historical and developmental path that is imposed on less-developed nations. In a typical scenario, traditional nations presumably follow the path of industrial societies as modern cultural values are diffused and internalized. This scheme does not recognize the historical legacy that has created the "traditional" societies as well as the national and world-economic structural constraints that make universal industrialization along Western lines highly unlikely. The qualitatively different nature of less-developed nations, a product of historical world-economic forces, suggests a very different future and developmental trajectory.

The evolutionary element in modernization theory stems from the "time-space fallacy" common to many models of social change. At any one point in time we will notice that significant differences exist between nations in gross national product, percent of the population living in urban areas, infant mortality, and other socio-economic dimensions. These are variations between spatial or geographic units. There is a tendency to impose a temporal causal logic to this kind of cross-sectional data. It is then assumed that the richer, more urbanized nations have been "developing longer," and that the poorer, less urbanized nations see, in the modern industrial nations, their inevitable future. Modernity becomes a function of time and the historical roots of contemporary problems of less-developed nations are disregarded. It is as if the process of development begins at some arbitrary moment when, according to modernization theory, less-developed nations are touched by modern values.

A number of additional criticisms of the individual-level modernization models can now be added to those identified by Portes. The first and most obvious concerns the *ethnocentric bias* that runs through most of the individual modernization accounts. This is the assumption that modern Western values are not only the exclusive source of development but that these cultural beliefs are also morally superior to those that exist in less-developed nations. What begins in this literature as a comparative description of cultural patterns and traits inevitably becomes a judgmental exercise about the moral goodness and correctness of these differential cultural systems coupled with an elevation of Western culture to a supreme status. The point here is not to argue for an extreme version of cultural relativism, one that precludes making value judgments about different cultural practices; rather, it is a reminder that one must be self-conscious of the extent to which ethnocentrism drives an analysis of the causal requisites for socio-economic development.

A second and related problem concerns the tendency to romanticize all aspects of modern society and degrade all features of less-developed society. The individual modernization literature is replete with comparative descriptions of modern and traditional societies that amount to little more than fictional accounts or invidious comparisons of ideal-type polar opposites. There is little empirical foundation for these comparative claims.

This tendency can be clearly seen in the previously cited work of Inkeles and Smith and is also applicable to the parallel formulation of Hagen, Lerner, and McClelland in the identification of particular character traits as "modern" (rather than traditional). For example, Inkeles and Smith believe that the modern person is characterized by: participatory political tendencies, a developed sense of efficacy, the ability to arrive at decisions autonomously and independently, and an open and flexible approach to new experiences and worldviews. Since this psycho-cultural mind-set is said to be not only related to, but the determinant of the level of modernization, we should find these character traits in ample supply among publics in modern industrial societies. However, in the United States, which is often held up as the embodiment of all that is modern, the most recent and best available evidence (Hamilton and Wright 1986) indicates that for the vast majority of citizens the major focus of life is the family, and the major concern is providing for the family and "making ends meet." Although typically associated with traditional societies, it appears that communal-kinship ties and basic economic concerns structure and shape the lives and routines of the world's most modern citizens.

Further, the characterization of the modern society and population as necessarily participant is also refuted by the evidence for the American polity: over half the eligible population in the United States does not even engage in the simplest of all acts—voting; most Americans are ill-informed about most issues and exhibit low levels of political sophistication (Converse 1964; Verba and Nie 1972); most prefer the "simple, concrete, or close to home" to the "remote, general, and abstract" (Converse 1964); and large proportions of the American population express feelings of political inefficacy, powerlessness, and distrust toward politicians and the political system (Wright 1976). All of this suggests that the modern participant society described by Inkeles and Smith, and Lerner, is a fictional account, or a utopian vision of some future citizenry and society. At minimum, this evidence casts doubt on the idea that participant personality traits are causally related to the level of socio-economic development. The modern person, as defined by these accounts, is a rare species indeed.

It should be emphasized that none of this is meant as an indictment of the American mass character structure. Nor is this a declaration of the traditional nature of American society. Rather, it is a statement about individuals that can only be understood within the broader context of the socio-economic organization of the society in which they operate. There is abundant evidence indicating that levels of participation and perceived efficacy and autonomy (the "modern" traits) are related to one's social class position. This suggests that the modern person is not a spontaneous creation, but a product of circumstance; that the opportunity for individuals to become modern in the sense described by Inkeles and Smith is not equally distributed within modern societies. Many of the praiseworthy modern traits identified by these theorists require resources of power, authority, and wealth. As these are unequally distributed and/or entirely absent for the vast majority of citizens; so too are many of the consequent personality traits. The same sort of stratification system that produces the differential socio-cultural experience across classes within a nation is mirrored at the cross-national level in such a way that variations in national-aggregate wealth and power are translated into personal experiences and attitudes that may appear either traditional or modern. The critical issue is the origin of these experiences and attitudes, how they relate to broader systems of power and inequality, and whether they determine socio-economic development.

This raises a related problem involving the values and attitudes that supposedly buttress modern institutions. Among these, again using the arguments of Inkeles and Smith, are the ability to accept and discharge responsibility without close supervision, to manifest mutual trust and confidence in co-workers, to subordinate special interests to the goals of the larger organization, to be flexible in the interpretation of rules. These alleged features of industrial organization are, in fact, rarely found, even in modern industrial societies. Rather, the organizational forms that have contributed to the development of modern industry involve hierarchy, inequality, supervision, and the rigid control of workers. In producing for profit and a world capitalist economy there has historically been little incentive to institute the participatory forms of industrial organization implied by Inkeles and Smith.

A third problem with these theories is that they are plagued by a *tautological* or *circular logic*. This logical problem is not confined to individual-level theories. It stems from a tendency to establish a tight and necessary relationship between two concepts or variables. Once this airtight relationship is established the two concepts become inseparable and the causal direction of the relationship is muddled. As an example, consider the following proposition: nations that industrialize possess the appropriate culture, those that fail to industrialize lack this culture. When nations decline, the culture is eroding; when they "take off," it is expanding. In this logical formulation the presence or absence of the requisite cultural value structure is determined a priori by the degree of industrialization and economic development—the effect (industrial development) automatically suggests the cause (appropriate culture). This kind of logic precludes the examination of alternative factors that might be equally or more important in explaining the phenomena in question.

A fourth problem, another causal fallacy, is the assumption that values and attitudes precede economic development. It is equally plausible that the psychological mind-sets of populations are the consequence rather than the cause of certain forms of development. It is the nature and course of socio-economic development that influences objective economic forces, material interests, and the proliferation of values and ideas. This point is related to the Weberian/ Marxist question concerning the primacy of ideas and/or objective material conditions. In the individual modernization models there has been a one-sided preference for the former.

A fifth and final criticism concerns the broad conceptual scheme used to organize the theories of socio-economic development in this book. It is vital that one recognize the *level-of-analysis fallacy* that is often built into the individual-level models. Individual-level theories are most useful when explaining differences between individuals. Theories of socio-economic development and social change, however, are primarily interested in explaining changes in the structure, organization, and level of economic output of nation-states. When one reduces changes in macro-level national units to the values, attitudes, and actions of individuals they are also leaping across numerous levels of analysis and reality that need to be integrated and incorporated into their explanatory model. One might choose to begin at the individual level in understanding socio-economic development, but this does not mean that a direct causal link can be advanced between individual-level cultural beliefs and values and the level of development and pace of change in the larger society. These values and beliefs play themselves out at organizational and societal levels of analysis which may accentuate, reinforce, negate, or modify their ultimate impact. Without considering how the cultural values and beliefs find expression in, or are in turn shaped by, these other levels of organization and social life, the model is incomplete. In short, the leap from the individual level of analysis to the large and broader national level omits too many important factors needed to understand the process of socio-economic development. This is a fundamental problem with many individual-level theories of development. In Andre Gunder Frank's (1969:67) critique of the individual modernization model, he states that it is:

inadequate precisely because the scale of their theory and hypotheses is already too small to treat adequately the dimension and structure of the social system which gives rise both to development and underdevelopment.

Or, as Valenzuela and Valenzuela (1984:112, 114) conclude:

Though there are variations in the literature, the *level of analysis* of a substantial tradition in the modernization perspective, and the one which informs most reflections on Latin America, is behavioral or micro-sociological. The primary focus is on individuals or aggregates of individuals, their values, attitudes, and beliefs. . . . And yet, precisely because modernization theory relies on a simple conceptual framework and a reductionist approach, it is far less useful for the study of a complex phenomenon such as development or underdevelopment.

While the above points have been critical of the individual-level models that stress the subjective/cultural determinants of socio-economic development, it is not the intent to argue that subjective/cultural forces are irrelevant for the study of social change. A legitimate and critical question involves the extent to which cultural factors support and influence objective social structures, organizational arrangements, and socio-economic policies. Note that in all of these instances the cultural values and sentiments are viewed in their interaction with other concrete levels of analysis. If we consider the latter—national-level development policies—one can make a case that differences in the socio-economic performance of nations can be attributed to distinct policies that are shaped by the historical cultural patterns of those nations. Of course, these policies find their expression in the actions of actors, organizations, and institutions. Nonetheless, they may be traced to a particular cultural orientation. Such an argument is suggested by Dore (1990) when he talks about the divergent developmental paths of East Asia versus Latin America. He notes that the East Asia nations, following the Japanese pattern, pursued a "model of collective effort to conquer foreign markets and move up the international pecking order of economic power." These nations also, according to Dore, possessed "purposeful states" that reflected a "will to develop," meaning "the salience of the achieving of sustained growth among the policy objectives of the people who were in a position to make policy decisions" (1990:358). Latin America, in contrast, is viewed as a region more heavily influenced by the American model that emphasizes "consumption patterns for individuals to strive for" and that the Latin American pattern represents "more of a drifters pattern, and countries with a substantial cushion of natural resources can more easily afford to drift" (1990: 358). Dore's comments suggest that particular policy choices and strategies are linked to particular cultural patterns, historical experiences, and the objective capacities of nations. Furthermore, the ability to legitimately pursue a development policy may be shaped by a nation's cultural fabric. Support for this argument is provided by a recent study by Sheridan (1996), who conducted in-depth interviews with Japanese officials from the Ministry of International Trade and Industry (MITI). He writes: "Japan's unique position cannot be overestimated for it derives from the historical need of the country to implement government planning to bring Japan into play as modern world economy. In so doing, its culture has supported the management of economic policy development" (Sheridan 1996:300).

Thurow's (1992a) analysis of Anglo-Saxon versus German and Japanese capitalism hinges on the notion that the former is based on "individualistic values" while the latter are characterized by "communitarian values." These differential value structures derive from the different historical experiences of the countries and their respective efforts to industrialize. While the Anglo-Saxon nations of Great Britain and the United States were on the leading edge of the Industrial Revolution, Germany and Japan were forced to play "catch-up." As a result, distinct national cultures were shaped that differed in the extent to which economic progress was viewed as either a collective or individual undertaking. In Germany and Japan the effort to make up lost ground was led by economic strategies that involved public and private cooperation and military-like mobilization of economic resources. In Great Britain and the United States, in contrast, economic development was led by individual entrepreneurs in the pursuit of self-interest or profit maximization. Today, according to Thurow, we find these historical paths have produced distinct national cultures—"individualistic capitalism" in Great Britain and the United States and "communitarian capitalism" in Germany and Japan. The strength of the various levels of Thurow's analysis is his linkage of these national cultures to institutions that indirectly and directly shape socio-economic outcomes. These include organizational management strategies, patterns of industrial organization, industrial and financial alliances, forms of government intervention, and levels of national administration planning and guidance. The tendency to establish and pursue, and the social legitimacy of, these various arrangements and policies are said to be shaped by the national cultures. Thurow (1992a:26) writes:

America and Britain champion individualistic values: the brilliant entrepreneur, Nobel Prize winners, large wage differentials, individual responsibility for skills, easy-to-fire-easy-to-quit, profit maximization, hostile mergers and takeovers . . .

. . . In contrast, Germany and Japan trumpet communitarian values: business groups, social responsibility for skills, team work, firm loyalty, growth-promoting industry and government strategies.

Thurow concludes that the communitarian forms of capitalism in Germany and Japan are more ideally suited to meet contemporary world-economic challenges. As we noted above in our discussion of the "functionality" of Western liberal culture, the assumptions made about the economic superiority of Western values is being challenged both by the economic performance of non-Western nations as well as observers who study the organizational and institutional manifestations of cultural patterns. Thurow clearly falls into this latter camp.

THE HUMAN CAPITAL APPROACH

Human capital is defined as an individual's productive skills, talents, and knowledge (Thurow 1970). Consistent with the work ethic and modernization approaches this theory is aimed at explaining growth and development by focusing on the characteristics of individuals. On the other hand, human capital theory recognizes that these traits are not inbred or cultural but developed and nurtured. Human capital theory has been used to explain wage differences between individuals (Becker 1964) but our interest is in the way investment in human resources promotes aggregate growth and welfare. Like physical capital, human capital can be improved, expanded, and made more productive through investment. Quite often this investment is undertaken by the government as there are society-wide benefits in expanding the educational, training, and health capacities of the population. In this view, then, the key to promoting productivity and economic growth is government investment in human capital (Psacharopoulos 1988). For example, Harbison (1973) contends that "the goals of development are the maximum possible utilization of human beings in productive activity and the fullest possible development of skills, knowledge and capacities of the labor force. If these goals are pursued, then others such as economic growth, higher levels of living, and more equitable distribution of income are thought to be likely consequences" (cited in Adelman and Morris 1973:101).

This basic idea is translated into the commonly held view that Third World poverty could be alleviated only if the people in these nations possessed modern technical skills and training. It should also be noted that the emphasis on education has links to the individual modernization models presented above. That is, through educational institutions individuals can be exposed to modern beliefs and values which, in turn, presumably affect their orientation toward work and achievement. Since we have already pointed to the limitations of this logic as an explanation for growth, we shall discuss the more direct economic role played by educational expansion.

Studies by the World Bank (1980:ch 5) suggest that there may be some payoff from investing in the expansion of primary education. Comparing farmers having four years of primary education with those who had none indicated that farm output was greater for the educated farmers. According to the authors of the report, "primary schooling is a training in how to learn, an experience in self-discipline and in working for longer-term goals" (1980:257). Apparently, this experience can be applied to the actual organization and management of agricultural production and have measurable consequences. In spite of the self-proclaimed strong and consistent support for their hypothesis linking primary education and agricultural productivity, the relevance of these findings for the broader population and economy is quite limited. This particular study was of self-employed farmers who owned and controlled their own productive resources. For the vast majority of the population, who own no productive property, the educational payoff is contingent, first, on employment (that is, finding a job), and, second, on the capital technology applied to the labor process. Neither of these conditions should be taken for granted. In short, the central question is whether and how expanding education and skills to the larger population will actually yield aggregate economic benefits.

The economic significance of skilled and educated labor lies not in the intrinsic social goodness of such a policy but in the potential "multiplier effects" of human capital investment. The conventional economic logic sometimes runs as follows: Skilled labor is more productive; productive labor produces goods more efficiently; efficient production results in higher profits and wages; higher wages stimulate demand; production to meet demand stimulates economic growth.

As applied to less-developed nations, there are a number of problems with this simple chain of causation. First, one must consider what incentives exist for expanding educational opportunities. For many poor nations that continue to specialize in the export of primary products there is no rational reason to expand mass educational facilities in any significant way, since job opportunities for the newly educated are quite scarce. It is important to take the structure of the economy into consideration when assessing what role education might play in the development process. If the economy cannot absorb educated labor, the educated are likely either to emigrate or create political difficulties for the existing regime. If the economy is unable to meet basic family subsistence needs, then it is unlikely that the young will have the luxury of investing in human capital, since they must spend the majority of their time working in order to support family members.

Further, education cannot, by itself, create productivity gains; it must be joined with appropriate machinery, technology, and material inputs. It is here that a number of problems and contradictions emerge. Many forms of productive technology reduce the skill requirements of the applied labor and thus counteract the demand for skilled and highly trained workers. There is also a tendency for modern technology to reduce the amount of labor required for production. This means the typical labor surplus found in less-developed nations goes unabsorbed and underutilized.

All of this suggests that human capital expansion is as much a consequence as a cause of certain forms of development. The positive association between aggregate educational attainment and level of development is suggestive, but the causal direction of this relationship is open to question. Does a supply of human capital create its own demand, or is the supply stimulated and effectively utilized under particular economic conditions? As with the individual modernization models, it is useful to consider what might happen if a poor nation suddenly possessed a highly educated, technically trained population. Would the economy automatically begin to grow rapidly? What countless adjustments would have to be made? Would the leaders of these countries be rejoicing or fleeing? While we can only speculate on the possible consequences, it is probably safe to say that many political, economic, and social structures would require modification and transformation. These changes would likely be opposed by privileged elites who have an interest in preserving the existing arrangements. In short, a simple change of individual capacities from uneducated to highly skilled is hardly a sufficient condition for development. Some may even argue that such a change will generate social regression and ''political decay'' (e.g., Huntington 1968).

The enthusiasm that originally accompanied the idea of educational expansion in less-developed nations has turned to frustration as the limits to such strategies have been realized. In spite of increasing educational enrollments and spending, poverty has not been reduced and equitable growth has not been achieved. There are many reasons, in addition to those above, for the failure of education to serve as the motor of development (see Simmons 1979). Much of the skepticism already expressed about the ability of education to serve as a motor of development is echoed in the observations of John Simmons, who has studied extensively international education policy:

The experience of the past 30 years indicated that most education strategies have failed to promote development, if development is conceived primarily as a process of improving the lives of the deprived majority of the world's population. . . . That the poor are becoming discouraged is revealed by falling primary-school enrollment rates in countries like Egypt, Nigeria and Pakistan. . . . In a few countries that got an early start, the nightmare of rioting students demanding jobs and a new government, or of a third of the school budgets being spent on children who drop out of primary school before reaching the third grade has become reality. (1983:263)

Simmons' illustrations from the Pakistan experience are equally sobering:

Unemployment rates appear to be significantly higher among the educated than among the uneducated; forty percent of vocational school graduates are unemployed for 2–4 years after graduation; nine out of 10 pharmacy graduates leave the country. (1983:265)

His basic conclusion is that one cannot understand the consequences of individual exposure to education and training without a consideration of the broader levels of analysis that include the political, social, and economic systems of a nation. Studies confirming this position indicate that the translation of human capital expansion into economic growth requires, at minimum, the active intervention of the state coupling the educational system to the needs of the economy (Hage et al. 1988).

Placing these conclusions in the context of a levels-of-analysis framework, the point is that changing an individual's, and by extension the population's, level of educational attainment cannot be expected to automatically produce dynamic productive economic activity at either the individual or larger collective level. Work organizations and societal institutions must facilitate and channel individual human capital into productive and innovative directions. It should be noted that contemporary analyses of national economic growth and global competitiveness are reasserting the importance of human capital. The critical role played by technological innovation, and the rise of the knowledge economy, have served to place human capital in a leading position as a predictor of national socio-economic success (Reich 1991; Thurow 1992b; Romer 1986). We shall examine this factor in the context of broader levels of analysis in the chapters to follow.

NOTES

1. The relationship between the Protestant ethic and the rise of capitalism is a long-debated issue in sociology, and in social theory more generally. For further discussion of the issue and a systematic critique see Hamilton (1996:ch.3).

2. On the question of the relationship between individualism and capitalism, see Abercrombie et al. (1986).

3. For a very different perspective on human behavior see Etzioni (1988).

4. For a discussion of the work ethic concept, see Barbash et al. (1983).

3

Organizations and Development

> Although organizations are only one type of institution . . . they are critical to economic development. Most goods and services are produced by organizations and most development projects are implemented by them. In fact, the production function actually takes place in organizations, because capital, labor, technology, human capital, and materials are utilized by organizations and transformed into goods and services. Therefore, if organizations can be made more productive, the economy will grow and people will be better off generally. (Hage and Finsterbusch 1987)

In this chapter we shift to the organizational level of analysis as an explanation for socio-economic development. If we consider the level-of-analysis scheme outlined in Chapter 1, there are two directions in which organizations can exercise an influence—downward on the individual level and upward on the societal and international levels. Since we have just reviewed the individual-level models, and noted that a major shortcoming involves insufficient attention to the impact of broader structural forces, we should begin by noting that most productive human economic behavior takes place in an organizational context. Organizations specify, implicitly and explicitly, obligations, duties, roles, functions, tasks, specialties, means and ends, and rules and regulations. Thus, individual interests and motives are shaped by organizational forces and these may have further consequences for broader forms of social and political change. One of the purposes of this chapter is to fill in some of the gaps left by the individual-level models by examining organizational structures and organizational arrangements, as well as the interests that are served and shaped in work organizations.

The upward influence of organizations has a more direct connection to socio-

economic development. The efficiency and productivity of formal work organizations contribute to the gross national product and the rate of economic growth.
The primary focus is on organizations that have been deliberately formed for
the production of goods and services for direct consumption and/or sale in a
market.

We begin with a discussion of agricultural organizations and their impact on
socio-economic and political behavior. The second section takes up the question
of the transition from agricultural to industrial organizational forms and some
of the consequences of this transformation. This is followed by a review of
organizational theories and techniques that have been linked to economic development in industrial societies as well as less-developed nations. The chapter
concludes with a consideration of the transnational corporate organization.

AGRICULTURAL ORGANIZATIONS

Agriculture, as a sector, accounts for well over half the labor force in less-
developed countries. Among the nonindustrial developing countries an average
of 58% of the labor force is employed in the agricultural sector. For these
nations, the organization of agriculture is a central determinant of individual-
level motives, interests, and behavior, as well as a critical factor influencing the
growth rate of the economy. Where agricultural organizations produce for export
they are linked to international market forces and serve as a leading source of
foreign exchange. Changes in the organization and productivity of agriculture
also will affect the migration of human populations from rural to urban areas.
In short, many of the forces of social change in less-developed nations are tied
directly to the organization of agricultural enterprises.

Land Tenure Systems and Socio-economic Development

Individual-level modernization models have been used to explain the agricultural performance of less-developed economies. The logic should now be
familiar: The traditional and backward beliefs of farmers discourage productive
agricultural development. Agricultural development requires modern entrepreneurial values that not only promote the utilization of modern productive technology but also encourage a shift from subsistent to surplus agricultural
production. In the absence of such a value structure, agricultural producers will
be unable to respond to dynamic market opportunities, and agricultural development will stagnate.

In this chapter organizational forces and structures are introduced as causal
factors shaping work-related values and behavior. This represents a first step in
transcending narrow, individual-level models of development and social change.
From this perspective, if we look beyond the presumably deficient cultural values held by farmers, we may discover that the structural organization of work
explains a good part of their economic behavior. A student of agricultural ec-

onomics provides one alternative explanation for the risk-averse behavior of subsistence farmers, "the economic advantages turned out to be illusory—the landlord secured all the gain; the moneylender skimmed off the cream; the government guaranteed price was not in fact paid; the cost structure made the new innovation unprofitable" (Wharton 1983:235). In short, economic experiences and associated property systems can create disincentives and uncertainties that reduce the likelihood of entrepreneurial adventurism. Rather than blaming agricultural producers and subsistent farmers for holding the wrong values, we should interpret their behavior in light of existing organizational structures and economic experience. This requires an analysis of the effects of organizational arrangements. For the case of agriculture this means, first and foremost, a consideration of land tenure systems.

Land tenure systems refer to the ownership, reward, and utilization pattern of agricultural enterprises and the relationship between the owners and the producers of agricultural output. Patterns of land tenure have changed dramatically over the course of history and vary widely from country to country. It is clear, however, that land tenure systems exercise an enormous influence on the behavior of producers and the social, economic, and political development of nations.

What might first appear as irrational behavior in the face of economic opportunities is often, upon closer examination, rational and sensible within the context of particular land tenure systems and associated incentive structures. The incentive to invest time, money, and/or human energy will depend upon the system of land ownership and the way in which the fruits of labor are distributed and utilized. Under conditions of coercion, poor treatment, exploitation, or inequitable distribution, peasants are apt to behave in an "irrational," "unmotivated," or "unproductive" fashion. This behavior has less to do with any intrinsic cultural value system than the particular organizational arrangement governing agricultural production.

The relationship between the organization of production and the level of motivation among agricultural workers, known as the "tenure and incentive problem," is a fundamental fact of agricultural development. In a widely used economic development text, Gillis et al. (1987) point to the disincentives that emerge when farmers are unable to receive benefits from increased effort because they do not own the land. Under a wage labor system, where owners hire workers for a set wage, special techniques have to be devised to motivate the workforce. A "piece rate" method might be employed which pays workers by the number of units harvested. This system tends to be less successful in agriculture than industry, however, given the lag time between cultivation and harvest, the difficulties in supervision, and the inability to measure output accurately.

Other tenure systems, such as communal and collectivized agriculture, also have built-in incentive structures. Under communal systems there is common land ownership but a disincentive to improve the land because benefits are too widely distributed rather than directly returned to the individual. Collectivized agriculture combines common ownership with an accounting system of individual labor input that provides the basis for a distribution of output based on the amount of time and effort expended. In the end, many advocate the family farm as the system best able to motivate farmers, but the economies of scale make this system less feasible and inherently inefficient for large-scale agricultural needs.

The structure of land tenure can also serve as a central variable explaining social movements and political change. In a study of land reform and political development, Prosterman and Riedinger (1987) use variation in land tenure systems to predict revolutions and political upheavals in less-developed nations. Land tenure is said to influence the probability of civil violence through its effect on the individual-level sentiment of "relative deprivation," defined as "deprivation relative to one's own expectations for oneself" (1987:7). According to this model, tenure arrangements that fail to distribute a sufficient return to agricultural producers in accordance with their expectations can stimulate radical and oppositional political action.

Prosterman and Riedinger also link land tenure arrangements to labor productivity and the rate of economic growth. They divide land tenure systems into three major types: tenant farm/agricultural labor systems, small owner-operator farming systems, and collective farming systems. With few exceptions, the authors conclude, based on their cross-national data, that the owner-operator systems are the most productive followed by collective farming and, as the least productive, tenant/labor systems. These differences in productivity are attributed to the differential incentive structures of the tenure systems. The incentive to invest time, energy, and resources in enhancing the productivity of the land is strongly related to the perception that these investments will be rewarded by a fair and proportional share of the output. Under the owner-operated system, expected and actual returns are greatest and most certain. Under sharecropping and tenant systems the returns are both smaller and less certain.

A more elaborate typology of land tenure systems is found in Stinchcombe's (1961) model of agricultural enterprises. Stinchcombe confines his analysis to commercial agriculture and describes five types of enterprise. Four of these are considered here: the manorial system, family-size tenancy, the family smallholding, and the plantation. Stinchcombe's purpose is to demonstrate that each of these enterprise types gives rise to distinct rural class systems. The rural class systems can then be distinguished by the class differences in legal privileges, style of life, knowledge of the technical culture, and political activity between owners and producers.

The *manorial* or *hacienda system* is characterized by feudal social and political arrangements. The manor lord is bestowed with legal rights over the land, the peasant population, and the agricultural product cultivated by the peasants. Peasants are given access to small plots of land that provide for subsistence consumption needs. The landed elite pursue an aristocratic style of life influenced by international fashion and the conspicuous consumption of material goods. The landed elite also tend to be heavily involved in political affairs and depend on the political apparatus to enforce their rights over land and peasants. The peasants, in contrast, are isolated and excluded from national affairs and are politically weak and unorganized. The one asset possessed by the peasantry is knowledge of cultivation practices and techniques, but the independent exercise of these skills is not widely entertained.

In the *family-size tenancy* enterprise, labor is carried out by an extended family unit but the land is owned by rentier capitalists. Thus, the agricultural laborers pay a rent in the form of money or a portion of the agricultural product. Prosterman and Riedinger (1987) have suggested that levels of relative deprivation may be most pronounced under this type of system. Stinchcombe (1961) emphasizes that this enterprise is the most politically unstable. A number of structural features contribute to the political volatility of this arrangement.

First, the division of the agricultural product is clear and apparent, in that the rent paid to the landowner is a direct deduction from the farmer's potential income. Second, rental arrangements usually include provisions ensuring that the risks of failure are borne by the farmer rather than the rentier. Although many conditions affecting the agricultural yield are beyond the control of farmers, they are under constant pressure to meet their rent obligations. Third, there are sharp distinctions between the farmer and rentier styles of life and residential location. Rentiers are absentee in the sense that they tend to live in urban centers and have little direct contact with tenants. Finally, under this system the farmer is perfectly capable of performing all required agricultural tasks independent of the rentier, who is regarded more as a parasitic than productive force. For all these reasons, the political interests of the two classes tend to diverge sharply and the farmer has a visible object toward which to direct discontent. As Stinchcombe remarks, "it is of such stuff that many radical populist and nationalistic movements are made" (1961:168).

The *family smallholding* can be distinguished from the family tenancy enterprise in that the farmer is able to secure all or most of the agricultural product. As indicated above, this system is most likely to create the greatest incentives among the direct producers for enhancing productivity and output. Since there are no lords or rentiers to skim off the surplus, the primary concern of farmers under this system is the market price of their agricultural commodities. There are, however, creditors who may have loaned the small farmers significant sums. Thus, stable prices are often necessary in order to meet regular debt payments. Politically, then, these farmers can be quite active in pushing for stable commodity prices and opposing banking interests. Differences between family farmers and the rural upper classes in legal rights and style of life tend to be small.

Plantation agricultural enterprises are typically found where labor-intensive crops are cultivated, such as coffee and sugar. The plantation system comes closest to approximating the industrial factory. Workers are hired and paid a wage (though in some instances slave labor may be used) and they are directed by managers and administrators. In this sense the actual laborers do not possess the technical know-how required to cultivate and harvest the crop. The large-scale nature of plantation agriculture also involves substantial capital investment. Landowners under this system have a direct interest in and make a direct contribution to the productive and efficient use of resources. There are sharp divisions between the landowner class and agricultural laborers. The latter often come from racial/ethnic minority groups who are highly exploited and systematically excluded from urban industrial job opportunities. Where the labor force is recruited from other regions or nations, and employed on a seasonal basis, they may also lack basic citizenship and residence rights. Landowners, in contrast, usually possess considerable political clout and, as capitalists, may own enterprises in a variety of other industries.

Stinchcombe's typology of rural enterprises provides a useful framework linking organizational structures with socio-political behavior. Some of the basic elements of Stinchcombe's typology are found in the rich and sophisticated study of export agriculture and political movements by Jeffery Paige (1975). Paige examines the social relationships between, and the sources of income for, rural cultivators (farmers) and noncultivators (landowners) in the export sector of less-developed economies. Based on the income source of the two classes, Paige offers some expectations about the likely form of political conflict and development.

Paige's theoretical and empirical account is an exemplary model of multilevel social science research. Individual-level motives, forms of land tenure, socio-economic systems, and world-economic forces are brought together in his theory of rural class conflict. Rural relations and conflict are empirically examined using both cross-national and case study data. In its most simplified form, Paige's theory of rural class conflict hinges on the different income sources of cultivators (agricultural workers and/or peasants) and noncultivators (landed aristocrats or capitalist property owners) and the political interests and motives that stem from these organizational and social class positions.

Table 3.1 summarizes the four forms of land tenure that emerge from the land-wages/land-capital income basis of cultivators and noncultivators, and the likely course of socio-political movements. For the commercial hacienda, land is the income source for both cultivators and noncultivators and this determines their respective political behaviors. The noncultivators derive their income from land and tend to be economically weak. They therefore must rely upon extra-economic or political forms of intervention and coercion in order to control cultivators and maintain their privileged position. They are also likely to view conflict in zero-sum terms. This means that any gain by or concession to cultivators in the form of land or income is regarded as a direct loss to the noncultivating class. The cultivators or peasants, who depend on access to land for their survival, are hesitant to take political risks, are more prone to competition than cooperation with other peasant cultivators, and are

Table 3.1
Paige's Model of Agricultural Organization and Social Movements

	Source of Income for:		
Type of Land Tenure System	Labor/ Cultivators	Owners/ Noncultivators	Political Outcome
Commercial Haciendas	land	land	Agrarian Revolt
Sharecropping/Migratory	wages	land	Socialist/Nationalist Revolution
Small Holding	land	capital	Commodity Reform
Capitalist Plantation	wages	capital	Labor Reform

Source: Adopted from Paige (1975:11), figure 1.1.

more closely integrated with and dependent on noncultivators than their fellow cultivators.

All this adds up to a peasant population that is unlikely to engage in collective political organization and struggle. However, the combined effect of a peasantry heavily dependent on access to land, and an intractable landed elite, creates a certain form of conflict, "the form of social movement most common in the commercial hacienda system might be best described as an agrarian revolt—a short intense movement aimed at seizing land but lacking long-run political objectives" (Paige 1975:43).

In contrast with the hacienda, the plantation is an agricultural system where cultivator income is derived from wages, and noncultivator income from capital investments. These income sources also have consequences for political behavior. Noncultivators who rely on returns from capital investment in machinery and factories do not define conflict in a zero-sum manner. Capital investments typically increase labor productivity such that wage concessions can be granted out of an expanded agricultural surplus. Because the noncultivators rely on wage labor, they tolerate the free movement of cultivators and assume that labor market forces will ensure an adequate supply of workers. In this way they are less dependent on the direct coercion of the state to maintain an adequate labor supply. The wage-labor cultivators under this system can also be distinguished from their hacienda counterparts by their inclination to take greater political and economic risks because they do not depend on access to land and are not involved in direct competition with their fellow cultivators. The net result is a greater incentive and likelihood for political organization and solidarity.

Paige notes that the agricultural organization of the plantation satisfies many of the very conditions that Marx associated with the development of proletariat political action.

Payment of wages in cash or in kind, . . . creates economic incentives for collective political action, intense class solidarity. . . . The agricultural export economy . . . creates a homogeneous, unskilled labor force with little or no internal stratification and no prospect for upward mobility. Economic gains can seldom be realized at the expense of other workers but rather in most cases, only through economic pressure on the employer. . . . The agricultural wage laborer seems to illustrate the characteristics that Marx believed were essential for the mobilization of the industrial proletariat. . . . While it has become commonplace to observe that Marx's revolutionary prediction remains unfulfilled in industrial societies, this fact does not invalidate his original hypothesis concerning economic conditions and class consciousness. . . . In the agricultural export economy, however, these economic conditions have persisted long after they have disappeared in industrial societies. The homogeneous poorly paid, concentrated mass of workers that Marx saw as the vanguard of the revolution are found not in industrial societies, but in commercial export agriculture in the underdeveloped world. It is in such societies that the greatest incentives for class-based organization and class conflict exist. (1975:33–34)

In order to understand why a more radical outcome does not actually occur, we must consider the interests and behavior of the noncultivating class. The expected form of political social movement emerging from the plantation is what Paige (1975:49) calls the "reform labor movement because the powerful noncultivating class in this agricultural system is in a position to make economic concessions to a well-organized agricultural proletariat."

For the "mixed types" of agricultural organization, the smallholding and sharecropping systems, there are also distinct political movements. In "smallholding" agriculture, where labor continues to receive income from control and access to land, and noncultivators receive returns from capital, a reform movement also emerges. However, the conflict is not distributional but over agricultural commodity markets and prices.

In the sharecropping system, the most explosive results are nurtured because it pits a rigid noncultivating class against a politically mobilized agricultural proletariat. The result is "agrarian revolution" where the demands of cultivators can be met only through the forceful appropriation of land and political power from the noncultivating elite.

The study by Paige is just one especially outstanding example of the relationship between land tenure systems and socio-political development. The results of his case study and cross-national analyses indicate the significant influence of organizational arrangements on individual motives and interests, political movements, and social change.

The Transition to Capitalist Agriculture

Much of the writing on the changing organization of agricultural production in less-developed societies employs the standard traditional-modern dichotomy, or what is often called the *dual society thesis*. This perspective views less-developed nations as transitional—they contain both distinct modern-industrial and traditional agricultural economic sectors. The traditional agricultural sector is assumed to be backward, feudal, subsistence-oriented, stagnant, and archaic.

The feudal landowning elite are, in this model, inefficient in their use of the surplus appropriated from the peasants. Excessive consumption and minimal capital investment are the twin character flaws of the feudal elite. Their behavior, and that of the peasants, is tied to the precapitalist organizational structure that dictates near-subsistence production by peasants and the squandering of surplus by feudal landowners.

The solution to the problem of inefficiency in agriculture, according to the dual society thesis, involves the diffusion of capitalist market forces. These will stimulate the efficient use of productive resources. Landowners will reduce costs, introduce modern productive techniques, expel redundant peasant labor and, overall, expand both the size of the agricultural surplus and the rate of profit. This scenario and prescription parallel the logic of the cultural diffusion or modernization model, only here it is applied to economic sectors within a single nation. Agricultural development and expansion is fueled as capitalism penetrates the feudal sectors. The spread of capitalism transforms traditional and stagnant agriculture into a modern, prosperous, and productive economic sector.

While there are many critiques of the dual society thesis (some of which lay the groundwork for dependency theories examined in Chapter 6) the feudal/capitalist division, as we have seen, informs many of the existing typologies of agricultural organization. Studies of Latin American agriculture typically draw the distinction between the hacienda and the plantation (Wolf and Mintz 1957; Stinchcombe 1961). The hacienda is the large estate that maintains vestiges of feudalism in the social relations between the large landowners and the dependent peasant labor force. The labor force is not free and mobile but "tied to the land" and in a servile relationship with the landowning elite. The hacienda is viewed, in this typology, as a highly inefficient form of production that directs a large portion of the surplus to conspicuous forms of luxury consumption in order to bolster the aristocratic image of the feudal elite.

At the other end of the typology are the plantations which more closely resemble capitalist forms of organization in that the labor force is hired for a wage, owners are oriented toward the maximization of profit through modern cultivation techniques, and the surplus is reinvested in production. For these reasons the plantations are said to be more efficient and dynamic.

In addition to differentiating the capitalist versus feudal nature of land tenure systems, there is the issue of how agricultural organization evolves from feudal to capitalist forms, and the consequence of this process for political and economic development. Lenin (1964) presented a model of two roads to capitalist agricultural development based on experiences in Prussia and the United States. In the former case, known as the "junker road," feudal landowners become capitalists as they convert production to large-scale commercial purposes, evict peasants from the land, hire wage laborers, and modernize production techniques. This account is based on the history of the Prussian junker class.

A different path to capitalist agriculture is represented by the "farmer road." In this model capitalist agriculture emerges from the activity of small farmers who gain access to land through social revolution, land reform, or redistribution programs. In the United States small farmers gained a foothold through the colonization of westward territories and the homesteading acts that encouraged the movement of individual farmers to previously remote and uncultivated locations. This is usually considered the most progressive and productive road.

The various roads to commercial agriculture have also been linked to national political development. Perhaps the most elaborate theoretical and comparative historical account of the various "roads" is provided by Barrington Moore (1967). Moore explains the political outcomes in a number of different nations (Britain, United States, France, Japan, India, Germany, and China) with reference to the class structure and the class alliances that existed and emerged in the transition to commercial agriculture. He identifies three major routes.

The first path is the "bourgeois revolution," which was followed in nations like the United States and Britain. The bourgeois road involves a fairly thorough transformation of the landed elite into capitalists such that they dissolve feudal peasant relations and apply rational production methods to agriculture production. These conditions are said to promote the flowering of liberal democratic institutions.

The second path, the "revolution from above, is associated with the historical experience of Germany and Japan. This path entails a strong landed elite who resist liberal reforms and maintain their hold over commercial agricultural production under conditions of serfdom or slavery. The strong and repressive political methods required to enforce this system, typically in alliance with a weak bourgeoisie, are said to lay the groundwork for the associated political system of fascism.

The third path, represented by the experience of China and Russia, is labeled "peasant revolutions." The absence of a commercial revolution in agriculture initiated by a landowning elite results in the persistence of feudal peasant institutions. These institutions, unchallenged by a significant bourgeois sector, are unable to manage the stress and strains of prolonged repression. The end result is said to be a peasant revolution and the institutionalization of Communism.

A more recent and comprehensive analysis of the relationship between capitalist development and democracy by Rueschemeyer, Stephens, and Stephens (1992) has largely supported the work of Paige and Moore. While their study examines a wide range of comparative cases and societal-level explanatory factors, the authors place considerable emphasis on the forms of agricultural organization, both capitalist and precapitalist, and the dependence of agriculture on a large supply of cheap labor. "Large landlords, particularly those who depended on a large supply of cheap labor, consistently emerged as the most antidemocratic force in the comparative studies" (Rueschemeyer et al. 1992:270). In this scenario it is less the reaction of the agricultural laborers to a repressive labor system than the pressure by landlords to maintain a nondemocratic state apparatus that drives the long-term political outcome.

The Formal Subordination of Labor and Functional Dualism

One of the preconditions for capitalist agricultural production is the *formal subordination of labor*, the process by which individuals are separated from control over and access to productive property. This process is also referred to as "proletarianization," meaning that a proletariat, or working class, is created as the number of people who own or control productive property declines. Without any independent means of survival, individuals are forced to work for someone else or "sell their labor power for a wage." Capitalist production for profit requires a workforce that can be hired and exploited. In the rural context, the formal subordination involves the dismantling of the hacienda, the eviction of peasants from their plots of land, and the demise of small independent farmers who are bought out or driven out of business. A labor force of workers is then created who can be hired by capitalist landowners interested in agricultural production.

If we confine our attention to the rural context, the formal subordination of labor can produce three possible outcomes. First, there might be a *labor equilibrium*, in which all the workers released from hacienda and independent agricultural arrangements find work and are absorbed by the plantation system as wage labor. A second possibility is a *labor shortage*, in which the plantations are unable to find significant sources of labor and therefore must recruit workers from other areas either voluntarily or coercively. The third and most common experience is *labor surplus*, in which the number of formally subordinated individuals exceeds the number of jobs in plantation agriculture. This result is an extended transition to capitalist agriculture and a system of *functional dualism*.

The system of functional dualism is described by deJanvry (1981) in his analysis of the transformation and crises of Third World agriculture. Based primarily on the experience of Latin America, deJanvry notes that a significant portion of the evicted peasant population, unable to find employment in rural areas, is forced to settle on unclaimed plots of land in proximity to capitalist plantations. On these plots, peasant families cultivate crops for home consumption and, if a surplus is produced, for sale in a local market. Some family members may be employed in the plantation, while others devote their labor to the family plots. DeJanvry describes this as a form of "dualism" because capitalist plantation agriculture and family subsistence agriculture exist side by side.

In contrast with the dualism described by dual society theorists, under functional dualism the capitalist and peasant forms of production are mutually dependent and closely linked. This dualism is regarded as "functional" in the sense that profit levels in capitalist agriculture are enhanced by the existence of the family subsistence sector.

DeJanvry describes the labor force in capitalist agriculture as only *semiproletarianized* because many of the workers and/or their families have access to, and derive income from production on, subsistence plots. They are not fully proletarianized because they have access to and control productive agricultural property. This allows wages in the plantation sector to be kept very low because the workers and/or their families grow much of their own food and therefore do not require money income to purchase foodstuffs. The "subsistence" plots may also produce a marginal surplus which can be sold in local markets. This further contributes to low wages in the capitalist plantation sector because relatively cheap food is available to those workers who purchase food from local producers. Finally, the settlement of peasant families in proximity to the capitalist plantation sector creates a "reserve army of labor" that undercuts the bargaining power of plantation workers and further reduces wage levels in the capitalist sector. The local peasant subsistence economy, therefore, serves to subsidize wage costs and increase profit and is therefore a vital ingredient in the logic of the transitional rural economy. The long-term effect of this arrangement, however, is the eventual and total subordination of the rural masses and abject rural poverty.

This outcome is based on the behavior of rural producers, which is a consequence of the survival strategies dictated by the system of functional dualism. There is constant pressure to increase the volume of production on the subsistence plots to create a surplus that can be sold in local markets. This provides access to cash income and allows the purchase of various market goods. Over time, however, the intensive use of the soil produces progressively smaller yields, as the land becomes less and less fertile.

Human fertility, on the other hand, is quite high because children are required as part of the family labor force that produces for home consumption and, where possible, the local market. Again, it is imperative to note that the fertility behavior of peasants is in large part a consequence of the economic organizational arrangements under which they live. DeJanvry describes it thus:

> Individual economic rationality does not exist in the abstract—it is conditioned by the social position of the household relative to productive resources and to the social division of labor. It is also conditioned by the absolute income level relative to the consumption and security needs of the couple. In peasant agriculture, poverty implies pressure to seek control over additional productive resources. Since producing children is often the only means whereby peasants can secure access to additional resources, more children are raised in order to increase the labor applied to a fixed piece of land so that it not fall below subsistence level. (1981:89)

The human population expands as the economic carrying capacity of agriculture declines. As deJanvry clearly documents, the net result of this process is rural overpopulation, impoverishment, and misery.

The lesson to be learned from the various studies of land tenure systems and the transition to capitalist agriculture is that the organization of production is an important explanatory variable for understanding human political-economic behavior and socio-economic and political change. Cultural values and motivational systems cannot be taken as given but must be linked to the conditions of material existence and modes of economic survival. It is difficult to isolate these factors from the broader structures of national social systems or the forces of the world economy. A complete and systematic analysis requires that connections be made both downward—to the individual level—and upward—to the level of social institutions and the international economy.

INDUSTRIALIZATION: FROM RURAL TO URBAN ORGANIZATIONS

The process of industrialization involves the geographic migration of the population from rural to urban areas and the organizational shift from agricultural to industrial employment. There are many neat and abstract theories that describe these processes as smooth and self-regulating, in which workers migrate from rural labor surplus to urban labor shortage sectors of the economy, in which labor supply and labor demand reach equilibrium. There are also expectations about the relationship between industrial development and urbanization.

What should first be emphasized is that the allocation of labor from rural to urban economies in less-developed nations has not conformed to the conventional models. A great deal has been written about the population explosion in the less-developed world, the crowded cities, the massive squatter settlements, and the urban shantytowns. The term *overurbanization* refers to excessive urban population growth relative to the carrying capacity of the industrial urban economy. At one time it was common to equate urbanization with progress, modernization, and development. This association was based on experiences in Western Europe and North America during the major phases of industrial expansion. However, for the contemporary Third World, industrial development and employment has not kept pace with urban population growth. In many less-developed nations, particularly middle-income countries, urbanization rates approach or equal those found in the advanced capitalist states, but it is "urbanization without industrialization." In Peru, for example, 71% of the population resides in urban areas but only 12% are employed in industry. Most observers agree that this type of "hyperurbanization" is the result of massive rates of rural-to-urban migration alongside the sluggish growth of the urban industrial economy.

Standard models of population migration explain the geographic shift of human population as a combination of "push" and "pull" factors. *Push factors* are those forces at the point of departure that encourage the population to leave a geographic location. In rural-to-urban migration these are characteristics of the agricultural economy and rural enterprise, such as the mechanization of agriculture, the erosion of the soil, rural poverty, the eviction of peasants, the shift to export cash crops, and rural overcrowding. These factors affect the ability of the rural population to work and survive in the countryside.

Pull factors are those features of the urban environment, such as "city lights," income opportunities, higher wages, industrial jobs, and kinship ties, that encourage and attract population settlement in urban areas. While the explanation for migration involves some combination of these push and pull factors, the failure of the rural economy is one necessary condition facilitating excessive rates of rural-to-urban migration. Where prospects for rural survival are deteriorating or have evaporated, labor is forced to migrate to areas where work and income opportunities exist. These are usually the towns and urban centers.

Once migrants arrive at their urban destination, they must deal with the problems of finding employment and housing. Expectations for employment are often dashed because the urban labor market is unable to generate a supply of jobs to meet the swelling demand. Survival in the urban economy often requires, therefore, innovation and resourcefulness. This is reflected in the informal economic activities that are engaged in by a substantial portion of the urban population. Studies of these activities in less-developed nations indicate a massive, vibrant, and highly functional informal sector. Estimates of the share of the urban labor force engaged in informal sector activities in Latin American cities range from 60% in urban areas in Peru to 24% in Rio de Janeiro (Brazil) (Sethuraman 1981).

The rural "functional dualism" identified by deJanvry, which promotes the eventual migration of labor from rural to urban centers, is reproduced at the urban level. The "urban dualism thesis," described by Portes and Walton (1981), delineates a dual urban structure made up of "formal" and "informal" economies. In the formal sector workers are hired by employers and paid a wage or salary. However, the large-scale rural-to-urban migration creates a labor surplus in the city that the urban formal sector is unable to absorb. This means that a substantial portion of the urban population, falling outside formal sector economic activity, must devise alternative means of survival.

The proliferation of these urban survival strategies contributes to the burgeoning informal sector. The *urban informal sector* is made up of myriad street vendors, peddlers, and hucksters who offer various goods and services to the urban cash market. These goods are produced cheaply with individual and family labor and are sold under conditions of intense competition. Consequently, the price of informal sector goods is quite cheap. The existence of the informal sector, then, is functional to the profitability of the formal sector. It supplies cheap wage goods (the basic goods that urban workers consume, such as food and clothing) to formal sector workers at very low prices. This reduces the cost of living, allowing employers to pay lower wages than would otherwise be the case. In this way informal sector activities serve to subsidize the wage costs of formal sector employers. Further, the informal sector serves as a huge reserve army of unemployed and underemployed labor that weakens the bargaining position of formal sector workers and drives down wages. Thus, many rural-to-urban migrants experience a shift from formal and/or informal rural production to informal urban production. Whether this represents a loss or gain in living standards is difficult to assess.

Both classical and contemporary social theory have a great deal to say about the social-psychological and political effects of the rural-to-rural transformation. Durkheim (1966) believed that this transition would threaten the foundations of social order unless new modes of social solidarity developed in the industrial setting. In Durkheim's relatively optimistic view, the mechanical solidarity regulating members in traditional societies on the basis of social similarity is superseded by an industrial version, organic solidarity, based on the division of labor and functional interdependence among members. Anomie and alienation are, therefore, minimized and social order is maintained.

For the less-developed economies, where urbanization outstrips industrialization, one might plausibly expect a less harmonious scenario. Effective organic solidarity can hardly be established where the mass of migrants exist outside the formal economy. *Mass society theory*, applied to less-developed nations, has offered a modern version of the Durkheimian obsession, but with a more explosive outcome. In this contemporary account, the transition from traditional to modern economies creates social-psychological strain due to the breakdown and absence of social control mechanisms. The severed communal and kinship bonds of traditional society are not replaced in the modern urban setting. Thus, the masses are said to be isolated, atomized, unattached, and poorly integrated. The net effect is the creation of a politically volatile population. Crowded into urban areas, lacking employment, discontented, the urban masses will presumably engage in unconventional and disruptive political activity as a means to redress their grievances. Less-developed nations, therefore, will inevitably and perpetually be plagued by mass political uprisings, riots, revolution, crisis, and political paralysis.[1]

The apocalyptic visions of mass society theory have not come to pass. In most cases the Third World urban masses have been relatively quiescent and politically conservative. Their moderate political behavior can be attributed to their organizational location in the informal urban economy and the nature of their economic existence (Petras 1970). The urban residents engaged in informal sector activities are organizationally isolated and individually competitive in their day-to-day struggle to eke out a living from the cash economy. There is little basis for collective political action. Many aspire to and identify with the position of the petty bourgeois shopowner who has achieved a relatively secure station in the urban economy. When political demands are made they tend to be rather modest, involving access to basic services. Studies of the political movements of urban squatters (Cornelius 1975) indicate that the major issues revolve around legal titles to squatter lands and permits to construct housing, and access to water and sanitation services. In short, the scenario of the urban powder keg, ready to explode at the slightest provocation, though a plausible expectation, must be qualified in light of the actual behavior of the masses in question. In most cases, urban survival strategies preclude revolutionary and collective forms of social disruption.

A different perspective on the transition to industrial society is offered by *convergence theory*, which assumes that the process of industrialization requires the application of modern technology, trained labor, and rational planning to industrial organizational tasks. As industrial capital penetrates less-developed societies, or governments make conscious efforts to launch national industrial ventures, these features of industrialization are regarded as necessary and inevitable. In this view, the process of industrialization has a single logic that results, over time, in a convergence across societies in patterns of production, decision-making, conflict resolution, and technological application. An important consequence of this process, which weds the organizational and individual levels of analysis, is the impact of industrial employment on individual workers. Not only is there a convergence in organizational practices under the industrialization process, but there is also an assumed convergence in the subjective beliefs of industrial workers. A study by Form and Bae (1988) attempted to assess the validity of this component of convergence theory, which they label the "industrial worker hypothesis." This hypothesis states:

that the exposure of workers to industrial technology and organization socializes them everywhere to adopt similar patterns of behavior and beliefs. Whatever their cultural socialization, they will respond to machine technology and industrial organization in much the same way. . . . The more workers participate in organizations in work and outside organizations, the more they internalize the urban-industrial milieu and their place in it. Thus, industrial working classes everywhere emerge with some common political dispositions and world views. (1988:621)

A key question guiding Form and Bae's research is whether exposure to modern industrial technology will have an independent influence on adaptation and acceptance of modern urban life and political ideology, above and beyond the effects of traditional origin and socialization. Based on a sample of South Korean workers employed in a Hyundai auto plant, their results support many of the expectations of the industrial worker hypothesis. Those workers exposed to the most complex technology, and for the greatest duration, were also the best adapted to industry and the most likely to participate in organizations outside the factory. It was also found that despite the traditional Confucian ethic that legitimates hierarchical authority patterns, the workers in this plant tended to support strong unions, and expressed an oppositional, working-class consciousness.

These findings point to the role of organizational forces, in this case a modern industrial complex, in shaping the attitudes and beliefs of workers within the formal sector. Locations and experiences within organizations can "create" people who fit the image, at least partially, of the "modern human." The reaction of workers to these industrial conditions, however, does not necessarily conform to the overly optimistic expectations of convergence theory. Rather than ideological consensus over the organization of production and the distribution of rewards, a "modern" working-class consciousness can develop in opposition to the industrial system. This less functional feature of industrialization has required, in the case of South Korea, a repressive state apparatus. One might wonder, given the international prevalence of such authoritarianism, whether this, too, is part of the package deal of industrialism.

Frederick Deyo's (1982) research on export-oriented industrialization (EOI) is instructive on this question. Examining the cases of Korea, Taiwan, Hong Kong, and Singapore, Deyo notes that all four nations are under pressure to impose controls over the cost and political organization of labor. This is because much of the production is labor-intensive and foreign investors are attracted to these nations because they can gain access to a cheap and reliable labor force. The export-oriented strategy pursued by these nations hinges on the availability of cheap, highly competitive labor, and smooth, depoliticized labor relations. This strategy typically requires the political repression of workers.

However, the relative levels of state repression vary significantly across the four countries. Deyo attributes these differences to the nature and strength of the labor movements prior to the institutionalization of the export-oriented strategy. In Hong Kong and Taiwan the labor force is quite docile, conservative, and intensely anti-communist. Immigrants from mainland China make up a significant portion of the workforce in both nations. The pattern of industrial organization also militates against collective labor organization. Deyo describes the system of industrial production in Hong Kong and Taiwan as "dispersed EOI," meaning that production is dispersed across a large number of smaller enterprises. This fragmentation of industrial workers makes labor organization more difficult and allows for greater employer control over the workforce. The net result is a less militant, politically weak, and poorly organized labor movement that, in turn, does not require heavy-handed state repression.

Singapore and South Korea represent the contrasting cases where there is a historical legacy of left-leaning labor organization and political involvement and where, in response, the state has been quite authoritarian. The pattern of industrial production, "consolidated EOI," further encourages a more cohesive labor movement. Under this form of export industrialization, production is carried out in large enterprises, bringing thousands of workers together in a single factory. Levels of worker communication and consciousness are enhanced under these conditions, and political action is more likely. For this reason the governments of Korea and Singapore have been forced to play a major role in the regulation of labor relations.

A consideration of these different cases suggests that, first, the process of industrialization in less-developed nations is driven by a different logic than in the developed states, due to the heavy dependence on foreign investment and foreign markets; and, second, the pattern of industrial organization, in this example whether it is dispersed or consolidated, has a significant effect on the development of industrial worker consciousness.

In sum, the historical process of the decline of agriculture and the rise of industry, and, accordingly, the movement of labor from rural to urban organizations, has been a critical part of the development process. As a number of studies indicate, this transition has been anything but smooth. The integration of the labor force into industrial organizations involves periods of conflict and economic dislocation. In order to illustrate further the role of organizations in the development process, we turn to the patterns of industrial organization and labor control in the advanced capitalist states.

INDUSTRIAL ORGANIZATIONS AND WESTERN DEVELOPMENT

The Rise of Bureaucracy

The best-known theory linking organizational structure with economic development is Weber's theory of bureaucracy (Weber 1947). While the bureaucratic system existed under ancient Roman and Chinese empires, it is with the rise of industrial capitalism, Weber emphasizes, that its superiority as the most efficient organizational arrangement compared to traditional forms of social organization became clear: "Experience tends universally to show that the purely bureaucratic type of administrative organization . . . is, from a purely technical point of view, capable of attaining the highest degree of efficiency" (Weber 1947: 337).

Weber developed the conceptual notion of the "ideal-type" to emphasize the most salient characteristics of bureaucracy. The fundamental features of the bureaucratic organization are: (1) a division of labor of specialized positions and tasks occupied and carried out by experts; (2) a hierarchical structure with authority flowing from the top down and each position responsible to a higher-level supervisor; (3) formal rules and regulations outlining official procedures, responsibilities, and relations between positions; (4) recruitment, promotion, and treatment of personnel based on universal rather than particular criteria.

These characteristics need not be an operative part of all bureaucratic organizations. Weber's point was to show that together they advance efficiency and that under capitalism, where production and economic decisions are based on the rational calculation of profit, the tendency to employ bureaucratic methods is enhanced.

capitalism in its modern stages of development strongly tends to foster the development of bureaucracy, though both capitalism and bureaucracy have arisen from many different historical sources. Conversely, capitalism is the most rational economic basis for bureaucratic administraion and enables it to develop in its most rational form. (Weber 1947: 338)

In addition to the objective structural characteristics of bureaucracy, Weber placed a great deal of emphasis on the system of legitimate authority or "voluntary submission." Systems of authority cannot simply be imposed on a reflective and conscious labor force; they must also be accepted to some extent as fair, just, and legitimate. Weber notes that bureaucratic *rational-legal* systems differ qualitatively from earlier traditional and charismatic forms. In a bureaucracy, differences in power and authority, and the fact of subordination, are accepted because the hierarchical authority structure is regarded as formally *rational*. That is, members of an organization, who presumably share the same goals and objectives, view the hierarchical arrangement as a necessary means to achieve the desired ends. If the ends (goals) are agreed upon, and the best way to realize these is to institute some type of hierarchical structure, then this will be regarded as acceptable by the members of the organization.

The *legal* side of this authority system involves the explicit rules and regulations that define the relations between positions and offices. Authority relations are formalized in a legalistic way and thus they do not reflect the personal tastes or whims of supervisory personnel. This lends further credence to the fundamental rationality and fairness of the organizational system. The importance of subjective legitimacy for the operation of objective organizational structures will be emphasized throughout our discussion of various industrial organizational systems.

The explanation for the rise of bureaucracy as an organizational system cannot be reduced exclusively to its relative efficiency. It must be understood as an effective system of control and exploitation which the emerging system of capitalism also required (see Clawson 1980). As Weber also noted, the ability to exercise hierarchy, control, and discipline over workers, which profitable production requires and bureaucracy assists, was facilitated by the rise of the free labor market and the dependence of labor on capital. We now turn to the development of this industrial system and the organizational strategies designed to maximize profit which, in turn, contributed to the course of socio-economic development.

The Labor Process and Capitalist Development

It is usually taken for granted that in order to survive and make money people must work for someone, and that once they agree to work in that organization they follow the rules laid down by owners and managers. However, prior to industrial capitalism, this was an entirely foreign concept, and one which produced a great deal of resistance and stress among industrializing populations. As already noted, the process of the formal subordination of labor involves the progressive loss of control over land and productive property by rural laborers, peasants, and independent artisans. As these populations are forced off the land, denied access to fertile soil, outcompeted by larger producers, and cut off from markets, they can no longer exist independently. They must now sell their labor power to an employer for a wage. That is, they must depend on the owners of the means of production for income and survival. The resulting wage–labor relationship ushers in the capitalist mode of production and the development of the primary social classes—the capitalist class who hires labor, and the working class who is hired by capital. The formal subordination of labor is a precondition for capitalist production and accumulation.

Once workers are within the confines of the capitalist work organization or factory, the *real subordination of labor* begins. This involves the organizational methods and techniques that are applied to the task of extracting the greatest work effort from employees. It should be emphasized that these techniques were (are) aimed at increasing the organization's level of productivity and profit margin. In the aggregate, this translates into economic growth and development.

Scientific management, popularized by Frederick Winslow Taylor (1939), was one of the first systematic attempts to carry out the real subordination of labor. Simply bringing workers into the factory did not solve the problems of control for owners and capitalists because craftspersons, and the workers they hired, still retained the knowledge and the know-how regarding the methods of production. While workers could be watched by the owners, there was still no way to determine whether they were producing as fast and efficiently as possible. A great deal of control, and with it power, remained in the hands of workers.

Frederick Taylor developed a system whereby each production process could be studied and dissected scientifically using basic principles derived from engineering. The aim of these studies was to show that there existed a ''one best way'' to organize production, and that managers could impose these techniques on the factory workers and thus gain control over the labor process. Using what came to be known as ''time and motion studies,'' Taylor demonstrated that the logic used to design a machine, involving repetitive motions, could be applied to the production of a product.

This organizational innovation weakens the power of workers and increases the rate of output. The basic stages of this process involve the division of production into a sequence of simple tasks. Workers are then assigned to these tasks and given basic instructions by the managerial stratum. With this latter process, conception and execution, or mental and manual labor, are distinct and separate activities. This organizational division of labor can be seen as an integral part of the development of capitalism.

A number of contemporary studies of the labor process place great importance on the role of scientific management as a major stage in the process of capitalist development. For example, Harry Braverman (1974:86–87) argues that:

> It is impossible to overestimate the importance of the scientific management movement in the shaping of the modern corporation and indeed all institutions of capitalist society which carry on labor processes . . . its fundamental teachings have become the bedrock of all work design.

The struggle over these organizational systems, and the new conditions that emerge from these conflicts, are also a fundamental part of capitalist development. There are many examples of this dynamic. The factory system, where workers are brought together under one roof so that they can be monitored by the owners, lays the basis for working-class communication, solidarity, and union organization. The struggle by labor to limit the length of the workday forces owners to develop more sophisticated technological methods to increase the rate of productivity. The struggle over control of work, and the imposition of scientific-management-type systems, creates a permanent strata of managerial employees and excessive hierarchy in the organization.[2] In short, each organizational "solution" or outcome contains problems and tensions that ultimately emerge as obstacles to continued production and development. The history of the development of industrial capitalism is replete with many instances of this "dialectical" process.

Richard Edwards (1979) has documented the historical evolution of organizational "forms of labor control" designed to maximize levels of work effort, productivity, and profit. The three systems are simple, technical, and bureaucratic control. *Simple control* is typified by the direct supervision and oversight of workers within an organization. In this personalized system the managerial role is one of immediate sanctioning and reward. This system is associated with the early stages of industrial production where the owner might have also carried out the managerial duties of oversight, encouragement, and discipline. *Technical control* replaces direct managerial supervision with a machine-based accounting system of the labor process. Technological innovations, most notably the assembly line, are introduced as nonpersonal methods of pacesetting. Labor is forced to adjust to the mechanical and technological tempo of production. Under *bureaucratic control*, work effort is extracted through the use of systematic rules and procedures for promotion, wage increases, and job security. These bureaucratic incentives are said to promote consent, satisfaction, and commitment which, in turn, should increase individual and collective work effort.

The evolution of organizational strategies is driven by a fundamental contradiction inherent to all productive systems—the pressure to rationalize as much of the production process, on the one hand, and the need to elicit human cooperation, on the other.

Rational methods involving differentiation, specialization, chains of command, and evaluation/accounting systems limit the freedom and autonomy of employees. Where the negative subjective response of workers counteracts the potential advances in efficiency and productivity, efforts must be made to develop systems that placate workers and facilitate their attachment to the enterprise. This can be accomplished through material rewards, normative appeals, human relations strategies, or genuine systems of workers' control.

In advanced capitalist states today we see organizational developments that often seem inconsistent: elaborate technological systems of workplace accounting and surveillance alongside efforts to involve workers in decisions on quality and the organization of production. These tendencies are responses to different but coupled forces. The imperative to plan and control production encourages the drive to rationalize; the subjective response to rationalization systems often defeats the purpose and must be confronted with a human strategy. The ebb and flow of the socio-economic development process finds much of its source within this basic organizational-level contradiction (see Jaffee 1994/95).

MODERN ORGANIZATIONAL FORMS AND ECONOMIC SUCCESS

Contemporary organizational studies are concerned with emerging organizational strategies that facilitate profitable production in a complex, competitive, and uncertain world economic environment. "Open-system" theories emphasize the relationship between the environmental demands on organizations—such as shifting markets, the location of required resources, the rate of technological change, intensified competition—and internal organizational arrangements. It is assumed that internal organizational structures can be developed to cope with changing environmental conditions. We now turn to some recent trends in organization theory that address the environmental demands made upon the contemporary industrial organization.

The Transition from Fordism to Toyotaism

The American fixation with Japanese-style management techniques is a striking acknowledgment of the link between organizational structure and socio-economic development (see Boswell 1987). There is now a vast business management literature based on the premise that American organizational practices have become obsolete and must be modified if the United States is to remain a globally competitive economic force. The Japanese system serves as one logical role model for industrial success given Japan's remarkable economic record over the past twenty years and its exceptional ability to compete in world markets. We now have a case where sustained Western economic development may require the adoption of Eastern patterns of industrial organization (Ouchi 1981).

The American model of industrial organization that fueled the rapid economic expansion of the 1950s and 1960s has apparently outlived its usefulness. Often referred to as "Fordism" (Aglietta 1979), this industrial model emerged alongside the transition to a mass production economy and is associated with the innovative production techniques introduced by Henry Ford and the Ford Motor Company. The organizational system of Fordism has two central ingredients. First, it extended the principles of Taylorism to the mass production of commodities. The driving technological innovation was the semiautomatic assembly line, which created a rigid division of labor, with job position and work pace determined by locations on and the speed of the assembly line. As with the principles of scientific management, Fordism involved a distinct separation between manual and mental labor as well as specialized and repetitive work tasks. These features of Fordism have long created problems with employee motivation, commitment, and satisfaction.

A second ingredient of Fordism served to compensate for some of the more unpleasant aspects of this industrial system. This was the relatively high wage scales paid industrial workers and the ability of industrial unions to engage in collective bargaining. The mass production system required the enlargement of working-class buying power and a consumer market. Unions fought for and gained regular wage increases in accordance with gains in productivity as well as work rule and job classification systems that reduced the arbitrary discretion of managers. Overall, labor–management relations were regulated through institutional channels but they remained fundamentally adversarial.

Fordism has been contrasted with a presumably more appropriate form of industrial organization appropriately named "Toyotaism" (Dohse et al. 1985). A key element of Toyotaism is the organization of the labor process and the nature of labor–management relations. As most studies indicate, Japanese workers have a greater affective emotional attachment to their work organization. Levels of commitment, loyalty, and identification with the firm are greater than for Western workers. While much of this attachment has been explained as a cultural phenomenon, Japanese management practices are also clearly related to the positive orientation of employees. Key among these is the human relations orientation toward the labor force that engenders the involvement of workers in the tasks of production and quality control. Greater efforts are made to integrate production workers into areas of managerial concern and to spread the responsibility for productivity and quality among a broader cross-section of the workforce. The use of bonuses, lifetime employment guarantees, and long-term career ladders further serve to attach employees to their place of work. Under this general system there is a stronger likelihood that workers will view their interests as consonant with managers and thus comply with managerial efforts to promote greater productivity and efficiency.

A variant of the Fordism-Toyotaism model is the comparative analysis of Ronald Dore (1973). Dore focuses on the organizational and employment system characteristic of British/American industrialization versus the contemporary Japanese system. Dore uses the term *market individualist* to describe the Anglo system. The market individualist system consists of weak communal ties in the relationship between worker and organization. Workers are not emotionally attached to the enterprise and, therefore, *inter*organizational mobility is routine. Wages tend to be determined by the labor market rather than by intraorganizational factors which results in individualistic career planning where workers gravitate toward the highest-bidding enterprise. The market individualist system also gives rise to occupational and/or class forms of solidarity rather than enterprise-level forms of attachment.

Welfare corporatism describes the Japanese system which, in contrast to the Anglo model, is said to facilitate the necessary conditions for production and growth in the modern world economy. Welfare corporatism promotes *intra*organizational mobility and careers, internal labor market–based wage structures, and a high degree of company loyalty and consciousness. While welfare cor-

poratism has historically been associated with the Japanese system, Dore contends that its superiority as an organizational form encourages its incorporation
in Western societies. This claim is no doubt true, since Western firms have
incorporated many welfare corporatist mechanisms into their organizations.

The key components of welfare corporatist organizational structures are summarized by Lincoln and Kalleberg (1985). First are structures facilitating participation which involve expanded opportunities for input in the decision-making
process in an effort to gain consensus over the goals and methods of production.
Second, workers are integrated into the organization through numerous divisions
and hierarchies that tend to cut across class and status lines and thus defuse
potential worker solidarity and class polarization. Third, an elaborate constellation of mobility and career ladders is used as a bureaucratic control technique
engendering long-term organizational attachment, motivation, and loyalty. Finally, there is a broad sense of all organizational members as "corporate citizens" with legal rights and obligations within the organization, as well as social
and recreational ties outside the factory. Together, these structures are said to
foster diffuse and specific employee attachment to and support for the organization, and make for a highly efficient and productive workforce.

The glorification of the Japanese system implied in many of these accounts
must be balanced with a few critical comments. In reality, the Japanese production system is intensive and fast-paced, and workers are not well protected
from managerial abuse. Work loads are subject to few restrictions and managers
are able to distribute, transfer, and allocate workers across a variety of positions,
responsibilities, and tasks. While the organizational flexibility that results from
these arrangements may be a critical structural feature enhancing global competitive prowess, it is also one based on significant managerial latitude.

Other descriptions of Toyotaism (Dohse et al. 1985) emphasize the pressure
and stress created by heavy work loads, daily production quotas, individualized
wage systems, frequent evaluations, and intraorganizational labor market competition. Further, unions—the organizations most able to alleviate these negative
workplace features—are company-specific and exist as part of the larger administrative structure of the firm. They are based on the principle of integration
and consensus rather than the adversarial role typical in the United States. Thus,
they do not serve as viable political organizations able to represent the grievances of workers.

What we have, then, is a remarkably effective (at least temporarily) system
of labor control that is based on a set of organizational structures that are keenly
tuned toward facilitating consensus and organizational attachment. Many of
these mechanisms are regarded as progressive, and in comparison to historical
U.S. patterns this may be an apt description. Nonetheless, one should not be
blind to the basic fact that Japan is a capitalist economy engaged in production
for private profit; there are many features of the employment arrangement that
would be undesirable from the standpoint of American workers.

There are a number of additional structural features of the Japanese corporate organization, apart from the management system, that account for the positive economic performance. One of the most important is the size and scope of the major industrial corporate units. Major production in all sectors of the economy is carried out by industrial groups, or coalitions of enterprises, that are tightly integrated and include a symbiotic relationship with a major bank and trading company (Zimbalist and Sherman 1984:ch.2). The close relationship with a major bank promotes a unique lending pattern that is oriented toward long-term projects and gestation periods. This "patient capital" is said to facilitate entrepreneurial risk in projects that require large start-up costs (Thurow 1985). Given the world-market orientation of Japanese industry, the trading companies have also played an integral role in the provision of imports and facilitation of the export of goods to foreign markets. While it is the management and employment system that receives the greatest hype, it is these kinds of nonmarket coordination mechanisms that are an essential key to the industrial success of Japan.

This vertically integrated system is also characterized by a significant level of internal dualism that delineates a core and peripheral structure within the industrial group. So, for example, while Toyota maintains lifetime employment policies and the other organizational benefits/structures outlined above, the subcontractors in these industrial groups are the organizations that bear the cost of slack demand and, therefore, establish a much less secure relationship with their employees. In short, the costs of market fluctuations and uncertainties are passed on to the peripheral members of the industrial group while the core is relatively protected and is thus able to project the image of the stable, trouble-free organization.

The success of the vertically integrated Japanese system and the way in which these organizations deflect market uncertainty has not gone unnoticed by Western organizational theory. The work of Oliver Williamson (1975) is just one of the most influential examples of the ongoing trend in organizational theory and research analyzing managerial strategies designed to buffer organizations from the market uncertainty. According to the *transaction cost model*, markets are cost-efficient allocators of goods and services only when transactions are short-term, one-time, and transient. They are less effective where long-term commitment and exchange is required.

In a turbulent and complex environment, economic conditions can change quickly and it is difficult, if not impossible, to incorporate all these contingencies into a market contract. Thus, contracts can be broken, altered, or continued even after they have outlived their purpose. All of these potential uncertainties make market transactions costly and enhance the incentive for the construction of *organizational hierarchies* that incorporate the former market transaction within the planning apparatus of the firm. *Vertical integration* is the process whereby upstream (suppliers) and downstream (buyers) transactions and the associated uncertainties are coordinated and controlled within a single hierarchy. This involves the merging of buyers and suppliers into a single enterprise, or hierarchy. Quality, price, and supply are presumably more predictable, and long-term planning can be carried out with greater confidence within the organizational hierarchy.

This logic of the hierarchical solution to market transactions is also extended to the labor market in the relationship with employees. In order to reduce the uncertainty associated with the labor component of production, where workers may not be totally qualified or committed to the firm, *internal labor markets* are erected. These bureaucratic structures of control, noted by Edwards and included in the welfare corporatist model, allow the organization to promote and select the known quantities that have also developed an allegiance to the firm. This presumably is the most effective way to reduce the transaction costs stemming from external labor market contracts that are based on incomplete information about the quality of the labor input.

Recent trends in organizational theorizing and corporation restructuring point to some major cost-efficiency limitations of the hierarchical organization. One major consideration involves the variation in costs across geographic areas and the ability to exploit advantageous market transaction conditions. In the employment relation, for example, rather than internalize the labor market within the hierarchy of the firm, it may make more economic sense for a firm involved in routine unskilled production to shift to a location or country where the labor market is characterized by less militant unorganized workers (Clark 1981). The spatial or geographic separation of the various functions of the firm can take advantage of existing labor market conditions in particular areas. It can also eliminate the "demonstration effect." This refers to the tendency of less-skilled production workers to demand the level of compensation and benefits of more highly skilled technical workers. While functions of the firm may be under a single corporate hierarchy it may be most advantageous to spatially decentralize the various functions (see also Massey 1985).

In terms of the relationship with suppliers, it may also be more cost effective to acquire supply inputs from independent producers located in low-wage, unregulated environments. General Motors provides a striking example of this situation. In an effort to become totally integrated along hierarchical lines General Motors expanded into parts production for its line of automobiles. These part producers came under the bargaining umbrella of the United Auto Workers, thus raising costs for parts. Foreign competitors, on the other hand, obtained parts through low-wage, peripheral producers. The ensuing crisis in the auto industry and the recent efforts at restructuring have prompted moves toward eliminating the General Motors' parts production and sourcing out of these functions to low-cost foreign and/or domestic producers. The whole movement toward off-shore production in cheap labor countries is part of the spatial logic of organizational restructuring. It also represents a more general trend toward creating organizational structures that have the flexibility to restructure the organization of production in response to changes in market competition and consumer demand. We now turn to these most recent developments.

The Flexible Organization: Alliances and Networks

The 1990s have seen a heightened interest among development theorists in the socio-economic impact of organizational strategies. There are a number of reasons for this. First, the geographic movement of capital and corporate facilities has been accompanied by an equally intense and extensive restructuring and reorganization of organizational forms. A major component of restructuring has involved "downsizing." This refers to the reduction in the size and number of functions carried out by the organization and, accordingly, the number of jobs. Unlike layoffs, which have historically been viewed as temporary adjustments to changes in market forces, downsizing entails the permanent elimination of positions as part of a corporate restructuring strategy. The impact of these forms of restructuring on people and communities has attracted a great deal of attention in both the academic literature and mainstream media.

Second, the focus on organizations may be part of a general shift toward "middle-range" levels of theorizing (Sayer 1995) that are less deterministic and better able to integrate some of the socio-economic processes operating at the individual level and societal/international levels of analysis.

A third related reason for the focus on organizational arrangements may be linked to the demise of socialism in the Soviet Union and Eastern Europe and the subsequent domination of market-based development strategies. This has resulted in a closer examination of the variation among capitalist regimes generally (see Chapter 5) and their organizational configurations and corporate governance structures in particular (Thurow 1992b; Gerlach 1992; Fukao 1995; Kester 1996; Roe 1994). This is a variant of the Fordism versus Toyotaism analysis. Fourth, as we shall examine more closely in the next section, transnational corporations (TNCs) are viewed as a major actor shaping national and global development. As Dicken (1992:95) has argued, "the globalization of economic activity is the manifestation of the internationalization and globalization of capital in the form, primarily, of the transnational corporation. The TNC is undoubtedly the primary force shaping and reshaping the geography of the contemporary global economy."

The central question driving the analysis of organizational forms in the development literature is: What forms and strategies enhance the competition ability of organizations in an increasingly globalized production system? There is also the more general issue of how these organizational changes aimed at enhancing competitive advantage contribute to the socio-economic development of an organization's nation of origin. There is clearly a growing sense that these two objectives—corporate competitiveness and national socio-economic welfare—are not mutually supportive and an organization's competitive strategies may have a negative impact on certain features of a nation's socio-economic development (Harrison 1994).

If there is a single term that describes the objectives of contemporary post-Fordist organizations it is *flexibility* (Clegg 1990). The desire for flexibility is largely the result of national and global environmental forces that entail high levels of competition and rapidly changing technologies, product designs, and market tastes. Together, these factors undermine the viability of the Fordist style of production. Fordism relied upon the large industrial complex, the mass production of standardized products, a rigid, vertically integrated organizational structure, long-term collective bargaining agreements with labor, sunk costs in fixed geographic locations, and an emphasis on economies of scale. Today these organizational features are viewed as strategically detrimental, since they tend to lock organizations into a particular system of production or production relations.

Flexible systems of production, in contrast, are characterized by decentralized and disintegrated production facilities, production in short runs for smaller specialized markets, a greater variety of products and designs, less hierarchical control over supplies/distribution and labor, flexible employment relationships, and economies of scope. There is a great deal that can be said about each of these changing production dimensions. To some extent they represent one end of a dichotomization that is more conceptual than empirically accurate. While there tends to be a shift from Fordist to flexible systems, organizations can be found at a variety of different points between the two polar extremes on each of these dimensions. Nonetheless, the dualistic strategic choice between ''market versus hierarchy'' has largely been transcended. Most organizational theorists and managerial strategists believe that the current environmental conditions demand an organizational arrangement that represents a new and distinct form of economic activity (see Powell 1990).

When observers speak of an alternative to the market versus hierarchy duality, they are usually referring to some form of network or alliance structure that connects organizations and coordinates economic activity. In order for hierarchical organizations to achieve this flexible structure they must shed units and divisions of the enterprise at the supplier and distribution ends of the production process. Rather than directly own and control these organizational units, as in the hierarchy, the organization will now enter into strategic alliances, joint ventures, or temporary subcontracting agreements with independent firms for the supply of particular components and/or the distribution of particular products for particular market segments. This differs from a pure market transaction system because the firms are embedded in a social relationship that involves collaboration, the sharing of technical information, and some degree of extended obligation. Rather than entering into a permanent relationship, or vertically integrating the units into a single corporate structure, the network alliance is a temporary arrangement that is formed for a particular purpose and dissolved once a market opportunity has been exploited and penetrated.

This type of network or alliance strategy serves two critical functions that are consistent with the environmental pressures noted above. First, it allows firms to respond quickly to changing product markets and production processes. Second, it eliminates a portion of the sunk costs in capital, inventory, and labor that characterized the vertically integrated, hierarchical, Fordist approach.

One specific account of this organizational arrangement is provided by Michael Gerlach (1992) in his study of Japanese business enterprises. Gerlach uses the term *alliance capitalism* to describe the institutional pattern of relationships among corporations and other organizational actors. At the center of this particular form of capitalism is the *keiretsu* which is an intercorporate alliance characterized by "institutionalized relationships among firms based on localized networks of dense transactions, a stable framework for exchange, and patterns of periodic collective action" (Gerlach 1992:3). The keiretsu style alliance of firms is characterized by a number of distinctive tendencies. First, the enterprises are linked by *affiliational ties* that promote preferential transaction and exchange. However, there is no unified chain of authority nor do the exchanges take place under anonymous market conditions. The relationships exist in the space between market and hierarchy. Second, the relationships among firms are built up over a long period of time and rely upon a diffuse set of obligations. Third, the relationships among firms are characterized by *multiplexity*. This means that the interfirm ties extend beyond production-related transactions and include "overlapping transactions" such as equity investment and personnel interlocks that further consolidate economic ties. Fourth, the firms are situated in an *extended network* or family of affiliated firms that share information and equity capital. Fifth, the intercorporate alliance is infused with *symbolic signification* based upon a shared culture, organizational mission, and set of objectives that substitute for legal contractual arrangements. Together, these five features of the keiretsu-style organizational structure distinguish it from U.S. or Western variants of intercorporate systems and are said to enhance the competitive prowess of the Japanese economy.

A concrete example of this phenomenon is instructive. The largest Japanese keiretsu, and one of the largest industrial groups in the world, is Mitsubishi. A closer look at this corporate behemoth will provide some further insights into the operations of and relations among a network of firms. In 1995, Mitsubishi's total revenue was $36.5 billion. The core resource base of the Mitsubishi group is made up of 36 factories and 15 research facilities. About one-third of the firms engage in "process manufacturing"—the production of materials such as cement, chemicals, plastics, and synthetic fibers—that supply the manufacturing units of the group. Another third of the companies are devoted to "fabrication manufacturing"—the production of products such as air conditioners, automobiles, computers, electronic components, and telecommunication devices. The remaining companies provide various services and specialized functions such as financial management, banking and insurance, construction, and global marketing.

A report in *Business Week* (1990:100) on the Mitsubishi phenomenon noted that:

Figure 3.1
The Mitsubishi Group

Mitsubishi Paper Mills 32%
Mitsubishi Kasei 23%
Mitsubishi Plastics 57%
Mitsubishi Petrochemical 37%
Mistubishi Gas Chemical 24%
Mitsubishi Steel Manuf. 38%
Mitsubishi Cable 48%
Mitsubishi Metal 21%
Mitsubishi Aluminum 100%
Mitsubishi Mining & Cement 37%
Mitsubishi Construction 100%
Nippon Yusen 25%

Mitsubishi Estate 25%
Mitsubishi Oil 41%
Kirin Brewery 19%
Mitsubishi Warehouse 40%
Asahi Glass 28%
Tokio Insurance 24%
Mitsubishi Rayon 25%
Mitsubishi Electric 17%
Mitsubishi Trust and Banking 28%
Mitsubishi Motors 55%
Nikon Corp 27%
Mitsubishi Kakoki 37%

Percentages refer to shares of each company held by other members of the group.

Source: Business Week, September 24, 1990, p. 99.

The Mitsubishi group is not a single corporate entity with a central "brain." The cross-shareholdings, interlocking directorates, joint-ventures, and long-term business relationships—all underpinned by common educational and historical links—create a family of companies that do not depend on formal controls, but rather recognize their mutual interests. . . . In a keiretsu no single company predominates. Since one core member of a keiretsu rarely owns more than 10% of another, it doesn't do business with another unless it makes economic sense. . . . But the financial cross-holdings among companies in a keiretsu do weave a dense fabric of relationships that can be exploited when mutually beneficial. In effect, companies in the keiretsu enjoy a family safety net that encourages long-term investment and high-tech risk-taking.

As the graphic in Figure 3.1 demonstrates, many members of the core group carry the Mitsubishi name, yet, as indicated by the percentage figures, cross-shareholding is extensive. However, in this particular network, as noted above, affiliational ties are very tight and the use of regular but not wholly dependent firms for materials and services creates a highly flexible organizational arrangement. This network-based arrangement, and the contribution of various firms to the final product, can be seen in one of Mitsubishi's automotive facilities in the United States, established in partnership with Chrysler. The vertical supply network is dominated by Mitsubishi and Mitsubishi-related firms. On the other hand, each of these suppliers is free to forge connections and establish contracts with other non-Mitsubishi companies.

In the context of the level-of-analysis framework, the Mitsubishi phenomenon represents more than simply a particular type of organizational structure or management strategy; it is a system of interorganizational relationships that enhance flexibility and reduce costs for the core group members. Further, according to Gerlach, it may also contribute to national economic performance in several ways. First, the intercorporate alliance produces an economic system that is more resilient in the face of rapid economic changes. Key business relationships among firms are both more stable and more adaptable under the keiretsu arrangement. Second, this interorganizational system encourages, and is based upon, cross-shareholding, which provides mutual equity investment capital for a large number of firms, and also draws investment capital into productive activities due to the shared interests that are built into this arrangement. Third, the keiretsu system sets up structural barriers that prevent encroachment by foreign firms that might be interested in replacing domestic suppliers. As the automobile industry example above clearly demonstrates, the affiliational ties and long-term relationships bind suppliers and manufacturers to the exclusion of alternative supply sources. This has been a major complaint of U.S. auto parts producers who have been shut out of Japanese automaker supply networks, even within the United States. On the other hand, from the Japanese perspective, this system sustains the economic viability of a diverse array of Japanese companies.

While U.S. firms have complained about the size and competitive strength of the Japanese keiretsu, and have been unable to replicate (practically or legally) the keiretsu organizational structure, a more recent development suggests a potential niche for U.S. firms within the kieretsu apparatus. A number of large U.S. firms—including IBM, GE, TRW, Hewlett-Packard, and Caterpillar—have entered into strategic alliances with various Japanese keiretsu (see *Business Week*, 1996b:52–54). This appears to be the latest global phase in the movement toward alliance forms of capitalism:

The deepening web of relationships reflects a quiet change in thinking by Japanese and U.S. multinationals in an era when keeping pace with technological change and competing globally have stretched the resources of even the richest companies.

. . . And while Uncle Sam and U.S. companies with grievances have attacked Japan's system of big industrial groups, called keiretsu, as exclusionary, other chieftains of Corporate America have quietly become stakeholders of sorts. (*Business Week*, 1996b:52, 54)

The connections between U.S. firms and Japanese keiretsu have a number of significant implications. First, they complicate the debate over the Japanese trade surplus with the United States. Official trade statistics are unable to account for the U.S. contribution and role in the production of Japanese products that are based on cooperative arrangements between U.S. and Japanese firms. For example, while IBM and Toshiba compete in the laptop computer market, they have joined forces in the development and production of a key component of this product—the liquid-crystal display panels (monitors).

This points to a second implication of these intercorporate and international alliances—the conflict between corporate and national interests. Or, to put it another way, international competition in global product markets between firms is no longer a purely zero-sum game. The sale of a Toshiba rather than an IBM laptop is no longer viewed as a total loss for IBM given its role in the production of a Toshiba component.

Third, the keiretsu structure represents a prototypical case of an organizational arrangement combining interorganizational networks with flexible forms of production. However, this system is not easily replicated, and in the United States questions have been raised about antitrust implications of the Japanese keiretsu network. Nonetheless, there is a clear movement among U.S. corporations toward similar flexible models of production that draw on a diverse assemblage of firms both within and outside the United States. A recent analysis of the changing corporate structure and landscape, by Bennett Harrison (1994:127), discusses the attempts by U.S. corporations to develop various new strategies to cope with the competitive pressures of the global economy and argues that:

> The most far-reaching may well turn out to be the creation by managers of boundary-spanning networks of firms, linking together big and small companies operating in different industries, regions, and even countries. This development . . . is the signal economic experience of our era.
>
> Managers everywhere have responded since the 1970's in various ways—all of which can be characterized as a search within large and small firms alike for greater *flexibility*: through reorganization and technological change, in labor-management relations, and in the reconfiguration of each firm's (and establishment's) transactional and in long-term relations to other companies and operating units. In other words, firms are becoming more *integrated* into one another's orbits.

The reorganization of corporate production systems, according to Harrison, rests on four central principles and practices. First, managers are reducing the number of corporate activities in an effort to identify and focus on the central core competencies of the organization. Other less central and peripheral activities are eliminated and left to other firms. This produces what Harrison and others have referred to as the *lean* organization.

A second key element in the move toward a flexible system involves the application of computer technologies that make possible the coordination of "spatially far-flung" production activities as well as alterations in product design and production processes.

Third, in a manner similar to the keiretsu, corporations are constructing strategic alliances that incorporate a network of smaller firms supplying various components and services.

Fourth, at the human resource level, there is a concerted effort to elicit the active collaboration of the remaining and most highly trained and highly paid employees in the organization through corporate culture strategies and organizational mission statements (see e.g., Kunda 1992).

Some additional features of the flexibility strategy include management efforts to restructure and redesign work tasks so that workers can be more easily deployed across a variety of job categories; increasing the level of competition among workers and, accordingly, reducing the level of long-term job security associated with tenure and seniority; outsourcing and subcontracting various activities previously performed in-house; and reconfiguring relationships among suppliers and distribution networks. While each of these flexibility-enhancing strategies has different consequences for different groups, they are all designed to reduce the rigidities, sunk costs, and long-term constraints that prevent organizations from responding quickly to changing environmental conditions. However, as the keiretsu model has shown, the object is not to reduce the organization to an isolated entity that secures resources through spot market forms of interaction; rather, as Harrison (1994:131) notes, ''the solution to private industry's search for greater flexibility has, in one way or another, increasingly come to entail the creation of *networks* among producers.''

In the United States, unlike Japan, there is not a long tradition supporting the kind of close-knit alliances that characterize the Mitsubishi-style network. There are also many unanswered questions about the antitrust implications of organizational strategies designed to emulate the Mitsubishis of the world. As Teece (1992:20.15) has observed:

Strategic alliances appear to be an attractive organizational form for an environment characterized by rapid innovation and geographical and organizational dispersion in the sources of know-how. . . . Unfortunately, in the United States, strategic behavior is often uncritically viewed as anticompetitive, with negative effects on economic welfare assumed. While such behavior may be ''anticompetitive'' in the sense that it limits the entry of competitors, strategic behavior can sometimes enhance national if not global economic welfare.

In the U.S. context, therefore, while there is a trend toward the proliferation of networking, much of it takes the form of outsourcing various organizational tasks to firms that have little symbolic connection or financial link to the core firm. The multitude of subcontracting and outsourcing arrangements has recently led *Business Week* (1996a) to ask, ''Has Outsourcing Gone Too Far?'' Among the issues raised were the union response to outsourcing which can provoke strikes and shutdowns, the unreliable supplier that can delay or disrupt the launching of a new product, and the possibility of being locked into a long-term contract with an uncompetitive supplier. These latter two points are the very issues that prompted advocating the hierarchical organizational form. What should be noted here is that much of what is labelled an alliance, a network, or a collaboration is really simply a more elaborate set of market contractual exchanges among a wider range of firms providing more specialized services and inputs. For this reason, there has been a great deal of organizational analysis aimed at identifying the key elements that make up a strategic alliance and signal a unique interorganizational structure able to exercise flexibility in product and process technological development (Teece 1992; Powell 1990; Dicken 1992:ch. 7).

THE TRANSNATIONAL CORPORATION

The transnational corporation (TNC) might be considered the single most influential organizational structure due to its international reach and global power. The TNC is also the major force responsible for the internationalization of economic activity. Dicken (1992:47) outlines three of the most significant defining features of the TNC:

1. its control of economic activities in more than one country;
2. its ability to take advantage of geographical differences between countries and regions in factor endowments (including government policies);
3. its geographical flexibility, that is, its ability to shift its resources and operations between locations at a global scale.

The impact of TNCs on national development can be viewed from a variety of perspectives. Nations that headquarter these large firms are placed in a relatively powerful international position given the ability of TNCs to dominate international markets, contribute to a favorable trade balance, and influence social and political events worldwide. However, it is also the case that these firms, being multi-national or transnational, have no loyalty to any single nation-state and thus act to advance their own narrow self-interest, often at the expense of the economic health of the nation of origin.

The impact of TNCs on the nations they invest and operate in is also a source of heated debate. Most conservative political economists view the spread of multinational capital as a positive development and one which can improve the economic performance and quality of life of less-developed nations. Third World nations should, therefore, encourage and accommodate foreign investment. Neo-Marxist theorists, with few exceptions (see Warren 1980), regard TNCs as exploitative, profit-maximizing firms that dominate and distort less-developed economies, hamper independent forms of development, and, ultimately, retard prospects for long-term economic growth. Some of these issues will be reviewed in Chapter 6. For the moment, it is worth considering the organizational characteristics of the TNC that allow it to function as a leading source of capital investment and accumulation.

Stephen Hymer's (1972) influential and insightful analysis of the TNC viewed this organizational form as the logical product of the tendency toward ever larger units of production. This evolutionary process dates to the Industrial Revolution and involves a movement of productive forces from "the workshop to the factory to the national corporation to the multidivisional corporation and now to the multinational corporation" (1972:113).

Efforts to deal with the problem of market uncertainty and flux promoted, according to Hymer, the precursor of the TNC—the multidivisional corporation. The strength of this organizational structure is its ability to produce for various markets simultaneously, expanding and contracting divisions as the market dictates while leaving the larger corporate structure intact. The essence of the TNC phase involves the *spatial expansion* of the multidivisional corporation to foreign locations that serve both as sources of supply and outlets for demand. Through the mechanism of direct investment the TNC secures control over those environmental resources that were formerly acquired through world-market exchange. Hymer describes something akin to the hierarchical strategy advocated by transaction-cost theory, but on a global scale. As Hymer suggests: "multinational corporations are a substitute for the markets as a method of organizing international exchange" (1970:441). The combination of size and international scope allows TNCs to coordinate production and exchange worldwide, produce in cost-efficient locations, and extend markets beyond national boundaries. In this way, TNCs "enlarge the domain of centrally planned world production and decrease the domain of decentralized market directed specialization and exchange" (1970:443).

The various functions of the TNC also undergo a systematic spatial distribution. Hymer applied the basic insight of location theory, along with a model of administrative levels, to depict a spatial division of corporate tasks. Level I activities, the highest level of management and strategic planning, will be located in the world-class cities and capitals that also house the centers of finance capital and governmental support structures. Level II—the intermediate administration level composed of middle management, white-collar, professional, and information processing tasks—deals with the coordination activities which also tend to be located in the larger international cities. At the lowest level, Level III, the actual operational management of production is carried out and this is located where appropriate raw material and labor market conditions exist. This means that the TNC system represented at Level III is decentralized and spread widely across the globe. In short, the internal hierarchy of the firm is reproduced spatially and internationally which, according to Hymer, "represents an important step forward over previous methods of organizing international exchange. It demonstrates the social nature of production on a global scale. As it eliminates the anarchy of international markets and brings about a more extensive and productive international division of labor, it releases great sources of latent energy'' (1972:133).

A broader question is how these organizations, international in scope, affect the development of their nations of origin and those that they penetrate. As we shall see, dependency theory has a great deal to say about this latter question. Hymer's assessment of the developmental role of the TNC is based on the application of a marketing cycle model to the international economy. In this model, innovation and new product development originate at the center of the international administrative hierarchy—the advanced capitalist states and the central international cities. Production and consumption patterns are then transferred to less-developed economies by TNCs interested in expanding the market for their products. These products then trickle down to other groups and locations giving the sense of material advancement when, in fact, their relative position remains unchanged.

In this scheme the less-developed economies serve as a source for the extension of the cycle. Hymer's analysis of this process is related to that advanced by Vernon (1966), who used a *product life cycle* model to analyze the changing nature of international production. According to this thesis, product development begins in the advanced industrial economies and, therefore, the economically dynamic effects and positive spinoffs are also felt in this location. Once these areas have reaped the benefits of product innovation, satiated center markets, and routinized production methods, the products and techniques are exported outward to less-developed nations. In both cases it is implied that the spatial extension has sustained the cycle while diffusing fewer of the dynamic by-products.

Given this view of the process, Hymer argues that TNC activity in the less-developed nations is not particularly beneficial and may actually reduce developmental options. He notes that TNC-generated forms of industrial development create little demand for highly trained and educated labor in the host country. In addition, TNCs tend to contribute little government revenue as they either avoid significant taxation through transfer pricing or are granted major tax concessions as a condition for locating in the less-developed country. Hymer concludes that ''a regime of multinational corporations would offer underdeveloped countries neither national independence nor equality. It would tend, instead, to inhibit the attainment of these goals. It would turn the underdeveloped countries into branch-plant countries, not only with reference to their economic functions but throughout the whole gamut of social, political and cultural roles'' (1972: 129).

TNCs can also have a negative effect on the development objectives of the advanced capitalist nations from which they originate. Hymer (1970) cites as the major contradiction the fact that the international scope of TNC operations precludes effective nation-state control or regulation of the most significant source of capital investment. Economic policy instruments are unable to capture much of the economic activity that takes place outside the borders of the nation-state. There are no international governmental institutions capable of or willing to control these giant corporations.

More recently, it has also become clear that the internationalization of capital contributes to the mobility of foreign investment, jobs, tax revenue, and industries from the advanced to less-developed nations. While this was, for a long time, part of the product life cycle and trickle-down process, it is now clear that the industrial base is not being replenished and other, significantly less dynamic, sectors have taken the place of manufacturing industry. The current consequences of transnational corporate mobility and disinvestment have stimulated debate over the net impact of deindustrialization and the question of a national industrial policy.

It should be fairly obvious, at this point, that a consideration of the role of the TNC moves us beyond an organization, and even national/societal level of analysis, and into the realm of the *global* level of analysis. In our original formulation at the beginning of this chapter the organizational level of analysis was introduced as a way to identify the way in which work organizations shaped individual-level patterns and also contributed to the economic output of a nation. Determining the precise impact becomes more difficult as the various economic operations are geographically dispersed across the globe. For this reason we take up the TNC in Chapter 6 when we turn to the global level of analysis. For the moment, however, it is important to note that the TNC strategy of owning and controlling all phases of an increasingly internationalized system of production is giving way to the kinds of networks, alliances, partnerships, and interfirm relations described in the previous section. As these trends pertain to the TNC, the most significant changes involve (1) a shift from the vertically integrated, hierarchical organizational structure to a global chain of production that contains a greater number of independent firms; and (2) a movement from global chains of production dominated by the large industrial producers to chains directed by large retailers (Gereffi and Hamilton 1996). Both of these trends suggest a greater number of organizational players involved in international production in an increasing number of countries. It also means that the strategic decisions of TNCs and large retailers will center less on the internal organizational arrangements of production and more on the interfirm configurations as a means to organize production and enhance the rate of profit.

Since most of the current literature linking organizational strategies and socioeconomic development is heavily influenced by the concepts of vertical disintegration, flexibility, and globalization, the anticipated trend is a further structural and geographic decentralization of production. It is worth concluding this chapter with a consideration of several factors that suggest either some constraints on this process or some possible countertendencies.

There are and continue to be many regional economies characterized by relatively dense webs of sustained transactions that are of the network variety. These regional economic networks, composed typically of a central core firm and a configuration of supplier and distributor peripheral firms, establish long-standing relationships that are based on more than rational economic cost considerations. Familiarity, ease of communications, intimate knowledge of each other's operating procedures, and material needs all combine to embed the large and potentially mobile core firms in a regional environment that constrains either migration of the core firm or replacement of peripheral firms with lower-cost suppliers (see Romo and Schwartz 1995).

The effort to improve the product quality and competitive position of a core firm may depend more upon the ability to work closely with this familiar peripheral firm network than the relocation or alternative sourcing strategies that have received so much attention. The importance of regional economic networks suggests geographic stability for some firms and the prospect for a return to territorialized production systems.

A related factor is the increasingly widespread use of just-in-time inventory control in relation to input supplies. Since the just-in-time system relies on frequent deliveries of supplies and component imports, there is good reason to establish connections to suppliers that are in geographic proximity to the manufacturing or assembly operation. Short-term alterations in product and/or process design may also necessitate a need to establish tighter connections to proximate suppliers.

The standard structural and geographic flexibility strategies that have been widely touted for their competitive enhancing features may actually produce some significant disadvantages. In the most dynamic and innovative economic sectors, such as semiconductors and computers, flexible restructuring has often involved a spatial division between the research, development, and design functions and the manufacturing operations. A number of observers (most notably Florida and Kenney 1990) have argued that this spatial division of labor, widely practiced by U.S. high-technology firms, overlooks an important form of integration that is vital for high-technology industry—the need to create close internal linkages between innovation (R & D) and manufacturing. Florida and Kenney (1990:235) advance the concept of "structural flexibility" to describe the Japanese method of restructuring in the high-technology sector involving "the integration of a number of dimensions of the new flexibility identified in high-technology districts within a highly structured and stable institutional framework." The integration and highly structured linkage between innovation and manufacturing is viewed as a critical necessity if smooth and timely alterations are to be made in product design and process reorganization. More specifically, there must be constant and ongoing communication and interaction between the research design and manufacturing units or firms. The structural and geographic separation of the "mental" and "manual" labor eliminates the possibilities for the firm to "capitalize on shop-floor innovation and/or to create synergies between innovation and production" (Florida and Kenney 1990:237). As high technology becomes an increasingly important sector of the economy and a source of socio-economic development, we may witness a structural and geographic reintegration of innovation production units.

The question is not only whether but also where this geographic reintegration will occur. Ideally, from the perspective of national employment and income levels, firms would geographically reintegrate production units within their nation of origin and in areas and regions that can benefit from industrial and economic revitalization. However, the advantages of reintegrating production, research and development, and supplier units will likely be weighed against the higher cost of labor in the industrialized nations. NAFTA-style free trade agreements between conjoining nations can also produce regions that allow firms to exploit advantages related to geographic proximity of production, development and design, highly skilled technical labor, and cheap semi- and unskilled assembly workers. The U.S.–Mexican border provides many of these benefits in a single location and has become a region that combines a variety of economic activities with widely varying levels of economic compensation (see *Business Week*, 1997).

NOTES

1. See Wright (1976) and Hamilton and Wright (1986) for critical assessments of the mass society theory.

2. For a contemporary version of this argument, see David Gordon (1996).

4

Societal-Level Explanations I: Structural Modernization and Economic Growth Models

The societal level of analysis contains the greatest assortment of explanatory models of development. This is because it is commonly assumed that national development is a function of national (or societal-level) characteristic. In societal-level theories the causal factor, some national characteristics or policies, and the effect, socio-economic development, are observed at the same level of analysis. Development, according to this framework, is the result of the organization of political, economic, and social institutions, or national socio-economic policies. The review of these theories covers two chapters. This chapter considers the influential structural modernization approach to development as presented by sociologists and political scientists. This is followed by an examination of economic growth and alternative development models.

STRUCTURAL MODERNIZATION AND SOCIO-ECONOMIC DEVELOPMENT

Chapter 2 considered the individual modernization approach that explains socio-economic change in terms of the diffusion and adaptation of Western values and beliefs. Closely related, but aimed at a different level of analysis, is the *structural modernization* approach which identifies a set of social and political structural characteristics that define and are required for the realization of economic development. Like the individual-level approach, many of the requisite structural features represent ideal-typical patterns of social organization found at the modern end of the traditional-modern continuum. To the extent that less-developed societies can incorporate these elements of modernity the potential for sustained development is presumably enhanced.

Structural Functionalism and Social Change

The structural modernization model, like the individual-level version, is heavily influenced by structural functionalist theory. While the role of functionalism's value-normative factor loomed large in the individual-level model, the functionalist logic is even more pronounced in the structural renditions given the converging levels of analysis—the social or national system. Many elements of Talcott Parsons' (1951) structural functionalist systems theory have been incorporated into structural modernization models. We will not consider all the aspects of Parsons' work, but rather restrict our attention to those concepts of structural functionalism used in theories of social, economic, and political development.

One of the central concepts in Parsons' evolutionary model of social systems and social change is differentiation. This refers to the proliferation of new structures and roles that emerge out of previously multifunctional structures. For example, in traditional societies the family structure combined a multitude of functions and roles—biological reproduction, economic production, education, medical care, and so on. In the course of modernization, and indicative of the process of development, there is both structural and role *specialization*. Specialized institutions and structures develop for the purpose of producing goods and services, training the population, and providing health care, and these institutions are composed of highly specialized and expertly trained personnel.

''Structural differentiation'' is one of the leading indicators of socio-economic development in Smelser's (1963) widely cited model of structural modernization. He defines structural differentiation as the process whereby ''one social role or organization . . . differentiates into two or more roles or organizations which function more effectively in the new historical circumstances. The new social units are structurally distinct from each other, but taken together are functionally equivalent to the original unit'' (1963:106). Contributing to the process of structural differentiation, according to Smelser, are a number of fundamental transitions: technologically, the shift from simple traditional techniques toward the application of scientific knowledge; economically, the evolution from subsistence to commercial farming and the transition from human/animal to industrial power; ecologically, the migration from farm to urban areas. Each of these changes further serves to differentiate various structures and systems. Smelser cites numerous examples. Scientific knowledge provides the basis for new forms of secular rational understanding promoting the differentiation and specialization of religious systems. Commercial farming contributes to the differentiation of the kinship-family-community unit as specialized economic units emerge and are directed toward market production. The rise of the urban industrial system contributes to the decline of the multifunctional extended family unit, leaving it as a more specialized structure formed by choice and providing for expressive needs.

Establishing the causal ordering of these various processes, or the precise determinants of socio-economic development, is no easy task in Smelser's functionalist model. Causes and consequences are routinely confounded. While scientific knowledge, commercial farming, industrial power, and urbanization are seen as harbingers of economic progress and expansion they merely describe the most common stereotypical elements of modern society. The socio-economic origin of these modern characteristics are not clearly delineated. Referring to these as "interrelated processes" that "frequently accompany development" sheds further darkness on the causal priority of the different forms of differentiation and modernity.

A second popular application of structural functionalist theory is the employment of Parsons' pattern variables. These define the fundamental forms of social interaction and organization in social systems and borrow heavily from Weber's ideal-type bureaucracy. The three variables most often selected and used to compare and differentiate modern and traditional societies are: *specificity-diffuseness, achievement-ascription*, and *universalism-particularism*. These three polar concepts have been used to describe value systems, interaction patterns, modes of organization, and social systems. Consequently, there is a great deal of ambiguity in the meaning of these terms. For the present purposes, however, we can consider the three variables as defining the different ways in which roles are organized, allocated, and evaluated in traditional and modern societies. The pattern variables are correlated with the level of differentiation and specialization.

Specificity-diffuseness refers to the extent to which roles are either narrowly or broadly defined. It is assumed that in modern differentiated societies people occupy specialized roles that carry formal and explicit expectations and responsibilities. In a modern society, with a complex and interdependent division of labor, role specificity contributes to the effectiveness of the larger system. This is contrasted with diffuseness, which is presumably common in traditional societies, where people perform many roles simultaneously. Diffuseness is said to create difficulty in defining and accounting for areas of authority and responsibility.

Achievement-ascription, a second pattern variable, embodies two of the most widely used sociological concepts defining the basis for role allocation and reward. In modern societies achievement is regarded as the primary means by which positions are rationed and rewarded. People achieve positions in society through education, the development of skills, competent performance, and experience. In this way the specialized roles are carried out by the most able, and the society, as a result, is more productive. This is contrasted with role reward and allocation on the basis of ascription which involves recruitment to positions and the distribution of rewards on the basis of family background, race, sex, and other unachieved or ascribed characteristics. Traditional societies, in this model, employ ascriptive criteria, and this pattern of reward and allocation is seen as economically irrational and inefficient because positions are not filled on the basis of competence and merit.

The third pattern variable, *universalism particularism*, has also assumed the status of a classic sociological dichotomy and is used to differentiate traditional and modern organizations. In modern universalistic organizations all members are subject to the same rules and regulations. As a feature of modern bureaucracy universalism guarantees that universal and impersonal standards will guide the allocation of rewards and sanctions. Universalism is said to contribute to organizational effectiveness and legitimacy. Particularism, in contrast, is a system where rewards and sanctions favor some groups and individuals over others. The application of rules and regulations is not universal but selective and discriminatory. It is assumed that particularism characterizes less-developed societies and impedes the effectiveness of their social institutions.

The general argument of the structural modernization school is that less-developed nations must adopt the structural patterns of modern society—universalism, achievement, and specificity—if they hope to develop socially and economically (Hoselitz 1960). One illustration of the application of these concepts is found in the work of Theodorson (1966), who believes societies must move toward the modern end of the pattern variable continuum if they are to industrialize effectively. He used the pattern variables to define and describe the different orientation and interaction patterns of individuals. Theodorson contended that in a society driven by industrial machines—a "machine society"—people must conform to modern patterns of interaction. What most distinguishes the modern industrialized world from traditional societies is the location where people work—the factory. Thus, according to Theodorson, people must adjust themselves to the fact that work is no longer carried out with family and community members but rather with unfamiliar people who must be dealt with on a *specific* and *universalistic* basis. Relations and interactions with co-workers are explicitly and formally designed for instrumental purposes—to achieve organizational goals. Therefore, the diffuse, nonwork roles of workers are irrelevant in the machine society.

Theodorson further combined the pattern variables in arguing that, because machines are expensive and complicated, there is no room for anything but *achievement-based* recruitment to industrial positions. The ability to operate machines is a *specific* demand; diffuse or ascriptive standards of selection and evaluation have no basis in the machine society.

The machine society is also characterized by a complex division of labor, specialization, and considerable interdependence among producers of goods and services. Impersonal market exchanges are required in order for workers to secure access to food and clothing, and satisfy various other needs. Accordingly, individuals must approach these market interactions and exchanges with a *specific* orientation with regard to the buyer and seller of goods. The only relevant consideration is the adequacy of a person as a supplier of some product, and the ability of the buyer to pay for the product. Again, diffuse roles and ascribed characteristics are irrelevant. In Theodorson's model, then, the brave new world of the machine society is characterized and driven largely by instrumental rather than expressive interactions, secondary rather than primary groups, specificity rather than diffuseness. All of this fits squarely into classical sociological accounts of modern urban industrial life.

Theodorson included a fourth pattern variable, not defined above, in his analysis of the machine society—*affective neutrality–affectivity*. This further complements the instrumental-expressive distinction and refers to the extent to which one gives open expression to immediate desires or, in contrast, suppresses these desires for a long-range goal. The suppression of desires, according to Theodorson, is required in the industrial milieu because

One of the most serious problems facing the new factory in the underdeveloped area is that of absenteeism and labor turnover due to the reluctance of the workers to accept the new factory discipline. The worker must do his work regardless of his private desires of the moment. Gratification must be postponed. (Theodorson 1953:303)

In sum, structural differentiation and role specialization, which stem from the process of industrialization, require congruent patterns of interpersonal behavior and interaction. The expressive freedoms of multifunctional roles give way to the instrumental goal-directed constraints of role specialization. These social structural patterns both define and promote socio-economic development.

Problems with the Structural Modernization Model

Because the social-structural modernization models are based heavily upon the tenets of structural functionalist theory, an attack at the foundations of functionalism would go a long way toward a critique of structural modernization approaches. However, functionalism-bashing, while still a favorite pastime among many sociologists, has become somewhat passé.[1] Rather than restate the accumulated litany of charges against structural functionalism, it proves more fruitful to select those major shortcomings of the structural modernization approach that relate specifically to the question of socio-economic development, social change, and the level-of-analysis question.

One of the most forceful critiques of the modernization model is found in an article by Andre Gunder Frank entitled "The Sociology of Development and the Underdevelopment of Sociology" (see Frank 1969). In Frank's strident assault he takes the theoretical model to task on the basis of its empirical validity, theoretical adequacy, and policy effectiveness. Frank's "gloves-off" style makes for a stimulating and entertaining critique.

Frank directs a large part of his attack at the "pattern variables"—universalism-particularism, achievement-ascription, and specificity-diffuseness—outlined above. As already noted, the use of the pattern variable logic is consistent with the general tendency among modernization theorists to compare the ideal-typical traits of equally ideal-typical societies. Using this theoretical strategy, the modernization model leaves itself wide open to charges of empirical irrelevance and invalidity. Certainly, all theories are, to one degree or another, susceptible to the accusation that reality has been compromised and oversimplified. Such is the nature of theory construction. Yet modernization theory goes further. There is the clear implication that the ideal-typical characteristics of the modern society are superior to the patterns prevalent in traditional systems and social structures. The ethnocentrism of the modernization model incites critics and invites attacks as to the empirical validity of such invidious comparisons. If claims for the superiority and inferiority of societies are based on fictitious accounts, then the theory "deserves what it gets."

Frank, in his critique, wastes no time attacking the empirical weakness of the pattern variable system. He points to the indisputable fact that universalism and achievement are more accurately normative ideals than behavioral realities in modern industrial societies. The persistence in almost every empirical study of "statistically significant" effects for family background, race, and sex on life chances in all modern societies should put to rest the traditional-ascriptive versus modern-achievement societal comparison. The effects of ascription are especially strong, as Frank points out, in the recruitment to roles at the upper and lower reaches of the stratification system. The fact that particularism and ascription are pervasive facts of life in modern industrial societies, yet they remain ever modern and industrial, suggests that these factors are much less critical for development than structural modernization theorists assume. In fact, there may be many rational reasons to select people on the basis of particular and ascribed criteria. Institutions and organizations may benefit greatly from the appointment of personnel who have outside connections that can advance the goals of the institution (see Perrow 1986). In this instance their technical administrative competence is much less important than "who they know" and "where they have been." To put it succinctly "to deplore particularism is only to advance an ideal and to neglect the reality of organizational affairs" (Perrow 1986:11).

Further, as for the presumed necessity of "functional role specificity," Frank points to the common pattern of role diffuseness that exists in modern industrial societies at the highest and most critical institutional levels. He uses the example of the "power elite" who, as documented by C. Wright Mills (1956) and William Domhoff (1971), carry their power and influence across and into political, economic, and educational organizations. Indeed, it is their role in numerous spheres, but most notably the corporate, that often qualifies them for positions in other institutions. Role diffuseness, in this case, is an asset that legitimates role recruitment—it is viewed as a strength rather than a weakness. Likewise, in traditional societies, normative universalism holds considerable sway. Universalistic norms have had the effect of spawning, according to Frank, the radical anti-colonial and nationalist movements and protests that frighten the very modernization theorists who claim devotion to the universalistic ideal. Similarly, both normative and behavioral achievement patterns are apparent in traditional societies in the mobility and recruitment of comprador capitalists and military elites who have achieved their positions through extortion, speculation, exploitation, murder, and torture.

Frank also takes issue with structural modernization theorists for failing to identify which of the many social roles are the most decisive for socio-economic development. It is often implied that structural differentiation and functional specificity must characterize all institutions and social roles. Frank believes that certain political-economic roles are more important and should therefore be assigned greater weight in a model of development. Specifically, if one examines the top economic and political roles in modern societies, which have the greatest influence on socio-economic development, the claims of achievement, universalism, and specificity simply cannot be sustained.

An important level-of-analysis question is also raised by Frank. He accuses structural modernization theorists of moving from one set of variables or units of analysis to another. The version of modernization theory reviewed here is considered by its advocates to be a social structural and systemic model, yet it tends to identify smaller units (tribes and families), particular roles, and patterns of interaction, as explanatory variables suggesting that to ''produce development it is only necessary to change particular variables, roles or parts of the social system—that it is not necessary to change the structure of the system itself'' (Frank 1969:37). This, claims Frank, is a betrayal of the very structuralist model they seek to employ. Further, Frank (1969:35) contends that the selection of roles and interaction patterns is ''empirically unacceptable'' because it draws attention from ''the system whose characteristics are the determinant ones for development and underdevelopment.''

There are a number of points that can be added to those raised by Frank. The traditional-modern duality presented by structural modernization theorists, and the mutually exclusive polar traits associated with these ideal types, obscures the fact that a combination of traditional and modern traits coexist in all societies. This is true not only in the transitional sense but also in a functional sense, as the example of ''functional dualism'' in the previous chapter indicated. In deJanvry's account, family subsistence agriculture, with its likely constellation of traditional pattern variable traits, coexisted alongside modern rationalized plantation agriculture. The traditional kinship economic unit contributed to the viability and profitability of the modern sector. This mutually reinforcing system of traditional and modern elements is reported in many other contexts.

The critical point to emphasize is that there is no necessary reason why modernization and industrialization should automatically shatter traditional patterns based on particularism and ascription. This kind of teleological argument is difficult to sustain in the face of the various modes of industrial development existing in the contemporary world. The case of South Africa illustrates the point. South Africa is, by any measure, an industrialized society. Yet it is hardly driven by universalism—normatively or behaviorally. The racial caste-like system that existed in South Africa was ''dysfunctional'' but that did not lead to its demise. One of the major dysfunctions of the racial system of apartheid was its effect on the labor market. Excluding the black majority from higher status positions resulted in a severe labor shortage as well as an inflated wage structure for white workers who, having a monopoly over the best jobs, did not compete with black workers. The economic irrationality of such a system, from the standpoint of capitalist logic, has failed to create anything close to a universalistic-achievement–based society. Instead, alternative nonuniversalistic arrangements were devised. As Randall Stokes' (1975:131) analysis of the South African system indicates: "Racial particularism is the parameter within which rational solutions are sought." Any solution which involves the upgrading of the position of blacks to deal with the labor shortage problem is typically accompanied, according to Stokes (1975:132), by two general but unspoken principles:

First, the "principle of contamination" holds that whites must not be put in intimate contact with Africans unless there is a clear superiority of rank to insulate whites. . . . Second, the "principle of preserving relative position" holds that whites must retain their traditional income and status advantages over Africans.

In sum, the traditional-modern dichotomy, and the various social processes presumed to accompany the movement from one extreme to the other, offer little in the way of an analysis of the socio-economic forces responsible for development. The societies described by structural modernization theorists are fictional. The praiseworthy traits of modern society are not found in real-world industrial societies and the inferior traits of traditional society are equally difficult to find in most nations of the world. The assumed logic of industrialism and modernity has not inevitably resulted in universalism-achievement, nor are these required for economic development. The structural modernization perspective provides little more than a bundle of interrelated concepts that describe imaginary societies. The explanatory power of this model is severely limited.

Structural Functionalism and Political Development

The impact of structural functionalism is not confined to sociology. Political scientists have borrowed elements of structural functionalism to describe political structures, delineate the function of political institutions, and explain the way political structures contribute to socio-economic development. In the structural functionalist model, political institutions assume a critical role in the structural evolution of social systems. As societies become increasingly differentiated structurally, they require institutions that *integrate* and *coordinate* the differentiated structure. A number of subsystems emerge for this purpose and these permit the system to adapt and maintain continuity and stability (Smelser and Parsons 1956). One of these subsystems is the *polity* which is designed to facilitate the attainment of collective goals. Because these goals may be economic, there are direct links between the structure of the political subsystem and the process of economic development (Spengler 1966).

The language and logic of structural functionalism has become an integral part of comparative politics and the study of political development. Perhaps the most striking example of this interdisciplinary germination is found in the work of Gabriel Almond and his colleagues (Almond 1960; 1965; Almond and Powell 1978). The process of political development, according to Almond, involves *differentiation* and *secularization*. These terms mean for the political structure what has already been described for the social system—roles change and become more specialized and autonomous, social patterns of behavior are more oriented to cause and effect relationships, belief systems come under the sway of science and technology (Almond and Powell 1978). Almond's basic argument is that: "A structurally differentiated political system with a secularized political culture will have an increased capability to shape its domestic and international environment" (Almond and Powell 1978:20). Needless to say, modern political systems are characterized by high levels of structural differentiation and cultural secularization.

Lucian Pye (1968) offers a similar set of structural functionalist concepts. After reviewing all of the various definitions of political development, Pye reduces the concept to three key elements. The first indicator of political development is *equality* in the form of mass participation and citizenship. The principle of equality is said to ensure that the legal system is guided by *universalistic* laws and procedures and that recruitment into positions is based on *achievement* rather than ascription. The second element of political development, according to Pye, is an increased *capacity* of the political system. This involves the implementation of policy outputs, effective and efficient governmental performance, and a rational and secular orientation toward administrative matters. The final feature of political development for Pye is the familiar *differentiation* and *specialization* of political structures. Political development entails both the functional specificity of political roles and institutions and the integration of the various structures and specialties.

As with Smelser's model of structural modernization, the causal relationship between political development and socio-economic modernization is not clearly formulated. Political development is seen as both a cause and consequence of modernization. While political differentiation and secularization may promote socio-economic development, it is also the case that the forces of social change prompt further political development. For example, Almond and Powell (1978: 21) assert that: "Development results when the existing structure and culture of the political system are unable to cope with the problem or challenge without further structural differentiation and cultural secularization."

In identifying the source of "problems and challenges" for political systems, Almond incorporates additional elements of structural functionalism. Almond frequently conjures up the familiar "black box" image of the polity as a system receiving various inputs, converting and aggregating the inputs and, ultimately, manufacturing outputs in the form of government policies and actions. Inputs refer to both governmental supports (symbolic forms of support and loyalty, financial resources) as well as political demands. Problems and challenges are said to result when there is a decline in input supports, an imbalance between supports and demands, or the oft-cited "demand overload." These forms of disequilibrium are presumably less likely where the political system has developed the appropriate (read "modern") structures that carry out the necessary functions of political socialization and recruitment, interest articulation, interest aggregation, and political communication. Because modern political systems are structurally differentiated and culturally secularized they have developed a diverse set of institutional structures that serve these various and imperative functions.

Among the many challenges that might confront a political system, Almond and Powell cite three specific types: nation-state building, participation, and distribution. They note how each of these challenges contributed to the structural differentiation of Western political systems. Thus, the ages of "absolutism," "democratization," and "welfare" in the West are interpreted as structural responses to the challenge of nation-state building, participation, and distribution, respectively. However, as Almond and Powell indicate, there is no guarantee that these challenges will be handled as effectively by less-developed political systems. Where political systems are unable to develop sufficient levels of structural differentiation to absorb these demands, system maintenance is threatened.

This brings us to yet another concern of structural functionalist theory—"social disturbances." These refer to the potentially negative consequences of modernization such as hysteria, violence, religious outbursts, and political movements (Smelser 1963). These types of challenges to political systems are seen as a largely inevitable result of "social mobilization" (Deutsch 1966:493):

> Social mobilization is a name given to an overall process of change which happens to substantial parts of the population in countries which are moving from traditional to modern ways of life. It denotes a concept which brackets together a number of more specific processes of change, such as change of residence, of occupation, of social setting, of face-to-face associates, of institutions, roles, and ways of acting. . . . Social mobilization can be defined . . . as the process in which major clusters of old social, economic and psychological commitments are eroded or broken and people become available for new patterns of socialization and behavior.

While social mobilization might be regarded as a positive indicator of socio-economic development, both structural functionalist and political modernization theorists tend to place a greater priority and value on social order and stability. Therefore, social mobilization is not always a good sign because it may result in social and political disorder. Consequently, political development theorists informed by structural functionalism have devoted a great deal of energy attempting to identify the requisite political structures able to contain social mobilization and thus prevent instability. If such a political capacity is established it is believed that socio-economic development will proceed more smoothly.

The fear of instability has a long legacy in post-war American sociology and political science. The rise of fascism in Germany and Italy and the institution-alization of socialism in the Soviet Union shaped the pro-order bias of structural functionalist theory. This bias is reflected in the obsession with stability, order, integration, consensus, harmony, balance, and equilibrium. In the underdevel-oped world, modernization and social mobilization are feared because they may result in just the opposite—instability, disorder, disintegration, dissensus, dis-sonance, imbalance, and disequilibrium. Thus, a definition of a "modern," cor-rect, and adequate political structure must include the "capacity" to deal with social disturbances, prevent political chaos, and promote gradual, peaceful, and harmonious change.

It was in this context that Samuel Huntington produced his classic and con-troversial work *Political Order in Changing Societies* (1968). Huntington's model of political development incorporates not only some of the basic elements of structural modernization logic but also some healthy pessimism and appre-hension concerning the ability of nations to modernize in a smooth, painless, and orderly manner. In this latter sense his account departs in a constructive way from the naive optimism of evolutionary modernization models (on this point see Leys 1982).

Huntington's basic premise is that development and modernization are not necessarily progressive forces because they can breed instability and disorder. The essence of political development, therefore, is the creation of *effective states* that are able to authoritatively and legitimately govern in the face of social change. Huntington cites the United States, Great Britain, and the Soviet Union as effective political structures which differ from the "debile" political systems of Latin America, Asia, and Africa. His primary thesis is that instability and violence are due to "rapid social change and rapid mobilization of new groups into politics coupled with the slow development of political institutions" (1968: 4). The relationship between these two variables—social mobilization and political institutionalization—determines the pace of development and modern-ization. While social mobilization is viewed as a relatively inevitable feature of social change, political institutionalization is susceptible to active intervention by elites and nation builders. As structural requisites for development, then, Huntington cites those that promote the institutionalization of political systems and organizations.

It is Huntington's contention that highly institutionalized political structures, characterized by adaptability, complexity, autonomy, and coherence, are best able to handle social mobilization and, therefore, to provide for the smooth and stable modernization of their societies. However, for most less-developed nations such effective political structures are absent and this results in political instability and "political decay." Political institutions, under this condition, are unable to absorb the expansion in political demands and political participation. Huntington describes these societies as "praetorian"—combining low levels of institutionalization with high levels of participation. In praetorian societies a variety of socio-political movements, often resorting to unconventional methods, act directly on the political system. The political intervention of military, religious, and student groups are some common examples of the praetorian pattern cited by Huntington. "What makes such groups seem more 'politicized' in a praetorian society is the absence of effective political institutions capable of mediating, refining and moderating groups political action. . . . Each group employs means which reflect its peculiar nature and capabilities. The wealthy bribe, students riot, workers strike, mobs demonstrate, and the military coup" (1968: 196).

These activities are a common part of the "praetorian polity." This is contrasted with a "civic polity" where political institutionalization is high relative to political participation, stable patterns of institutional authority exist, political organizations such as political parties mediate the involvement of different social groups, and structures of political socialization are present. Under the civic polity the conditions for socio-economic development are enhanced insofar as political participation is institutionalized and managed, and political disruption is avoided. The praetorian–civic comparison is akin to the various other traditional-modern dichotomies that have already been discussed. In Huntington's model the explanation for development or decay resides at the political system level of analysis with the implication being that a civic polity is the most appropriate political structure for development.

Huntington's formulation has been the target of numerous critiques. One rather glaring logical weakness is its extreme circularity. Similar to individual modernization models and many renditions of structural functionalism, the empirical presence or absence of certain attributes determines the cause. In this case, the level of institutionalization is determined by the presence or absence of political stability. Systems that are politically stable are highly institutionalized; instability reflects low levels of institutionalization.

The high value placed on social and political order in Huntington's model and, more generally, in most versions of structural functionalism deserves critical comment. Order, as a developmental objective, may appear to be a perfectly reasonable goal. However, it is not, as many theorists would have us believe, an entirely value-free or unbiased objective. The political implications of the call for order have been most clearly elaborated in Alvin Gouldner's (1970:251-254) sweeping critique of structural functionalism. He argues that the political conservatism of a social theory can be gauged by the value placed on the maintenance of social order. This is indicative of conservatism not only in a literal sense—that is, *conserving* the existing society and order—but also in a more explicitly political sense. To express a preference for the maintenance of the status quo over some possible alternative is to endorse those features of the existing order and, the corresponding privileges accorded to some and denied to others. In this context, as Gouldner's argument clearly implies, the defense of social order is a political position. Not all parties have an equal interest in the maintenance of social order. Those who benefit from the existing arrange-ments—the elite or ruling class—have an interest in preserving the system. Those at the bottom do not share equally in this interest. They may, in fact, prefer a major structural overhaul where the rules are changed and their chances of obtaining valued resources are enhanced. In short, the advocates of social and political order are defending the privileged position of the existing elite. This is obviously not a politically neutral or value-free undertaking.

It is also worth considering Gouldner's argument about the source of disorder. In many models of political development "social disturbances" are said to arise out of the mass "mobilization of excessive demands." Thus, those who make demands and seek change are regarded as the agents of disorder, chaos, and disruption; the change-seekers are "the problem." As Gouldner notes, "it takes two to make disorder." One must consider not only the demanders, but also the resisters of change. Elite rigidity and inflexibility in the face of political demands often force insurgent groups to utilize "unconventional" political tactics. These disruptive and sometimes violent strategies are not the result of inadequate po-litical institutionalization, or the failure of effective political socialization, but rather the direct product of deliberate attempts by elite segments to deny political access to particular groups or outlaw more "conventional" forms of political expression.

These kinds of tensions and conflicts often play a more important role in progressive (and regressive) socio-economic development than the employment of a particular set of institutional arrangements.

The potential for mass opposition, resistance, or mobilization has prompted the employment of a "bureaucratic-authoritarian" state. The model of "bureau-cratic-authoritarianism," developed by O'Donnell (1973), differs from Huntington's in that it is based on a number of specific historical cases (Brazil and Argentina) and is more explicit about the class interests that are served by this particular political development strategy. However, the model of bureau-cratic authoritarianism is mentioned here because it is informed by elements of structural functionalist logic and is seen as an anecdote to Huntington's nemesis, political disorder.

O'Donnell, tying the case histories of Argentina and Brazil to major currents in political development, relies heavily on the concepts of differentiation and integration. He argues that industrialization creates a pattern of social differen-tiation which has as its political expression *political pluralization*. Out of the proliferation of political actors and social units comes "competing interests, conflicting normative claims, and divergent behavioral expectations. Insofar as some 'fit' is not achieved among these aspects and across social units, social integration lags behind social differentiation" (1973:76). All of this contributes to a "demands-performance gap," there are "low levels of social cohesion," the "capacity" of the political system is diminished—the net result is "mass praetorianism."

The political tendency, thus, was toward a highly authoritarian political system, but the specific characteristics of such authoritarianism, as well as the major goals of the winning coalition, were deeply influenced by the degree of [high] modernization and the type of [mass] praetorianism. (O'Donnell 1973:87–88)

The authoritarianism to which O'Donnell makes reference is defined as an exclusionary coercive system that seeks to deactivate the masses and allow for governmental autonomy unconstrained by mass demands. At the same time, the system lacks any coherent ideology or solid basis of legitimation. Because the model is based upon the experience of the more modernized Third World states, O'Donnell adds the "bureaucratic" dimension to his political system type. The implication is that the authoritarian state system is, like other parts of the modernized social system, highly differentiated and composed of greater role specificity. He emphasizes the emergence of technocratic roles in all institutions, including the state. The value orientation of these role incumbents is said to be toward rational and efficient solutions to economic and social problems. This rational orientation, which O'Donnell links to the diffusion of technical expertise from the advanced to less-developed nations, leads to a technocratic alliance in opposition to mass political participation:

technocratic role-incumbents in situations of high modernization are likely to act in contrast to their usually politically liberal role-models, and to constitute the core of the coalition that will attempt the establishment of an authoritarian, excluding political system. . . . This coalition will aim at reshaping the social context in ways envisioned as more favorable for the application of technocratic expertise and for the expansion of the influence of the social sectors that the role incumbents have most deeply penetrated— i.e., an "excluding" authoritarian system. (1973:87–88)

It is here where O'Donnell employs the kind of language, akin to Huntington, that obscures more than it illuminates. With all the talk about "technocratic role incumbents," it is implied that the disdain for democracy is nothing more than a desire for efficiency. It is also suggested that exclusion and coercion are pursued because they facilitate the efficient formulation and implementation of government policy, allowing technocrats to "get things done." The banning of unions and strikes, the curtailing of consumption, and the abolition of government social programs, however, must be linked to the interests of particular class segments and the enhancement of the rate of private profit. O'Donnell makes this connection quite explicit in his case studies but the theoretical model, with its propositions and hypotheses, lapses into the obscurantist jargon of structural functionalist system theory. As Petras (1981:126) has put it: "In some ways, the bureaucratic structure is a facade, an alibi that disguises the multiple forms of repression and the arbitrary nature of the state. In this sense, the notion of bureaucratic authoritarianism itself is an ideology that serves to mystify the violent and arbitrary nature of the state.

In fairness to O'Donnell, it should be mentioned that his later work (1978; 1979) points directly to the foreign and political class interests served by the authoritarian regime. This "political economic" perspective shall be discussed in greater detail later in this and the next chapter.

Capitalist Development and Political Democracy

Any analysis of the relationship between socio-economic development and political institutions must address one of the most consistent findings in the cross-national research literature—the positive relationship between economic development and democracy or, more specifically, the relationship between capitalist development and formal democratic institutions.

This important question is addressed in *Capitalist Development and Democracy* (1992) by Rueschemeyer, Stephens, and Stephens. They accept the validity of a wide assortment of cross-national quantitative studies reporting a statistically significant positive relationship between economic development and democracy. The central question concerns the intervening social and economic processes that link capitalist development with the rise of democratic institutions. A statistical correlation cannot explain the reasons for an association between two societal-level variables. This task is assumed by Rueschemeyer et al.'s theoretical model that incorporates social-class dynamics, civil society, the role of the state, and the impact of transnational structures of power as intervening variables linking capitalist development and democracy. The theoretical model incorporates various levels of analysis and social life, and is applied to comparative historical case studies of both industrialized and less-developed nations.

The impact of capitalist development on the social-class structure may be the single most important factor determining the direction of political institutions. The rise of capitalism involves the emergence of two social classes—the capitalist class and the working class who, according to Rueschemeyer et al., together, act to weaken some of the anti-democratic forces. The capitalist class becomes the dominant social class in opposition to, and eventually substituting for, the less democratic feudal and absolutist social class and political elements. While this may represent a necessary condition, it is insufficient for the rise of democratic institutions. The movement toward democracy requires, according to Rueschemeyer et al., the additional presence of a "counter-hegemony of subordinate classes and especially the working class" to counter the exclusionary class interests of the capitalist class. The organization and mobilization of the subordinate classes is facilitated by the existence of *civil society*, defined as the "totality of social institutions and associations, both formal and informal that are not strictly production-related nor governmental or familial in character" (Rueschemeyer et al. 1992:49). These associations provide the opportunity for interaction and communication among the subordinate social classes producing the mobilization and articulation of pro-democratic forces and demands. The ability of mobilized and organized segments of the population to have an impact on the openness of political institutions is further contingent upon the existence of a "potentially autonomous" state. Here we see some overlap between the conceptual models of Rueschemeyer et al. and Huntington. "[I]nstitutional differentiation—in some measure characteristic of all modern societies—gives government and politics a certain autonomy from social power and privilege, but it certainly does not make structured inequality irrelevant" (1992:63).

The final factor shaping the prospects for democracy is the "transnational structure of power." This takes us to the international level of analysis with a focus upon the position of a nation in the international division of labor and the geopolitical and economic relationship between nations. As we shall examine in greater detail in Chapter 6, certain international economic forces may shape capitalist development. In Rueschemeyer et al.'s model international forces may act in a manner that "weakens the two effects of development on the class structure most favoring democratization: an expansion and strengthening of the working class and a reduction of the large landowning class in size as well as political power" (1992:72). A less favorable class configuration, with powerful foreign capital in alliance with the feudal elite, will typically create a nondemocratic state structure closely tied to the interests of the landowning class.

Rueschemeyer et al.'s elaborate theoretical model of the relationship between capitalism and democracy links institutional changes (the political and economic), places class dynamics at the center of the political development process, and includes levels of analysis ranging from associational organizations to the international system. In applying this model to a variety of nations and historical periods, Rueschemeyer, Stephens, and Stephens arrive at a central conclusion:

> The contrasting posture of the landed upper class and the working class contains the core of our argument of why capitalist development and democracy are related: capitalist development weakens the landed upper class and strengthens the working class as well as other subordinate classes . . . capitalism creates democratic pressures in spite of capitalists not because of them. Democracy was the outcome of the contradictory nature of capitalist development, which, of necessity, created subordinate classes. . . . Capitalism brings the subordinate class or classes together . . . it strengthens civil society and facilitates class organization. (1992:271–272)

Rueschemeyer et al.'s analysis provides further insight into the intricate and highly complex interrelationship between political institutions and socio-economic development. While the political development theorists, informed by structural functionalist models, have emphasized the necessity of having particular political structures in place in order to facilitate economic development, Rueschemeyer et al. point to the impact of capitalist economic development on the establishment of democratic political institutions. The lesson to be learned is that the mobilization and articulation of social class demands and interests are an important component of the social change process that mediates any deterministic relationship between the economic and political spheres.

ECONOMIC MODELS OF DEVELOPMENT

We now turn to economic models of development that operate at the societal level of analysis. These typically focus on, as explanatory variables, national economic structures, economic processes, aggregate measures of economic behavior, and financial conditions. The major dependent variable, or indicator of development, is the level of and change in the gross national product (GNP). Many of these economic models are quite technical and complex. The presentation is confined to theories and arguments accessible to readers unfamiliar with formal micro- and macro-economic theory.

The GNP Growth Model

Among conventional economic models, development is defined simply as an increase in the GNP—the change in the value of the output of goods and services between two points in time. If the development objective is to expand the GNP then one must identify those factors that have the greatest influence on this measure. The problems of the less-developed nations are often framed in this way. Their economies do not produce enough commodities and services, enough value, or enough income. The key to expanding the value of output involves the manipulation of a set of other factors.

Most GNP models place the greatest weight on the role of *capital formation*. This is defined as the net investment in capital assets such as factories, machinery, and productive equipment. Holding many variables constant, the basic GNP model assumes that economic growth is a direct function of the amount and rate of capital formation (Domar 1946). In this theory of ''capital fundamentalism'' (Gillis et al. 1987:253–254) the solution to underdevelopment involves an increase in the volume and rate of capital investment.

Like much of economics, however, the causal chain extends further backward such that the level of capital formation is itself a function of the *rate of savings*. The rate of savings refers to the level of available financial capital that can be used for investment. The rate of savings is based on the degree of surplus at the governmental, corporate, and household levels. Government savings requires that revenues exceed expenditures; corporate savings are based on the retention of earnings and profits; household savings are based on the remaining income after consumption expenditures. Where a surplus exists and saving occurs, resources for capital formation are available. The ability to produce surplus income, however, requires advances in the *level of productivity* such that the level of output increases with constant inputs of labor. In turn, and it is here where the model comes full circle, the level of productivity depends upon the rate of capital investment and formation.

We have sketched some of the basic elements of Ragnar Nurkse's (1962) famous ''vicious circle'' model. The deficient state of each factor in the model is the product of the insufficient level of some other factor. There appears to be no way out of this developmental trap. Poverty breeds poverty. We have outlined the "supply-side" of the dilemma, but there is also a "demand-side" (Smelser 1963). On the demand-side the incentive to invest in capital formation is weak because the internal market (domestic buying power) is too narrow. The lack of buying power is due to the low level of productivity which, as we have seen, is due to insufficient capital investment. And so the cycle is complete.

The trick is to somehow break the cycle by intervening at some point in the chain. The level or quantity of one of the variables must be increased and this will then generate expansion of the other factors and, ultimately, the gross national product. This requires the intervention of some exogenous force. Nurkse suggests a variety of solutions. For example, production can be geared for export which gets around the problem of insufficient internal demand. Or nations can borrow investment resources from international lending agencies to build the stock of capital formation. Each of these proposals—export-oriented growth and a reliance on external capital—have been instituted, in some form or other, in most less-developed nations. However, they have not entirely solved the problems of economic development and some theorists (see Chapter 6) argue that these policies have, in fact, reinforced the state of underdevelopment. Nonetheless, the logic of Nurkse's formulation necessitates the entry of some external force to break the circuit.

Smelser's (1963) treatment of Nurkse's model attempts to demonstrate the central role of sociological variables in the "vicious circle" problem. He notes that the problem of savings and consumption are intimately tied to the modes of social organization and social class. Thus, in feudal societies the controllers of the surplus—the feudal oligarchy—consume rather than invest savings and therefore do not contribute to advances in productivity. The unproductive use of labor is also due, according to Smelser, to the kinship ties in rural areas that discourage workers from moving to the geographic locations where they can be used most productively. And the entrepreneurial spirit, which would encourage capital investment and risk taking, is hindered by traditional religious beliefs and institutions. Here we see some of the modernization arguments linked directly to the GNP model and, more generally, to the idea that the circle can only be broken through the diffusion of Western capital, social organization, and culture.

Paul Baran (1957) also presents a theory of growth that revolves around some of the variables in the GNP model. In Baran's thesis the key factor in generating the expansion of per capita output is new net investment, or capital formation in the means of production. This depends on the availability of capital and savings which are drawn from a nation's economic surplus. The concept of economic surplus plays a major role in Baran's theory of economic growth. He distinguished between the actual and potential economic surplus. The *actual* economic surplus refers to "the difference between society's actual current output and its actual current consumption" (1957:22); the *potential* economic surplus is "the difference between the output that could be produced in a given natural and technological environment with the help of employable productive resources, and what might be regarded as essential consumption'' (1957:23).

Baran assumed that the difference between the actual and potential surplus could be realized under alternative forms of economic and social organization. This basic idea provides a useful way to conceptualize the fundamental problem of socio-economic development—organizing society in such a way that all available resources are productively directed toward economic production, while wasteful consumption is minimized. It is unlikely that many students of development would object to this definition of the development problematic. The battle would begin, however, over which factors are responsible for the inability to realize the potential surplus.

In Baran's view, the potential surplus is unrealized because of excess consumption, loss of output from unproductive workers, wasteful and inefficient organizations, and chronic unemployment and underemployment. These various explanations for the inability to realize the potential surplus, and their elaboration in Baran's work, extend across all levels of analysis. At the individual level there are the values and behavior patterns of the landowning elite and their tendency to squander surplus through the inordinate consumption of luxuries. At the organizational level Baran pointed to the lack of investment in modern technology which retards the productive use of labor. At the level of national socio-economic systems, Baran distinguished between Western European capitalism and the hybrid feudal/capitalism of underdeveloped societies. Baran also pointed to a number of world-economic forces that will be considered in Chapter 6. The multilevel scope of Baran's work distinguishes it sharply from conventional economic GNP-growth models.

The emphasis on the expansion of gross output or GNP as the ultimate developmental goal has a number of political and social implications that must be considered. First, it is often assumed that growth in per capita GNP will automatically trigger progress in the political and social spheres. In this scenario, an economy that expands its output of goods and services will industrialize, provide jobs, promote democracy, and improve the quality of life. While many of these economic deterministic claims have been called into question, the belief in economic growth as a panacea remains widespread. The universal faith in the inevitable benefits of growth has allowed national policy-makers to impose programs in the name of growth that impose significant costs on large portions of the population.

For example, advocates of the GNP-growth model often oppose policies of progressive taxation or those aimed at equalizing the distribution of income. This *growth-first/redistribute-later* approach is an integral part of the conventional GNP model (Lewis 1954). Redistributional policies should not be pursued, it is argued, because they will stifle growth. Taxes and restrictions on the income of the wealthy squelch the entrepreneurial spirit. The economic elite must retain their capital funds for the purpose of investment in productive property and technologies. In this formulation, income inequality is a necessary functional condition for economic growth. It is argued that these costs of growth, imposed disproportionately on the working classes, will eventually produce widespread dividends once the economy takes off and income begins to "trickle-down." There was a time when this prescription for growth was confined to the economies of less-developed nations. However, this ageless policy for capitalist growth periodically comes home to roost, most recently under the guise of "supply-side" economics. The same growth-oriented logic that has championed laissez-faire for the Third World has been used in advanced capitalist states to justify high interest rates, recession, unemployment, tax breaks for the rich, and a frontal assault on the living standards of workers.

While there is considerable evidence from the Third World experience that such policies promote economic growth, enhance profit rates, and enrich landowners and capitalists, there is less support for the presumed "trickle-down effect" on the incomes of the lower and working classes. A number of Third World nations have experienced remarkable growth rates while at the same time making little progress in alleviating poverty. In fact, in some cases we find a "trickle-up effect" where wealth is concentrated in fewer hands and the proportion of income accruing to the bottom wage-earners actually declines.[2] It is worth noting that such experiences are often accompanied by political regimes of the "bureaucratic-authoritarian" type. Social and political order by way of government repression often ensures the priority of growth over redistribution. One is hard-pressed to find a clearer illustration of the "political economy of growth."

The claims of the growth-first/redistribute-later policy, refuted by sustained expansion in GNP coupled with increasing income inequality, has necessitated a consideration of alternative growth strategies (Stewart and Streeten 1976). Growth may be necessary but it is hardly a sufficient condition for improving the overall standard of living. Rather, as Samater (1984:4) argues: "the problem of mass poverty is more one of the *pattern* of growth rather than the *rate* of growth per se. As a result, arguments for 'functional' inequality are now rarely heard, and we find a widespread acceptance of the necessity for new development strategies" (emphasis in original).

What has recently emerged is a series of GNP growth-oriented models that do not require income inequality as a prerequisite for economic development. One alternative is to reverse the causal ordering of the variables, thus, the *redistribute-first/growth-later* strategy. In this approach growth requires significant reforms or revolutionary changes in the distribution of wealth and property. Again, these involve not simply technical economic but fundamental political issues.

This growth strategy is often associated with socialist strategies, such as the experience of the People's Republic of China where the property of capitalists and landlords was confiscated and either redistributed among small producers or converted to collective enterprises. As with the growth-first approach, there are clear winners and losers under this economic policy. This development strategy, however, does not necessarily require the wholesale appropriation of property. Many nations have experimented with versions of land reform, which can take a variety of forms, but have as their basic objective the institutionalization of laws that enforce the right of workers' access to land. Such policies range from legal limits on the ability of landowners to evict and extract rent from tenant farmers, and the amount of land that can be controlled by a single landowner, to the actual confiscation of property and redistribution to small producers. These policies have many objectives. The reforms may ensure a more intensive utilization of land, reduce the rate of rural poverty and underemployment, prevent massive rural-to-urban migration, head off rural unrest, or encourage the production of foodstuffs for domestic consumption.

Another growth strategy which also challenges the assumption of a rigid-trade-off between growth and distribution is the *redistribute-with-growth* approach. This strategy involves a combination of policies ensuring that the gains of growth are distributed to the working and lower classes (see Weaver et al. 1978). Active government intervention is required in order to direct the use of human resources, encourage geographically balanced capital investments, expand the supply of human capital, enforce progressive forms of taxation, and subsidize the cost of basic necessities. Such policies may not only provide for more equitable growth but may further fuel economic expansion by improving the productivity of human resources and widening the internal market, encouraging further investment in production for domestic consumers.

Finally, there is what has come to be known as the *basic needs* approach. Advocates of this strategy question the ability of the growth-with-redistribution model to adequately meet the basic needs of the population. One of the most forceful advocates, Paul Streeten (1977), argues that the growth-with-redistribution approach relies too heavily on income policies intended to increase the buying power of the poor. This approach, according to Streeten, leaves a great deal to chance. Significant portions of the population may fall outside the income stream and many basic needs may be unprovided through market mechanisms. Therefore, what is advocated in the basic needs approach is direct governmental provision of basic services which usually refers to "satisfying minimum levels of material needs such as consumption of food, shelter, and clothing, and access to such essential public services as pure water, sanitation, public transport, health and education" (Samater 1984:4). The governmental provision of these basic services obviously requires both economic growth and available sources of revenue.

This points to a basic bind for capitalist economies. On the one hand, growth requires promoting the confidence and encouraging investment by private capitalists, which usually necessitates a restricted government role in the economy; on the other hand, the state must gain access to a share of the surplus in order to finance basic social needs. This "dilemma of the state" is hardly confined to less-developed nations and it plagues all capitalist economies. In this sense it is not surprising to find that socialist strategies are more successful at combining economic growth with the provision of basic needs. Evidence for this relationship is provided in a study by Jay Mandle (1980:186) who points to a basic distinction between the two kinds of systems as it affects the growth-equity question:

A shift of resources from the population generally to the public sector in order to finance welfare does not represent a reallocation away from would-be investors. The converse is true in the context of capitalist underdevelopment. . . . The financing of public sector-provided basic needs must therefore come from the relatively affluent. But these are the potential savers and investors in the community. It is recognition of this conflict which is the source of the belief that growth and equity are in conflict under capitalism.

Rostow and the "Stages of Growth" Model

Rostow's (1960) model of economic growth provides a greater elaboration of the precise factors and stages that must be present and completed as a nation becomes a modern industrial society. The "stages of growth" outlined by Rostow are based on the experience of the industrialized West. Because today's advanced capitalist states passed through a series of economic stages, these stages must be initiated and completed if less-developed nations are also to reach the promised land of a mass consumption industrial society. In this respect Rostow's thesis shares the ethno- and Eurocentric bias of countless other recipes for economic success.

The first stage of the model conforms to the standard descriptive category found in theories of modernization—the "traditional society stage." In this stage methods of production are backward and inefficient. There are no advances in the level of productivity and economies at this stage are relatively stagnant. Since things can hardly get any worse, the next stage, almost by definition, must entail sowing the seeds of growth. Rostow terms the second stage the "preconditions for take-off." The most outstanding feature of this stage is the emergence of a "leading sector" in the economy which has a positive influence on other economic sectors. It is usually assumed that an industrial sector or set of enterprises will emerge, encouraging expansion and productivity in the agricultural sector as well as improvements in transportation and other forms of infrastructure. In short, the leading sector stimulates the forces of supply and demand, and this sets the nation on the road to economic development.

The third and most important stage is the "take-off." It is during this stage that all the past obstacles to growth are presumably removed and overcome. Growth becomes a "normal condition" for all sectors of the economy, the ratio of savings and investment to national income increases, and political and social institutions support the growth mode. Rostow emphasizes the role of the entrepreneur during the "take-off" phase. He believes, like many of the individual modernization theorists reviewed in Chapter 2, that an elite segment of risk-takers driven by the profit motive is a requirement for "take-off." As income shifts into the hands of the entrepreneurial elite, spending is said to be more productive because it is ploughed back into new capacity and modern innovations.

Once the "take-off" stage is complete, the economy then moves into the home stretch—the "drive to maturity stage." In this phase there are long periods of sustained growth, with minor fluctuations, and 10–20% of national income is steadily reinvested. In addition to continuous growth and investment, new sectors emerge to replace the aging leading sectors.

The drive to maturity is followed by the terminal "age of high mass consumption stage." In this final phase, structural changes are less rapid and the leading sectors are those specializing in the production of consumer goods and services. In the end, once nations "take-off," they are essentially destined to complete the stages and follow the Western pattern toward a mass production/consumption economy. In Rostow's optimistic account all nations will eventually join the ranks of the advanced consumer societies. It is implied that this is the end of the line and, once having achieved mass consumption status, a nation's problems are solved and the society can shift into cruise control. The recent imposition of austerity-type policies in many advanced Western nations indicates that the joy ride may occasionally be derailed. There are future stages to confront.

Rostow's model had a major impact when first presented in the early 1960s—it attracted both praise and criticism. I shall focus on the shortcomings of Rostow's work since it is unlikely that even the most avid fans would today exhibit much enthusiasm for the model. The most obvious difficulty with Rostow's theory of growth is his assumption that all nations will travel along a single unilinear developmental path. On this count Rostow has a great deal of company as many of his contemporaries, equally optimistic and ethnocentric, believed that any nation was capable of following the industrialization model if they only adopted the cultural and economic patterns of the West. Today, given the vast historical case studies and the critical contribution of dependency theory, it is relatively easy to identify this fault. Yet it is quite pronounced in Rostow's stages of growth scenario. These stages effectively deny the non-Western, non-industrial world of their history. In 1960, when Rostow decided to proclaim them "traditional societies," still in the starting blocks, these nations had already run a few hundred laps under conditions that now distinguish their social structures from anything which ever existed in the presently advanced nations. This legacy, in essence, assures that they will pass through a number of qualitatively different stages on a very different trajectory (see Frank 1969). This point will be extended further in Chapter 6 when we consider the international level of analysis that links stages of growth in the West to the stages of underdevelopment in the Third World.

Perhaps the most thorough and devastating critique of the stages of growth thesis can be found in the polemical review by Paul Baran and Eric Hobsbawm (1961). Because a great deal of fanfare surrounded the release of Rostow's work, and it was hailed as an alternative to Marxist theory, Baran and Hobsbawm hold it up to a rather high standard and, on this basis, essentially conclude that Rostow's "manifesto" is worthless as an explanatory model of economic development. While Baran and Hobsbawm clearly have a larger axe to grind, they raise some very valid points on deficiencies in the stages of growth logic and theoretical strategy.

One of the fundamental weaknesses they identify is the wholesale inability of the stages of growth model to explain anything because it is more a descriptive account of an ideal sequence of economic changes than a coherent theoretical framework that allows one to understand how nations actually move from one stage to another. As the critics note: "There is no particular reason why the 'traditional' society should turn into a society breeding the 'preconditions' of the 'take-off.' . . . Nor is there any reason within the Rostovian stages why 'preconditions' should lead to the 'take-off' to maturity" (1961:236).

They also point to what is by now a familiar flaw with many explanatory models of development—circular logic. Once we assume that all forms of national development proceed along the path outlined in the stages of growth, a nation's "take-off" automatically presumes that the prior "preconditions" have been established and instituted. Effects determine cause. The claim for the existence of any stage implies a prior as well as a subsequent stage.

Baran and Hobsbawm further renounce the model for its lack of utility as a tool to illuminate the empirical world of underdevelopment. That is, placing a nation within any one of the stages proposed by Rostow hardly advances our understanding of the social, economic, and political forces responsible for the realization of that particular stage or the prospects for further development. This can only be done, according to Baran and Hobsbawm, by using the very historical materialist (Marxist) framework that Rostow seeks to transcend. Much of the review is an attempt to demonstrate that Rostow's rejection of the Marxist concepts of forces and social relations of production renders the model entirely useless. The social and political forces, and social-class behavior and motives, shaped by existing social structures, cannot simply be shoved aside and replaced by a deterministic sequence of stages that contain very indeterminate propositions or none at all about why it is that capitalists invest and exploit, why it is that workers struggle and rebel, why it is that elites resist change, and why it is that few nations ever actually travel on the "stages of growth" line. Finally, as Baran and Hobsbawm make clear, it is important to place the Rostovian edifice in its social historical context—"It demonstrates in a particularly striking way the low estate to which Western social thought has declined in the current era of the cold war" (Baran and Hobsbawm 1961:242).

Today, neither the structural modernization thesis nor the GNP/stages of growth models claim many adherents. The traditional/modern dichotomy guiding the modernization approach has lost its attraction as an explanatory framework. The increasingly important qualitative features of development have rendered the fixation on GNP obsolete. In place of these theoretical models one finds a preference for particular socio-economic arrangements and policies as the central societal-level dimensions responsible for development. These are examined in Chapter 5, where we continue our review of societal-level theories.

The New Growth Theory

Much of the criticism of the GNP growth model is based on the emphasis on gross national product, or economic output, as the leading measure of development. More recently, this model has been the subject of a different kind of critique and revision based on the GNP model's exclusive focus on the influence of external inputs on economic growth. The so-called "new growth theory" conceptualizes the process of economic growth in terms of endogenous dynamics, most notably technological innovation and change. Most closely associated with the work of Paul Romer (1986; 1994), the new growth theory adds an endogenous variable into the growth model designed to capture the role and impact of knowledge and ideas. Investment in scientific knowledge and research and development can have positive consequences for product and process technological development and, in turn, economic expansion and growth. Rather than viewing applied knowledge as another case of diminishing returns, requiring repeated external infusions to sustain growth, it is regarded as having increasing returns to scale. Technical knowledge that is communicated and applied will stimulate new ideas and innovations. It will also have broader positive external effects on competing firms and start-up enterprises.

It is not surprising that a theory emphasizing scientific knowledge and technical innovation as the engines of growth should emerge and take hold in the present economic context. There has been an enormous amount of attention devoted to the role of the computer and information technology sector as the driving force in the modern or post-modern economy. References to "the knowledge economy" (Castells 1993), "knowledge workers" (Reich 1992), and the "knowledge link" (Badaracco 1991), further substantiate the premises of the new growth theory. The role of knowledge and its relationship to the high-tech sector of the economy has prompted discussions of a "new economy" that is characterized by steady growth, low unemployment, and low inflation (*Business Week*, December 30, 1996).

The new growth theory also suggests a number of societal-level policy implications. First, it clearly provides support for expanded investment and commitment to human capital. In the second chapter we examined the human capital model and critiqued the argument that a highly educated population is the key to development. While it is possible that the human capital model can provide a more powerful explanation and set of policy prescriptions for development in the context of a knowledge economy, the same logical difficulties remain. Most critical is the need for highly educated labor, first, to be employed and, second, to be working in organizations that allow for the exercise, application, and communication of knowledge and ideas. With phrases such as the "jobless future," and the "end of work" (Aronowitz and Difazio 1994; Rifkin 1995) the first condition is far from guaranteed. The existence of the second condition also varies widely by occupational categories and economic sectors.

ALTERNATIVE MEASURES OF DEVELOPMENT

Sustainable Development

One of the most powerful challenges to conventional measures of socio-economic development, which have tended to focus on the growth of output or the distribution of material goods, is represented by the *sustainable development* movement. The growing and widespread awareness of the relationship between economic growth, the degradation of the environment, and the depletion of natural resources, has led to a new conception of development that gauges economic progress in relation to the natural resources consumed in the development process. Sustainable development has been defined as "development that meets the needs of the present without compromising the ability of future generations to meet their own needs" (World Commission on Environment and Development, 1987). In order for nations and international agencies to begin thinking in terms of long-term sustainability, measures of sustainable development are needed. The World Bank is now developing a series of indicators that provide a broad measure of the wealth of nations that incorporates the natural resource base alongside human capital resources and produced assets. These three components of a nation's, or region's, resource base are combined to produce a measure of the total stock of wealth and a more balanced assessment of the sustainability of the development process. The three-dimensional measure, according to the World Bank (1995:57), addresses a number of critical issues:

traditional economics gives disproportionate attention to finance and produced assets at the expense of natural capital and human resources. Measuring wealth, or the stock of capital, would help us to set aside the simplistic notion that sustainability requires leaving to the next generation the same amount and composition of natural capital that we found. Substituting for this notion would be the promising concept that the stock of capital that we leave future generations, defined to include all forms of capital, should be the same if not larger than what we found.

The three components of a nation's wealth are produced assets, natural capital, and human resources. Produced assets "include machinery and transport equipment and building and construction" (World Bank 1995:59). These forms of fixed capital formation are an integral part of standard economic analysis.

Natural capital is the component most directly related to the concerns of sustainable development theorists and also, not surprisingly, the most difficult to measure quantitatively. The central factors considered in developing a measure of natural capital are raw materials important in international trade, land, standing timber, and subsoil assets. *Human resources* are measured as "the future income pool that today's population might expect" assuming stability in per capita income and life expectancy.

Preliminary estimates of world wealth, using the World Bank methodology, indicate that produced assets make up 16%, natural capital 20%, and human resources 64%. Comparing "high-income countries" with "other developing countries," the largest differences lie in the natural capital and human resource areas. While the share of wealth accounted for by produced assets is 16% for both groups of countries, 67% of the wealth in the high-income countries is accounted for by human resources versus 56% for the other developing countries. On the natural capital dimension, the other developing countries have a larger share of total wealth in natural capital (28%) than the high-income countries (17%). In assessing these figures, and the relative contribution of each component to the total wealth of nations and the world, the World Bank concludes (1995:61) that it is time to devote as much attention to natural resources as has been devoted to produced assets "now that natural resources are becoming almost equally scarce, nations, the Bank, and others need to be equally concerned with this form of wealth."

If we shift to a measure of development that places the conservation of natural and environmental resources at the center, we should also ask what kinds of policies, programs, and institutions can best advance this form of sustainable development. While the World Bank report has little to say on this matter, there is considerable debate over the root cause of environmental degradation and, in turn, the most appropriate policy response.

On the one hand, there are those who argue that the greatest environmental threat is posed by the continuing poverty and squalor in certain regions of the world which results in large populations using natural resources, and residing in ecologically fragile areas, as a means for survival. The co-presence of rural poverty, high population density, and environmental resource degradation and depletion suggest a set of interrelated processes linking survival strategies and natural resource use. Studies in regions of Sub-Saharan Africa, for example, have pointed to the divergence between the private and social costs and benefits of resource use (Perrings 1996). Survival strategies that are necessarily driven by immediate needs produce a dilemma such that "the incentives confronting individual resource users induces short run behavior that is inconsistent with the long run interests both of the resource users themselves and of society" (Perrings 1996:4). The solution, according to this perspective, is more economic growth that will raise the standard of living and incorporate excluded populations into the formal economy, or identify the necessary conditions for the development of incentives that are compatible with the ecologically sustainable use of resources.

On the other side are those who argue that the greatest threat to the environment comes from the high growth, high consumption, affluent nations that systematically exploit and consume environmental resources as a routine part of the production process. The policy implications stemming from this argument are not more growth and economic expansion but, rather, a reordering of priorities that acknowledges the limited and dwindling resource base and the need for a reallocation and redeployment of resources that serves to preserve existing natural and environmental resources (Daly 1996). A corollary to the anti-economic-growth argument is the rejection of the neo-liberal free-trade doctrines that encourage the unfettered flow of not only goods but also capital. The competition for foreign capital investment may result in national level policies that sacrifice environmental standards in order to attract foreign capital investment. We will revisit this issue in Chapter 6. What needs to be emphasized at this point is the widespread acceptance, even among such institutions as the World Bank, of alternative measures of development that include and emphasize the value and long-term viability of the natural resource base.

Human Development

There is no longer much debate over the question of whether economic growth, as measured by GNP, should be the sole measure of socio-economic development. It is now widely acknowledged, in almost all academic circles, that economic growth does not necessarily bring with it improvements in other spheres of socio-economic life and that other dimensions of development must be measured. In response to the demands for measures that gauge the basic needs/human welfare dimension, the United Nations Development Programme launched a major research effort designed to establish a measure of *human development*. The first *Human Development Report*, published in 1990, proclaimed that ''People are the real wealth of a nation. The basic objective of development is to create an enabling environment for people to enjoy long, healthy and creative lives. . . . Human development is a process of enlarging people's choices.''

In an effort to measure human development, and rank countries on a human development scale as they have been ranked by GNP per capita, the UN report focuses on three dimensions of human development. First is *longevity* measured by life expectancy at birth. Second is *educational attainment*, which is based on combining adult literacy rates with primary, secondary, and tertiary school enrollment ratios. The third dimension to be included is *standard of living*, measured by real Gross Domestic Product (GDP) per capita. A standardized index is created for each of the three dimensions. They are then averaged to achieve a single human development score. While there are many alternative ways to conceptualize, and perhaps even measure, human development, the UN researchers are constrained by the availability of reliable cross-national data. The three dimensions of the human development index tap into three critical aspects of human existence—survival prospects, human capital, and material resources. Since the measures are aggregated for each country it is difficult to assess the distribution of these social goods. Nonetheless, the human develop-

Table 4.1
Human Development Index, Selected Countries

Rank/Country	Human Development Index	Real GDP per capita 1992 in PPP$[a]
1 Canada	0.950	20,520
2 USA	0.937	23,760
3 Japan	0.937	20,520
4 Netherlands	0.936	17,780
5 Finland	0.934	16,270
6 Iceland	0.933	17,660
7 Norway	0.932	18,580
8 France	0.930	19,510
9 Spain	0.930	13,400
10 Sweden	0.929	18,320
18 United Kingdom	0.916	17,160
31 Republic of Korea	0.882	9,250
52 Russian Federation	0.849	6,140
53 Mexico	0.842	7,300
58 Thailand	0.827	5,950
63 Brazil	0.804	5,240
111 China	0.594	1,950
148 Haiti	0.362	1,046
153 Cambodia	0.337	1,250
174 Niger	0.207	820

[a]The GDP per capita of a country converted into U.S. dollars on the basis of the purchasing power of the country's currency.

Source: United Nations Development Programme, *Human Development Report, 1995* (New York: Oxford University Press, 1995), p. 155, table 1.

ment index is a solid starting point for gauging the levels of human development and welfare across nations.

Some selected nations, with their ranking (a total of 174 countries were ranked in 1995), are listed in Table 4.1 along with the real GDP per capita. The latter measure is included to examine the relationship between the human development score (or rank) and the conventional economic measure of development. There is clearly a strong relationship between per capita income level and human development which can be seen if one follows the magnitude of GDP per capita from the top- to the bottom-ranked countries. On the other hand, it is also clearly not a perfect one-to-one relationship as the top-ranked country on the human development index (HDI), Canada, is the eighth wealthiest country as measured by GDP. The Northern European, or Scandinavian countries, which are well represented among the top ten on human development would rank somewhere between 20th and 25th on the GDP measure. In short, and as argued elsewhere, aggregate level of wealth can be considered a necessary but insufficient condition for ensuring high levels of socio-economic development. The question is not simply the aggregate level of wealth but how it is distributed and whether it is directed toward policies and programs that enhance the dimensions of human development contained in the index. In spite of the widespread anti-government rhetoric and ideology currently prevailing among development planners and theorists, human development requires a significant governmental role in the areas of educational expansion and health-related policies contributing to longevity.

Since the inaugural report (1990), the United Nations has refined the measurement of human development and advanced a human development paradigm that extends beyond the quantitatively measurable features of human development. In the 1995 report (1995:12) they present the human development paradigm as containing the following four main components:

1. *Productivity*. People must be enabled to increase their productivity and to participate fully in the process of income generation and remunerative employment. Economic growth is, therefore, a subset of human development models.

2. *Equity*. People must have access to equal opportunities. All barriers to economic and political opportunities must be eliminated so that people can participate in, and benefit from, these opportunities.

3. *Sustainability*. Access to opportunities must be ensured not only for the present generations but for future generations as well. All forms of capital—physical, human, environmental—should be replenished.

4. *Empowerment*. Development must be by people, not only for them. People must participate fully in the decisions and processes that shape their lives.

In keeping with the spirit of transcending a narrow economic growth perspective on human development, and identifying the qualitative and institutional factors that might contribute to or impede human development, the 1995 edition of the *Human Development Report* is devoted to an examination of *gender inequality*. As the report (1995:1) emphasizes, human development is the "process of enlarging the choices for all people, not just one part of society. Such a process becomes unjust and discriminatory if most women are excluded from its benefits." Therefore, human development requires that men and women enjoy equal rights that include: equal access to basic social services; equal opportunities to participate in political and economic decision-making; equal reward for equal work; equal protection under the law; elimination of gender-based discrimination and violence; and equal citizenship rights in all areas of social life.

The report contains some of the best available data on gender disparities in industrial and less-developed societies and includes one of the most comprehensive efforts to construct a cross-national measure of gender disparities. More specifically, the report contains a *gender-related development index* (GDI) which "measures achievement in the same basic capabilities as the HDI does, but takes note of inequality in achievement between women and men. The methodology

Table 4.2

Gender-Related Development Index, Selected Countries

Rank/Country	Gender Development Index (GDI)	Real GDP per capita 1992 in PPP$[a]	HDI rank minus GDI rank[b]
1 Sweden	0.919	20,520	8
2 Finland	0.918	16,270	3
3 Norway	0.911	18,580	3
4 Denmark	0.904	19,080	10
5 USA	0.901	23,760	-3
6 Australia	0.901	18,220	4
7 France	0.898	19,510	0
8 Japan	0.896	20,520	-5
9 Canada	0.891	20,520	-8
10 Austria	0.882	18,710	3
11 Barbados	0.878	9,667	10
29 Russian Federation	0.822	6,140	15
34 Spain	0.795	13,400	-26
37 Republic of Korea	0.780	9,250	-11
39 Argentina	0.780	8,860	-14
13 Cuba	0.768	3,412	10
57 United Arab Emirates	0.674	21,830	-20
58 Sri Lanka	0.660	2,850	117
100 Nigeria	0.383	1,560	3
130 Afghanistan	0.169	819	-4

[a]The GDP per capita of a country converted into U.S. dollars on the basis of the purchasing power of the country's currency.

[b]A positive figure indicates that a country performs relatively better on gender equality than on average human development achievement alone.

Source: United Nations Development Programme, *Human Development Report, 1995* (New York: Oxford University Press, 1995), pp. 76–77, table 3.1.

used imposes a penalty for inequality, such that the GDI falls when the achievement levels of both men and women in a country go down or when the disparity between their achievements increases. The greater the gender disparity in basic capabilities, the lower a country's GDI compared with its HDI. The GDI is simply the HDI discounted, or adjusted downwards for gender inequality'' (*Human Development Report 1995*:73).

The UN ranked 130 countries on the GDI. (The rankings of selected countries are presented in Table 4.2.) The top four countries are the Nordic nations of Sweden, Finland, Norway, and Denmark. As with the human development index, these nations have also tended to make a more concerted effort in the areas of social policy that protect and advance the rights of women. In each of these countries there is greater gender equality in the areas of literacy, combined school enrollment, life expectancy, and earned income than those ranked below. The data provided in the UN report also allow a comparison between the overall

HDI rank and the gender adjusted GDI. (See column 4 in Table 4.2.) This indicates the extent to which the elements of human development are distributed equitably between men and women. Some countries do much better in the area of gender development than would be expected given their level of resources and their overall human development ranking—Barbados, Cuba, Sri Lanka, and Thailand. Other countries do worse than would be expected given their level of resources and rank on the HDI—Argentina, Chile, Spain, The Netherlands, and several Arab nations. It should also be noted that income, as measured by GDP, is less tightly correlated with GDI than HDI. Countries such as China, Thailand, and Zimbabwe, for example, rank highly on the GDI in spite of their economic resources. As the UN report (1995:3) notes: "Comparing GDI ranks with the income levels of countries confirms that removing gender inequalities is not dependent on having a high income. . . . So, gender equality can be pursued—and has been—at all levels of income. What it requires is a firm political commitment, not enormous financial wealth."

In terms of the larger development process, there are several sound reasons for being concerned with the relative status, participation, and treatment of women, beyond the question of equity and fairness. First, many development programs designed to manage environmental and natural resources must recognize that women often play the central role in securing, managing, and using natural resources in many communities, regions, and nations (World Bank 1991; Braidotti et al. 1994). It is therefore imperative, for the success of the development project, that women not only be involved in the implementation of the project but also have access to the requisite resources. In the past, women have been excluded from both of these areas and the projects have been much less successful as a result. In order for women to be fully involved in these development projects it is important that women have access to property and credit, are able to form groups and associations to articulate and advance their collective interests, and are provided with the necessary information relating to natural and environmental resources.

A second critical area for the full participation of women is poverty reduction initiatives. While basic needs and human development approaches are concerned with the issues of collective and general welfare, there must also be some consideration of the differential impact of various programs on men and women. Public expenditure on social welfare and the provision of other resources may not have the poverty-reducing impact intended if the benefits and resources are not equitably distributed. It is important to recognize that poverty reduction and gender inequality do not necessarily go hand in hand. Thus, policies designed to improve general socio-economic welfare must attempt to include and target women. Over the past ten years there have been an increasing number of public and private sector policies designed to address the dual challenges of poverty and gender inequality. One of the most notable is Bangladesh's Grameen Bank project, which advances credit to rural women. In place of the requirement that the women have physical property collateral, the Bank provides credit to peer groups who serve to collectively enforce and encourage the sound use and re-payment of credit, a form of social collateral. The loans are relatively small, ranging from $25 to $250, but provide a sufficient sum for the purpose of developing micro-entrepreneurship among the women lendees.

While there have been some successes with the program, and a great deal of media attention, and repayment rates exceed 90%, there have also been some significant questions raised (see Baden et al. 1994; Neff 1996). For example, while the women may receive the loans, there appears to be considerable ap-propriation of the resources by male kinship members. Thus, women do not control the assets but are held responsible for repayment. Further, given the existing gender inequalities in most societies in the areas of access to markets and economic networks, those women who control the assets find fewer prof-itable opportunities than males. The program also fails to provide the various support services—such as financial and business training—that would place re-cipients, particularly women, in a stronger position to control the assets and realize significant economic gain. There is some indication, in fact, that many of the women ''served'' by the program are essentially occupying a ''middle-woman'' role as provider of credit to other, primarily male, members of the family and ensuring that the credit is repaid. Reports on other programs targeted for women—such as structural adjustment programs that shift resources from urban to rural areas and employment guarantee schemes—also indicate mixed results in terms of reaching and elevating the economic status of women (Had-dad et al. 1995; Buvinic and Gupta 1994). In all these cases there is the finding that the existing gender disparities in social, local, and family power, influence, authority, and connections work to reduce the effectiveness of the programs. This points to the societal-level constraints on policies that identify individuals, and even organizations and collectivities, as sources of socio-economic progress, change, and transformation. Clearly, in the case of gender-equitable socio-economic development, some larger social structural forces are at work. Na-tional-level programs must address these in order to facilitate the success of individual-, organizational-, and sectoral-based programs.

NOTES

1. For the best and most comprehensive critique of structural functionalism in general, and Parsonian functionalism in particular, see Gouldner (1970).

2. On the complicated relationship between economic growth and income equality see Adelmen and Morris (1973).

5

Societal-Level Explanations II: Comparative Socio-economic Systems and Strategies

Here and elsewhere, we must never forget that perfect systems exist only in books, that the real world in East and West abounds in irrationalities, misallocation, misemployment of resources, various forms of waste. In the real world, whether socialist or not, some intractable problems and contradictions will exist. Indeed, it is well that this is so, for a world without contradictions would be an intolerably dull place, and social scientists would be threatened with unemployment.... We must learn from the things that go wrong, in the hope that by doing so we will diminish the ill-effects of predictable troubles. (Nove 1983:141)

This chapter continues examining societal-level explanations for development within a comparative analytic framework. The first section is devoted to a review of theories of capitalism and socialism as systems facilitating socio-economic development. The second section of the chapter considers variations, and prescriptions for development, among the capitalist economies. The final section reviews some of the issues related to the demise of state socialism and the transition to market-based economies.

SOCIO-ECONOMIC SYSTEMS AND DEVELOPMENT: CAPITALISM

The most common comparison of socio-economic systems has been between capitalism and socialism, with claims made for the relative superiority and appropriateness of each system as a strategy for growth.[1] While almost all nations in the world are organized along some variant of capitalism, it is important to understand why nations have opted for or experimented with socialist principles.

Describing the fundamental characteristics of socio-economic systems, such as capitalism and socialism, is a difficult task for at least two reasons. First, there are no "pure" socialist or capitalist societies existing anywhere in the world. By "pure" we mean societies that conform to the abstract theoretical models of what capitalism and socialism are supposed to be. For this reason, as one lists the characteristics of these societies, many reservations and qualifications are in order. A second, related problem that often emerges is the tendency, when comparing different societies, to select the ideal features of one society and compare these with the actual and often undesirable features of the other (see Burawoy and Lukacs 1985). This "selection bias" frequently is politically motivated because it is often the case that comparative analysts have a (unspoken) preference for one or the other of the different systems. Students of comparative social science should be aware of this tendency and make efforts to present both the ideal-typical features of socio-economic systems and the day-to-day problems, inefficiencies, and inequities that emerge in all systems to one degree or another.

In an attempt to follow this lofty advice, we shall consider some of the theoretical arguments for the advantages of both capitalism and socialism, and then confront some of the real-life deviations from these abstract models.

Capitalism in Theory and Practice

Capitalism is a socio-economic system that allows the private ownership of productive property (property that produces goods and services). Individuals who own the means of production make up the capitalist class; those who work for capitalists make up the working class. Arguments favoring capitalism as the best socio-economic arrangement for development hinge on the role of markets and the concept of incentives.

Markets determine the production and allocation of goods and services in a capitalist society. Buyers and sellers come together to exchange goods, services, labor, and money. Prices serve as the leading piece of information in markets and determine how much of a good will be bought and sold. When the supply of goods exceeds demand, prices tend to fall; when demand exceeds supply, prices tend to rise. Thus, through the market mechanism goods are assigned a value or price, and this results in the most efficient allocation of resources. Where a commodity is in plentiful supply, the low price will stimulate demand for that good and it will be used; where a good is scarce, the high price will discourage demand and buyers will seek alternative goods. The use and allocation of resources are both efficient and noncoercive, requiring no direct government intervention. The "invisible hand" of the market directs the economy and, in the process, preserves liberty and freedom.

A second argument for capitalism rests on the inherent incentive structure that prevails in competitive market systems. Because individual capitalists and workers are able to control the profit or income derived from their economic activity, there is an incentive to invest money and energy, take risks, work hard, and, ultimately, create wealth. The competitive nature of capitalism gives it its dynamic efficiency. Capitalists are competing with other capitalists for profits and markets, so they are driven to be as productive as possible and as accommodating to buyers as possible. Innovative production techniques are constantly developed, pressure is exerted to use resources as efficiently as possible, and high-quality products are required if capitalists are to secure markets for their goods. In short, the incentives of market competition guarantee expanding investment, productivity, wealth, jobs, and quality products for consumers.

Let us now consider some of the common arguments *against* capitalism (Zimbalist and Sherman 1984:10–11). First is the issue of inequality between workers and owners. Only a small proportion of the total population in a capitalist society owns means of production and therefore is able to reap the profits from production. The vast majority are workers who are hired by capitalists. The same market competitive forces that result in dynamic efficiency may also provide an incentive for the severe exploitation of workers as a means to cut costs and produce efficiently.

Second, because decisions about production are based on supply and demand, the investment behavior of capitalists tends to fluctuate, and so the "invisible hand" creates periods of recession and depression that result in long periods of production well below the actual capacity of the economy. Production of goods based on market criteria—that is, the presence of demand backed up with cash—means that those with the most income have the greatest influence over which goods will be produced. The supply of goods is not determined by actual human needs.

Third, the process of competition inevitably results in some winners and some losers. Over time wealth and power become concentrated in the hands of the largest and strongest firms and thus competition, the motor of innovation, is replaced by oligopoly and monopoly. The liberty and freedom presumably advanced by competitive capitalism are threatened as the economy and polity are dominated by individuals and firms who use their economic muscle to advance their own ends, set prices, control supply, and dominate the economy.

It should be clear from these critical comments that the assessment of the desirability of different socio-economic systems rests not only on economic growth criteria but also on a set of other, equally compelling values and priorities. These include efficiency, fairness, equality, democracy, freedom, choice, control, and quality of life (see Bowles and Edwards 1985:20–24; Zimbalist and Sherman 1984:23–29).

There is one final critical comment that deserves mention. Capitalist economies do not always utilize resources in the most efficient manner. As was argued above, market-based prices are said to provide for the most efficient use and allocation of resources. A major problem arises, however, when resources have no price tag and can be used at no cost. In this sense they appear to be infinite and can be used in unlimited quantities. Air is such a commodity. Since it can be used by producers at no cost, it is rational and profitable to use, and in the process pollute, this environmental resource. There is no price disincentive to do otherwise even though the pollution of air exacts enormous social costs.

This is the classic case of a *negative externality*. An externality is an action taken by a firm in one location that affects other firms or parties in other locations. In this case it is negative because the effects on other areas, firms, or people are costs. Firms or individuals who did not participate in the original action or decision nonetheless incur *costs* (clean-up costs, health hazards, higher medical bills, death) as a result of the action. This is also referred to as an *external diseconomy*.

There are also *positive externalities*. These occur when the effect of an activity in one place or firm transfers not costs but *benefits* to other places and firms. For example, converting a burned-out factory into attractive condos may enhance the property values of surrounding buildings and homes. This is also known as an *external economy*. Externality is an important economic concept that can be applied to all forms of economic activity. The widespread negative externalities that result from the actions of private firms and corporations are a major reason for government intervention in the economy and the development of socio-economic systems that do not conform to the pure capitalist model. In the case of a negative externality such as pollution, the state must "internalize" the external cost by penalizing firms for air pollution through fines, or by requiring pollution control devices that increase the production costs of firms that despoil the environment. The necessary increase in the role of the state in capitalist economies is probably the single most important reason for challenging the ideal-theoretical depiction of capitalism. We therefore examine the question of state intervention in greater detail in a later section of the chapter.

SOCIO-ECONOMIC SYSTEMS AND DEVELOPMENT: SOCIALISM

We now take up the question of socialism as a societal-level strategy for development. We shall proceed in the same manner as in the discussion of capitalism. First we outline the standard theoretical arguments for socialism as a socio-economic system facilitating growth. Second, we review the usual criticisms against socialism. Third, and of greatest importance, we consider some of the developmental problems that have emerged within this type of system.

Socialism in Theory and Practice

Under the socio-economic system of socialism, the means of production are owned and controlled by the state. Decisions about production and investment, rather than being determined by market forces and private capitalists, are based on a central plan. The plan contains growth rate targets for the national economy and the means to achieve these targets. The state, in designing and implementing the plan, considers the needs of the entire society, and in this sense directs resources on the basis of collective rather than private interest. Planning is viewed as an advantageous developmental tool because it eliminates the uncertainty inherent in market systems. Supply and demand can be written into the plan, and therefore the society does not experience the vagaries of the business cycle that result when supply exceeds demand or demand exceeds supply. The twin evils of capitalism—inflation and unemployment—presumably are eliminated by socialist planning, and development proceeds at a smoother pace. It is also argued that state control of productive property ensures that society's resources are fully utilized and devoted to national developmental goals.

In addition to the economic advantages, arguments for socialism are based on a number of other values. For example, because private productive property is controlled by the state, there is no exploitation of workers by capitalists nor windfall megaprofits concentrated in the hands of a small elite. This ensures that the distribution of income will be more equal and that the state will not be controlled by a small group of capitalists. The provision of basic human needs is also more structurally feasible under socialism because production is not undertaken solely for the purpose of private profit. Development under socialism, then, is smoother, more rational, based on national needs and priorities, more equitable, and less wasteful than under capitalism.

These compelling theoretical arguments for the superiority of socialism can be countered by a number of equally convincing criticisms against socialism (Zimbalist and Sherman 1984). First, under socialism power and control of the economy are placed in the hands of state bureaucrats who may be totally unresponsive to the needs of the people, yet are in a position to decide, arbitrarily, what is best for the society, what goods should be produced, who gets what, and so on. In short, the replacement of capitalists with bureaucrats may result in greater economic inefficiencies and inequalities. Second, placing the entrepreneurial role in the public sector reduces the important private profit motive and incentive to invest, innovate, take risks, develop new products, and respond to new markets. If private individuals are unable to gain materially from their economic actions, the incentives required for dynamic efficiency are precluded. Third, socialism, by placing control of the means of production in the hands of the state, concentrates political power in the hands of those who are appointed as state managers or party bureaucrats. Finally, the absence of markets means that the central planning board is faced with the enormous challenge of determining supply, demand, consumer preferences, and prices. Without market-based prices the state is faced with an impossibly complex task that may result in the inefficient use and allocation of resources.

All of these charges against socialism, like those against capitalism, have a real-life basis. Some of these will be discussed in the next few sections. For the moment it is worth considering the last point: the absence of market-based prices under socialism and the resulting difficulties in efficiently allocating productive resources. There has been considerable debate over this issue (Lange and Taylor 1964; Hayek 1935; Elliott 1973).

One resolution to the pricing difficulty under centralized socialism has been the system of *market socialism*. Some market mechanisms have operated in all socialist economies. In Eastern Europe, Yugoslavia and Hungary relied heavily on the market, while in the Soviet Union there was greater reliance on centralized planning. Under market socialism there is an effort both to set prices in a rational way, ensuring the efficient use of resources, and to allow greater autonomy for and competition among firms as an incentive to reduce costs. On the important question of prices, Oskar Lange, the founder of market socialist principles, argued that socialist economies could establish meaningful prices just as easily as market capitalism, through the actions of a central planning board. The central planning board would keep track of the supply of and demand for any good and adjust the price accordingly, so that the good is consumed in greater quantities when it is in excess and in smaller quantities when it is in shortage (Lange and Taylor 1964). The other element of market socialism involves competition between publicly owned firms. Within a set of general guidelines, managers of state firms are granted decision-making autonomy over how they use the factors of production, where they secure the inputs for production, how much they should charge for their products, and to whom they send their output.

It is worth asking, at this point, why one would opt for socialism if efforts designed to enhance efficiency require the incorporation of market capitalist principles. One of Lange's major contributions was to show how, at least theoretically, a socialist economy could carry out market-oriented forms of production in a manner superior to capitalism. Lange believed that a central planning board would be able to establish the correct prices for products with greater ease and fewer trials than in a competitive market system because it would have greater information about the entire economy.

Further, Lange argued that a market socialist economy would have the capacity to consider the needs of all segments of society, and the social costs of actions that are often ignored by private firms under capitalism. In this way the central planning board could raise costs to firms that produce negative externalities. "Internalizing the externalities" results in a net reduction in aggregate waste and a more efficient use of all of society's resources. In theory these are important and compelling arguments. In practice, of course, the mix of plan and market has created some difficulties but overall, in comparison with the centralized model, the economic performance of market socialist societies has been quite positive (see Zimbalist and Sherman 1984:chs. 14–16). Market socialism may prove to be a viable model for a number of former socialist countries (see Pierson 1995).

According to many Marxist theorists (e.g., Brus 1975), the establishment of socialism requires two conditions. The first is that the means of production are collectively controlled, meaning that the processes of production, distribution, investment, and development are directed by public institutions. A second condition of the realization of socialism involves democratic control over these economic processes. To those who have studied the historical record of social practice in various nation-states, it is painfully clear that the second condition has not typically been instituted, and so one finds that the capitalist appropriators are appropriated but the masses have little democratic control over the centralized means of production. It is often for this reason that self-proclaimed socialists have been hard-pressed to identify a real-life example of the socialist ideal.

Under capitalism the organization of the economic sphere—private control of productive property—precludes democratic control over economic processes; under socialism the lack of political democracy precludes converting formal public control into real social control over the means of production (Brus 1975). Capitalist societies separate the economic and political spheres, thereby, at least partially, preventing the principles of democracy from encroaching on the property rights of private capitalists (but see Bowles and Gintis 1982).

The term *bureaucratic centralism* was used to describe the kind of socialist regime that faced the greatest difficulty in instituting the democratic condition (see Arato 1978; Luke and Boggs 1982). Most often associated with Soviet-style socialism, a bureaucratic centralist regime is characterized by extreme centralization and concentration of all basic economic decisions, a rigid bureaucratic structure, and a top-down hierarchical planning apparatus. This bureaucratically centralized structure undermines the basis for the self-management or participation of workers. A further result is the emergence of a socio-political system of stratification in which power and influence are based on one's position in the bureaucratic hierarchy.

The comparison between two economic systems—capitalism and socialism—is a largely theoretical exercise given the fact that there are no capitalisms that rely exclusively on the market for the allocation of resources and there are no longer any existing Soviet-style socialisms. Therefore, we now turn to a consideration of the various forms of coordination that are employed by different economies. This involves a consideration of the role of the state in capitalist societies, an analysis of comparative capitalisms, the debate over free-market versus state-directed strategies, and the demise of socialism and the transition to market-based economies.

THE ROLE OF THE STATE IN CAPITALIST ECONOMIES

The state plays a major role in the development of all capitalist economies. In this section we consider some of the theories offered to explain the expansion of the state apparatus in advanced and less-developed capitalist societies and the socio-economic effects of this intervention.

State Expansion in Advanced Capitalist Economies

''Theories of the state'' have proliferated over the past two decades (see Alford and Friedland 1985; Evans et al. 1985) with the major contributions coming from neo-Marxist theorists. While most of these theories claim loyalty to the intention, if not the writings, of Marx, there is considerable variation in the extent to which they employ a rigid *base-superstructure dichotomy*. The orthodox Marxist contention that the economic base (the forces and social relations of production) determines the form and nature of other social institutions (superstructure), such as the state, has thwarted the development of a Marxist theory of politics (see Miliband 1977 on this problem). In this base-superstructure formulation one need only examine property and production relations in the economic sphere in order to understand the role of the political system. As we shall see, this one-way determinism has been largely supplanted by a more realistic, some might say dialectical, approach.

As a point of departure, however, it is worth considering the Marxist proposition concerning the fundamental contradiction in all societies—the contradiction between the *forces of production* and the *social relations of production*. The forces of production are the buildings, machines, technologies, and organizational corporate arrangements devoted to the production of goods and services. The social relations of production are the relations that exist between the two major social classes—the owners of the forces of production (in capitalist societies, the capitalist class) and the actual producers of goods and services (the working class). These include the property and legal rights of the two social classes and the authority relations between them. During certain periods the forces and social relations of production are compatible and consistent. However, according to the Marxist logic, as societies develop, they come into conflict or become incompatible, prompting major societal-level transformations.

In the modern era we find a contradiction that prompts the expansion of government intervention. As capitalism has developed economically, the corporate units (forces) of production have grown enormously. Corporations control greater and greater proportions of the nation's wealth, and the size and scope of their actions affect larger and larger numbers of people. The increasing interdependence of the economy also means that the actions of larger corporate units will have ripple effects, or external effects, on the entire society, population, and economy. In this sense production takes on more and more of a "social character." In spite of the increasingly social character of production, and the wide-ranging social impact of corporate actions, decisions about production and investment remain in the hands of private capitalists—individuals motivated by self-interest and profit. As part of the social relations of production of capitalism, private capitalists exercise legal sovereign rights over the use of their property. Tension develops between the forces of production, as embodied in the immense corporate units that dominate the economy, and the social relations of production allowing private control over these socially influential units.

The expansion of the state can be seen as a means to resolve this contradiction. Given the wide-ranging impact of private decisions on significant sectors of the population and various communities, the government is compelled to act to ensure both that corporate decisions are not socially destructive and that certain segments of the population are cushioned from the negative effects of corporate actions. This represents one perspective on the growth of the state. The production-based concepts driving this thesis are important to understand, as are the tensions that result from the coexistence of a highly interdependent, complex economy and a legal apparatus that places the economy beyond the direct control of public or democratic forces.

O'Connor's "fiscal crisis of the state" thesis (1973) posits a somewhat mechanistic and functionalist account of the expansion of state activity in capitalist societies. His analysis, like the forces–social relations thesis, links the expansion of the state to the changing organizational forces of production, most notably the rise of the monopoly sector. It is the monopoly sector of capitalism, made up of the large, highly profitable corporate firms, that has the greatest influence on the actions of the state. The powerful role of the monopoly sector in the overall economic health of the system prompts state intervention to stimulate investment, enhance the rate of profit, and ensure the viability of this pivotal sector. O'Connor calls this the *accumulation function* of the state. Through subsidies, tax breaks, industrial development incentives, educational training, and the provision and maintenance of a physical infrastructure, to name only a few activities, the state assists in financing the accumulation of capital.

The consequences of capital accumulation, on the other hand, are not necessarily socially beneficial or distributed equitably. This prompts additional state activity in the form of the *legitimation function*. This refers to government spending and programs designed to create and maintain harmony, mass loyalty, and an image of fairness. Welfare services, progressive taxation policies, and redistributive programs are some of the major components that serve to legitimate both the state and the capitalist economic arrangements.

One of the major contributions of O'Connor's analysis is the connection drawn between the accumulation and legitimation functions and the inevitable crisis of government. His basic point is that the combined expenses of accumulation and legitimation exceed the revenue capacity of the state. Budget shortfalls are the direct product of a state apparatus that publicly finances capital accumulation but, at the same time, does not directly control any of the subsequent profit. In this sense his thesis is founded on the forces–social relations contradiction. The social property relations allowing private corporate units to control their surplus guarantees that state expenses and social costs supporting these units will not yield proportionate financial returns to state institutions.

Supply-side economic theorists in the United States have offered one way out of the fiscal crisis of the state, based on the now infamous "Laffer curve." This curve, graphing the relationship between tax rates and government tax revenue, embodies a fundamental tenet of supply-side economics: Less government intervention means more economic growth. It posits a curvilinear relationship between tax rates and tax revenues. The relationship at first is *positive*—the greater the tax rate, the greater the tax revenue. However, at some point (no one really knows where) tax rates become excessive. This results in a decline in capital investment by private capitalists because returns on investment, after taxes, are insufficient to serve as an incentive. Workers presumably will cease working as the government extracts too large a share of their income in the form of taxes. The net result of the excessive rate of taxation is a decline in economic activity, less income being produced and distributed, and, therefore, less tax revenue for government coffers. The relationship between the tax rate and tax revenue, therefore, becomes *negative* as tax rates reach too high a level.

The policy implications of the Laffer curve are clear: Lower tax rates not only will stimulate economic growth but also will increase state revenue. The best of both worlds is assured. This supply-side logic guided Reagan's economic policy during the early 1980s and, in retrospect, it is now clear that the supply-side claims were (and are) fraudulent (see Thurow 1983). The record budget deficits registered during the 1980s provides ample disconforming evidence for this component of supply-side economic doctrine (once labeled "voodoo economics").

The ability to sell supply-side solutions to capitalist governments is based on the fundamentally dependent relationship that exists between the state and the private economy. This relationship is often described in *structuralist theories of the capitalist state* (see Gold et al. 1975). In attempting to answer the question of why the state in a capitalist society tends to act in the interest of the capitalist class, structuralist theories point to the dependence of the state on economic growth and vitality. State managers have an objective interest in presiding over an expanding economy because economic growth and the accumulation of income and wealth result not only in greater amounts of tax revenue to fund state projects and programs but also in greater levels of public support necessary for winning reelection (see Block 1977). In order to ensure adequate revenue and public support, the state is "structurally constrained," regardless of its ideological predilections, to institute policies that advance economic growth. In a capitalist system economic growth is based, in large part, on the investment behavior of private capitalists, and so the state must act in a manner that is consistent with this economically critical constituency. To do otherwise is to risk disinvestment and capital flight, which, in the end, will create unemployment and recession. In this sense, most government policies designed to facilitate private capital investment are "supply-side" in nature.

Keynesianism and the Political Economy of Crisis

While the more recent economic crises of advanced capitalism, particularly in the United States, have prompted efforts to curtail state action, it is important to understand the historical forces responsible for state expansion in the first place. This brings us to a consideration of *Keynesianism*, named for the economic theories and policy prescriptions of John Maynard Keynes, a British economist. Keynesianism advocates state intervention as a means to prevent economic crises and promote sustained economic expansion. For Keynes one of the central problems of a capitalist economy was the tendency to periodic bouts of unemployment and recession. He believed that these economic problems resulted from the investment behavior of capitalist firms under conditions of insufficient aggregate demand for goods and services (Sidelsky 1979; Martin 1979). Fluctuations in mass buying power created disinvestment, layoffs, unemployment, recession, and depression. In order to prevent these economic cycles Keynes advocated state intervention as a means to manipulate aggregate demand, thus encouraging investment and employment. The major tools for ensuring growth in the Keynesian model are taxation, state spending, and the redistribution of income. These serve to stimulate demand and encourage capital investment. If levels of demand are adequate, firms will be motivated to invest in the production and supply of goods and services.

The economic depression of the 1930s is often viewed as a crisis of overproduction or underconsumption; that is, a crisis in which the supply of goods and services is not matched by a corresponding level of demand. During the expansion that preceded the depression, major advances were made in the methods and organization of production. The most notable development was the rise of the assembly line and the beginning of the mass production of consumer goods. The enormous gains in productivity associated with this organizational innovation, along with the relatively low wages paid to production workers, made for an attractive investment climate. Goods could be produced rapidly and at low cost, but the enormous profit embodied in each commodity went *unrealized* because there was insufficient demand for the products. What followed was disinvestment, layoffs, and economic crisis—a demand-side crisis.

The logic of Keynesianism dictates a solution that involves progressive taxation, the redistribution of income, the expansion of social welfare programs, support for labor organization, collective bargaining, and higher wages. These components, and the legislation supporting them, make up what Bowles and Gintis (1982) describe as the "power-war capital-labor accord." One of the remarkable accomplishments of Keynesian economics was to convince the capitalist class that economic struggle was not necessarily a zero-sum game. Higher wages to workers, while increasing the costs of production, were beneficial to the extent that they served to stimulate aggregate demand and mass buying power. Thus, a compromise between labor and capital came out of the post-depression–World War II period that linked gains in productivity to income gains for workers. As the pie expanded, each could secure a larger and larger slice. The "institutionalization of class struggle" (Lipset 1963), celebrated during the so-called "end of ideology" phase of U.S. capitalism, involved in effect the conversion of labor into an additional and viable interest group, making claims on the economic surplus through collective bargaining contracts and demands for social welfare legislation.

According to various neo-Marxist political economists, the economic crises of the 1970s and early 1980s in the United States were due to the success and logical extension of the very forces that provided the economic prosperity of the post-war period. The argument that contemporary economic crises are the unintended consequence of the Keynesian/labor-capital accord of an earlier period is to apply a basic Marxian premise concerning the way in which solutions to economic crises at one point in time emerge as obstacles and impediments to continued capital accumulation at a later point in time (see Harvey 1982:ch. 6).

Bowles and Gintis (1982) present one version of this general thesis. In opposition to the standard Marxist view that the capitalist state functions exclusively to counteract crisis tendencies and support the interests of capitalists, they argue that actions of the state also can precipitate and reinforce economic crisis tendencies. This is due, in particular, to the success of working-class demands for redistributional social programs and the institutionalization of collective bargaining agreements. These efforts have resulted in the expansion of the social wage or ''citizen's wage''—''that part of a person's consumption supplied by the state by virtue of his citizenship rather than directly by the sale of labor'' (Bowles and Gintis 1982:53)—and the ability to protect and expand wages and job security in the post–World War II period. While these two developments provided the basic foundation for the Keynesian-based economic expansion of the 1950s and 1960s, they have more recently served as impediments to sustained capital accumulation and economic growth.

Long-term labor agreements make it more difficult for capital to reduce wages and lay off workers. Even when they are laid off, unemployment benefits and other social welfare provisions allow workers to collect income without working or entering the labor market. This means that fewer workers enter the labor market than would be the case if there were no alternative sources of income available. The supply of labor is reduced, and this serves to keep wages higher than would be the case if public support were unavailable. Therefore, the normal wage-reducing impact of unemployment is significantly moderated. High unemployment rates do not have as strong a negative effect on wages as was true prior to the expansion of the welfare state. All of these factors, according to Bowles and Gintis, strengthen the bargaining power of labor vis-à-vis capital and reduce the rate of profit and exploitation. This discourages capital investment.

In this interpretation of the recent economic crisis, the institutionalization of Keynesian economic policy and the related economistic demands of labor, originally seen as part of the solution to the economic crisis of the 1930s, are held responsible for the economic stagnation of the 1970s and 1980s. Using a slightly different approach, Weisskopf et al. (1985:259) state: ''Capitalist economic crisis may occur either because the capitalist class is 'too strong' or because it is 'too weak.' '' Where the capitalist class is too strong, the supply-side prospers and the demand-side suffers; where the capitalist side is too weak (in a relative sense), the demand-side is vibrant and the supply-side is inadequate. It is the latter condition that is said to characterize the most recent phase of economic crisis. The reemergence to prominence of supply-side economics and the initial policies associated with Reaganomics are developments consistent with this interpretation.

This neo-Marxist interpretation (see Clegg et al. 1986 for a dissenting view) of the source of economic crisis—the product of expanding welfare expenditures and economistic demands of labor—converges with some conservative accounts. However, the political and policy implications of these respective analyses are quite distinct. Among neo-Marxists the lesson is that there are structural limits on the expansion of social welfare programs under capitalism. Therefore, the economy must be reorganized or transformed along socialist lines. Among conservative economists the recent economic crises vindicate their general opposition to government intervention, point to the bankruptcy of liberal Keynesian formulations, and justify the institutionalization of pro-growth supply-side policies. A basic axiom of this position is that scaling back the state and "getting government off people's backs" is the key to growth and prosperity.

In spite of the widespread acceptance of this latter claim, particularly in the United States, there is little empirical evidence to support it (Katz et al. 1983; Kenworthy 1995; Scharpf 1991). In fact, a cross-national analysis of the United States, West Germany, Japan, and Sweden since 1960 (Gorham 1987) indicates that the United States, with the consistently lowest level of public-sector spending among the four nations, ranks last in per capita economic growth, industrial productivity, average unemployment, and the "misery index," which combines unemployment and inflation rates. These and similar results from other studies clearly call into question the simple claim that less government intervention means more prosperity. What all the studies suggest (Katz et al. 1983; Kenworthy 1995; Scharpf 1991) is that under certain structural arrangements, state intervention can enhance not only the rate of growth but also the quality of life.

Statism in the Less-Developed World

The active interventionist state is not a phenomenon confined to advanced capitalist economies. In the less-developed world, state actions also are a major determinant of socio-economic development. The universal extension of governmental intervention and regulation has prompted one observer to describe the second half of the twentieth century as the "era of the state" and to argue:

> The active penetration of society and economy by agents of the state is as extensive as at any previous period in the several-centuries history of the modern state, including the so-called "age of absolutism." This situation is widely recognized and is true virtually of all countries. "Statism" is pervasive. (Duvall and Freeman 1981:99)

Explanations for the expansion of the state in less-developed economies differ from those offered for advanced capitalist nations. While in both cases the state is concerned, first and foremost, with facilitating the process of capital accumulation, in less-developed economies there is a greater tendency for the state to play the role of entrepreneur, hence the term "state entrepreneurship." This is defined as

the expansion of the state into *productive* sectors of the economy (as distinct from infrastructural provision), the *degree* to which (public) management conforms to standard capitalist performance criteria, and the general *commitment* of the state to capitalist development. These features—state ownership of noninfrastructure enterprises, the relative importance of capitalist performance criteria, and the extensive commitment to capitalism—define the entrepreneurial state. (Duvall and Freeman 1981:105)

The hyperactivity of the state in less-developed economies and its encroachment into productive sectors are developments best understood in the context of the global economic structure and the historical position of less-developed nations within this system.

The term "entrepreneur," as was seen in Chapter 2, is usually reserved for private individuals who are innovators and risk-takers, and, by virtue of these actions, stimulate economic growth and production. Public organizations are, if anything, seen as a hindrance to this entrepreneurial process. However, where no independent class of entrepreneurs actually exists or is willing to act according to the capitalist ideal, other institutions may be required to fill the void in order for economic expansion to occur.

According to dependency theorists (who are considered in detail in Chapter 6), an indigenous entrepreneurial capitalist class is largely absent in less-developed nations. The shortage of a national bourgeoisie possessing the economic and political autonomy to shape the development of less-developed economies is, in this view, the historical product of domination by, and subservience to, the international market and multinational corporations (Cardoso and Faletto 1979; Evans 1982). A national capitalist class is unable to emerge or exert itself in the face of domination by these external forces. The weakness of this class is reflected in its inability to initiate a truly bourgeois revolution and its lack of control over sufficient economic resources to transform the forces of production. In order for the economy to modernize, therefore, substitutes for the national capitalist class must be found. There are three basic options: (1) allow the economy to be developed and controlled by the external forces of multinational corporate capital; (2) use the state as an institutional substitute for the absent national capitalist class; (3) align the state with foreign capital in an effort to encourage and direct capital investment.

This developmental dilemma is not unique to contemporary less-developed nations. As Gerschenkron's (1962) theory of "delayed industrialization" outlines, both Germany and Russia faced a similar choice in their effort to "catch up" with England. In fact, Gerschenkron believes there are advantages to late industrialization because many of the painful evolutionary stages have been faced, and technological innovations developed, by the leading international economies. The state can then, as entrepreneurial substitute, select the proven and most productive technologies and organizational methods as strategies for economic growth.

Gerschenkron's thesis provides a rationale for the state as an institutional substitute for the capitalist class. Evans (1979; 1982) indicates that the actual situation for less-developed nations is somewhat more complex and usually involves a tripartite arrangement composed of the state, multinational corporations (MNCs), and the national bourgeoisie. His analysis of the Brazilian experience (1979; 1982) represents a major contribution to the development literature.

Evans notes that the precise configuration of the tripartite alliance varies at different historical moments, and there are periods when the state favors MNCs to the detriment of the national bourgeoisie. Such an alliance—between the state and MNCs—existed in its strongest form in Brazil during the post–import-substitution industrialization phase as part of the development of the bureaucratic-authoritarian regime (described above). At the height of the dual alliance version of the bureaucratic authoritarian state (in Brazil, from 1968 to 1973), government policy was aimed at establishing an attractive business climate for international capital by financing infrastructural projects that complemented the needs of foreign capital, and repressing popular political movements and working-class demands. During this period the national bourgeoisie exerted little impact on government policies, many of which were carried out at the expense of local capital. However, if the state appears overly subservient to foreign capital, it risks not only the opposition of domestic elites but also political disruption by anti-imperialist nationalist movements.

The course of events in Brazil, as described by Evans (1982), supports this theoretical expectation. The dual alliance was followed by a period of government activity designed to "reinvent the bourgeoisie." Policies included the expansion of loan capital at generous terms for domestically owned firms and projects, preferential interest rates for activity in particular industrial areas, and fiscal incentives. These efforts, however, met with limited success. Evans attributes the failure of these programs to a fundamental contradiction faced by less-developed states: the simultaneous attempt to maintain good relations with international capital and to strengthen the domestic capitalist class.

While the role of the state in less-developed nations has been widely analyzed, recent work has made an effort to distinguish between types of states and state roles in the development process. More specifically, we are interested in whether variation in state structures and roles, as societal level factors, can explain the variation in the pace and trajectory of socio-economic development.

Peter Evans (1995) has recently refined his analysis of the state in newly industrializing countries, and identified four major roles the state may play in stimulating and directing economic activity. He labels these various roles *custodian, demiurge, midwife*, and *husbandry*.

When the state plays the role of *custodian*, the primary intention is to protect, police, and prevent particular forms of economic behavior that are viewed as inappropriate. This role may be associated with a minimalist state approach that proscribes minimal government intervention in the economic sphere except where private capital may be engaged in activities viewed as detrimental to the general interest. These can include, for example, anti-competitive actions by firms, licensing and patent violations, the production of low-quality or unsafe products, or the despoilment of environmental resources.

The state role as *demiurge* involves the state in the direct production of goods and services. In contrast to the minimalism of the custodial role, the state plays a maximalist role when it takes over productive activities and replaces or competes with private capital. As we have noted above, there are instances in which the state may view the domestic capitalist class as incapable of launching the necessary investments required for industrial transformation. Thus, the "state as entrepreneur" becomes the model guiding state involvement, through state-owned and managed enterprises, in certain strategic economic sectors.

In Evans' view, neither the custodial nor demiurge role is the best means for ensuring and enhancing the transformation toward a vibrant, competitive, and industrial economy. "Both custodial and demiurge grow out of negative conceptions of the private entrepreneurial class: as primarily requiring restraint in the case of the custodial and as incapable of entrepreneurship in the case of the demiurge" (Evans 1995:80). The problem with the custodial role is the insufficient attention to the *promotion* of particular positive economic activities. The demiurge role suffers from expansion and overreaching into areas that the state is unable to adequately develop, compete, and perform. "Instead of substituting itself for private producers, the state can try to assist in the emergence of new entrepreneurial groups and to induce existing entrepreneurs to take on more challenging endeavors" (Evans 1995:80).

These approaches (assistance and inducement) are found in the midwife and husbandry roles. The role of the *midwife* may entail some skepticism about the abilities of private capital to identify and pursue the most profitable economic opportunities, but this is coupled with an equally strong conviction that private capital is malleable and can be induced to "play an entrepreneurial role that it would otherwise be reluctant to undertake, thereby creating organizational and institutional resources committed to new sectors or new kinds of endeavors" (1995:81). In this role the state assists in the emergence of new forms of economic activity while supporting and protecting these infant firms and industries.

The final role identified by Evans, *husbandry*, takes midwifery a step further by cajoling, assisting, and pushing existing private capital in ways that ensure long-term economic growth and the exploitation of global economic opportunities. In this role the state can provide the information required for the effective economic mobilization of firms, state resources, and organizations to carry out risky complementary tasks like research and development, and loan guarantees that leverage investment capacities. In Evans' overall assessment of these various state roles, he emphasizes the importance of "trying to create synergistic promotional relations with entrepreneurs or potential entrepreneurs. Combining midwifery and husbandry should work better than combinations that rely more heavily on custodial or demiurge'' (Evans 1995:14).

Evans' analysis of state roles is based on an examination of the relationship between the state, local private capital, and transnational corporations in Brazil, India, and Korea. It is important to note that the four state roles outlined above are not mutually exclusive and can be applied to specific economic sectors (rather than across all forms of national economic activity). Thus, any particular nation may pursue several different roles and these may vary across economic sectors. Evans' primary focus is on the information technology and computer industry sectors of the economies. Based on a detailed examination of these cases, Evans comes to some conclusions about the broad role of the state and the forms of state structure that are likely to advance industrial transformation.

The *developmental state*, according to Evans, is the ideal political institution for the purpose of industrial transformation and socio-economic development. The developmental state combines both the midwife and husbandry roles that nurture, direct, and support private capital. A central component of the developmental state, and one that defines both its internal structure and relation to society, is *embedded autonomy*. The strength of the developmental state rests on its ability to operate organizationally as a coherent and autonomous bureaucracy, in the Weberian sense, while also establishing strong external ties to strategic actors and social groups. The developmental state, as a bureaucratic structure, is able to take actions independent of the interest of any particular group and maintain an autonomous policy-making capacity. On the other hand, state actions are ''embedded in a concrete set of social ties that binds the state to society and provides institutionalized channels for the continued negotiation and renegotiation of goals and policies. . . . Only when embeddedness and autonomy are joined together can a state be called developmental'' (Evans 1995: 12).

The developmental state, as described by Evans, has been most closely associated with Japan (Johnson 1982) and the newly industrialized countries of East Asia, particularly Korea and Taiwan (Wade 1990). These countries represent the dynamic of export-oriented capitalism coupled with an integral state role in directing and assisting strategic industrial sectors. Evans' comparative study of Korea, Brazil, and India allows an analysis of the impact of variations in state organization and state-society relations on socio-economic development.

The *comparative institutional approach* employed by Evans is a direct challenge to the neo-utilitarian view of the state. *Neo-utilitarians* view the state as an institution composed of bureaucrats who are primarily interested in expanding the size, power, and resources of their organization. Public officials, according to this perspective, are driven by self-interest rather than a public spirit and will therefore pursue policies and take actions that can only advance the interests of state officials at the expense of the larger society. State involvement in economic affairs should, accordingly, be kept to a minimum, involving only the protection of private property and the legal enforcement of private contracts.

In spite of the economic success of East Asian nations, and the significant role played by the state in directing this socio-economic development, the neo-utilitarian perspective remains quite popular, primarily as an anti-statist ideology. Much of the popular hostility to state involvement rests on an image of the state as a vast, oversized and intrusive bureaucracy that is intrusive, inefficient, and wasteful. While the term *bureaucracy* is used pejoratively, Evans' thesis on the role of the state conceptualizes the state bureaucracy in Weberian terms (Evans 1995:30–31) as an institution that transcends individual interests, that requires some degree of insulation from the demands of the larger society, that confers a "distinctive and rewarding status," and that concentrates expertise and professionalism through "meritocratic recruitment and provision of opportunities for long-term career rewards." If the state, and its personnel, are guided by this bureaucratic ethos (see Sheridan 1996), the state has the potential to make a positive contribution to economic growth. As Evans (1995:40) puts it: "A comparative institutional approach turns the neo-utilitarian image of the state on its head. It is the scarcity of bureaucracy that undermines development, not its prevalence."

COMPARATIVE CAPITALISMS

With the demise of Soviet and East and Central European socialism, the study of comparative economic systems and development has shifted toward an analysis of different forms of capitalism. As noted in Chapter 3, one element of the focus on capitalist systems concerns the various modes of industrial organization and corporate governance. In this section we shift to the broader national institutional configurations of capitalist economies that are purported to influence the pace and pattern of socio-economic development.

Before an analysis and comparison of some of the varieties of capitalism, it is worth noting that the demise of state socialism, and the dominance of market-based capitalism, has produced a unique global situation that has even been described as "the end of history" (Fukuyama 1992). If historical dynamics are defined by competing economic systems and ideologies, the widespread embracement of capitalism is viewed as the end of a long historical struggle. At the same time, just as the market becomes the dominant global institutional apparatus, the weaknesses of the system are exposed and critiqued—excessive individualism, naked self-interest, the decline of community, corporate downsizing, the end of employment, the neglect of social investment, and so forth (Aronowitz and DiFazio 1994; Rifkin 1995; Bellah et al. 1985; Kuttner 1997). In short, the future of capitalism may not be as secure as many believe. History marches forward. One version of this message has been provided by Lester Thurow (1996) who believes competition is the key to the survival and adaptation of capitalism. Thurow cites many of the challenges that face capitalist economies—the end of communism, the rise of brainpower industries, a multipolar world—and he believes that these will require significant changes in the ideology and policies of contemporary capitalism. In fact, much of the analysis of different forms of capitalism implicitly assumes that not all forms of capitalism are equally viable and that particular forms possess considerable advantages that may enhance their adaptive ability.

Perhaps the most common comparison (made by Thurow himself) is between U.S. and Japanese or, more broadly, ''Anglo-Saxon'' (U.S. and Britain) and ''communitarian'' (Japan and Germany) capitalism. These distinctions, as noted in earlier chapters, operate at and manifest themselves at the individual and organizational levels of analysis. At the societal level, we are more interested in the institutional forces that produce these capitalist variants. One significant institutional difference concerns the role of the government in planning and promoting long-term growth and industrial strategies. In Germany and Japan the government is more heavily involved in economic planning, direction, and investment than in the United States or Britain. This is viewed by many observers as a comparative advantage that allows the government to take a pro-active stance in economic affairs and represents adaptive ability in the face of changing conditions. In the United States and the United Kingdom, on the other hand, there is a greater tendency toward laissez-faire, at least in terms of long-term planning and government investment, and a belief that market forces and signals are the best mechanisms to ensure a responsive and flexible economy. As Thurow describes it: ''Governments should protect private property rights, then get out of the way and let individuals do their thing. Capitalism will spontaneously combust'' (1992:29). If one examines economic success and global competitive prowess over the past fifteen years, there is considerable support for the view that communitarian capitalism possesses the clear advantage. Observers like Thurow believe this is especially the case given the changing nature of ''21st century capitalism'' which operates on international rules and man-made (rather than natural resource–based) comparative advantages. Further distinctions between the two forms of capitalism are captured in notions of *social market economy* and *consumer versus producer economics* (Thurow 1992).

The social market economy is exemplified by several institutional features of the German economy that include the holding of industry stock shares by state and federal governments, massive public investment in businesses such as Airbus Industries, a publicly funded training and apprenticeship system, and an extensive array of social welfare programs designed to reduce the inequalities associated with unregulated capitalist markets. These policies and institutions are viewed as reflecting a general concern for the social and collective impact of economic growth that allows a greater level of government intervention, direction, and social welfare support.

Thurow (1992) has also compared individualistic and communitarian forms of capitalism on the extent to which their economies are structured to encourage consumption or production. The United States is viewed as a classic case of consumer economics that assumes human satisfaction is derived from consumption and leisure. This assumption has implications for the institutional configuration and the strategic behavior of productive units. If return on investment and income flow are viewed as the primary objectives, and work and savings are nothing more than means to achieve these ends, then corporate strategy and the government policies supporting economic activity are also likely to be based on this rationale. In contrast, producer economics assume that humans are "social builders" who are willing to forego immediate consumption, and the accumulation of consumer goods, if it means building a highly competitive economy and accumulating production goods that can enhance long-term productivity. Thurow characterizes Japan as the prototypical producer economy and he believes the United States can learn a great deal from this philosophy. Successful capitalism, according to Thurow, must be built on a foundation that recognizes both components of human striving.

In comparing these two approaches, Thurow identifies some of the broader economic implications and he clearly suggests that producer economics is a critical element for success in a competitive world economy (Thurow 1992:124–151). The kinds of economic activity that are encouraged by this form of capitalism include:

• investment of profits into further expansion rather than individual consumption;
• an emphasis on expanding market share over profit maximization;
• reducing levels of consumption in favor of long-term savings and investment;
• accepting a lower rate of return on investment during the early stages of a project;
• patient institutional stockholders rather than those who are solely interested in immediate return and dividends;
• an obligation to the firm and the employees rather than shareholders;
• sustained investment in research and development even through periods of recession and declining demand for products;
• a national strategy for supporting long-term investment and major technology products.

Clearly, many of these economic activities are driven by organizational-level strategies. However, these organizational decisions regarding investment and consumption are embedded in a broader national system of government policies and programs that can either reinforce or discourage such behaviors and strategies. Tax laws, industrial policies, and institutional arrangements related to the ownership and control patterns of the corporation have an enormous influence and, according to Thurow, they can determine who wins and who loses on the global economic playing field.

Recent empirical evidence would seem to favor the long-run success of the empire-building firms. Firms based on the principle of producer economics are clearly on the offensive in international markets, while those based on profit maximization are on the defensive. Individualistic capitalism meets communitarian capitalism. Eventually, the

Table 5.1
Comparative Capitalist Institutions and Ideology: United States, Germany, and Japan

	United States	**Germany**	**Japan**
Political Institutions	Liberal Democracy; divided government; highly organized interest groups	Social democracy; weak bureaucracy; corporatist organizational legacy	Developmental Democracy; strong bureaucracy; "reciprocal consent" between state and firms
Economic Institutions	Decentralized, open markets; unconcentrated capital markets; antitrust tradition	Organized markets; tiers of firms; bank-centered capital markets; universal banks	Guided, bifurcated, difficult-to-penetrate markets; tight business networks/cartels in declining industry
Dominant Economic Ideology	Free enterprise liberalism	Social partnership	Technonationalism

Source: Pauly and Reich (1997), table 1.

winners will be known. In the end the winner will force losers to change and play by the winner's rules. (Thurow 1992:149–151)

There is a vast and growing literature in the area of comparative capitalism and Thurow's analysis represents only one particular but generally representative strand of thought.[2] A similar though more highly differentiated model is provided by Pauly and Reich in their research on variations in the behavior of multinational firms. While their primary focus is the organizational level of analysis, they emphasize the linkage to national institutions. Table 5.1 (Pauly and Reich 1997:7) provides a comparative framework for the institutional/ideological difference between the United States, Japan, and Germany. Politically, the nations are distinguished by the form of democratic organization and representation with the United States characterized by a highly decentralized and interest group–based system, Germany employing a corporatist model, and Japan a strongly bureaucratic system with a tight reciprocal relationship between major keiretsu firms and the state. On the economic institutional dimension the market structures are quite distinct with the United States having the ''decentralized'' open market structure, Germany a more ''organized'' and cartel-based system tied to industrial groups and banks, and Japan a ''guided'' market system that is highly dualistic and dominated by keiretsu networks of firms. The dominant economic ideology reflects, to a large extent, these political and economic institutional patterns. For the United States, free enterprise liberalism supports a decentralized political and economic system with the lowest levels of government intervention and planning. Germany is characterized as a "social partner-ship" which is consistent with Thurow's notion of a "social market" emphasizing the social welfare/cooperative system of industrial relations and state policy. Japan is described as a "technonationalist" ideology which implies a strong state-guided system of support for domestic firms in competition with foreign firms and nations. These capitalist variants, largely obscured in the du-alistic comparison of market versus state socialist economies, are becoming in-creasingly salient in the current era of global market competition among a large number of self-proclaimed market capitalist economies.

The Corporatist Variant

Another variant of the capitalist mode of economic organization is *corpora-tism*. This term is used to describe a political arrangement, defined by Katzen-stein as "the voluntary, cooperative regulation of conflicts over economic and social issues through highly structured and interpenetrating political relationships between business, trade union, and the state, augmented by political parties" (1985:32). Grant sees it as

[a] process of interest intermediation which involves the negotiation of policy between the state agencies and interest organizations arising from the division of labor in society, where the policy agreements are implemented through the collaboration of the interest organizations and their willingness and ability to secure the compliance of their members. (1985:3–4)

This two-part definition touches on the essential elements of corporatism for our purposes, though it should be noted that there is a great deal of debate over the precise meaning of the term (see Panitch 1980). Corporatism is as much a political arrangement as an economic strategy. It is a political arrangement with significant economic implications and, more directly in the current context, it is regarded as a political solution to potential economic stagnation and decline in advanced capitalist societies.

As the definition of corporatism implies, a corporatist political-economic structure involves relations, bargaining, and compromise between encompassing interest organizations. The contribution of this form of interest articulation to economic success is the subject of a number of studies, primarily of European political-economic systems (Esping-Anderson 1984; Katzenstein 1984; 1985; Schmitter 1981; and see Hicks 1988 for a review of some of this literature).

Katzenstein's (1985) detailed analysis of the "small states" of Europe (Aus-tria, Belgium, Denmark, the Netherlands, Norway, Sweden, and Switzerland) and their success in dealing with the rapidly changing international economic conditions is a direct endorsement of the democratic corporatist system. Ac-cording to Katzenstein, these systems have been able to respond in a flexible manner to changing economic demands. This can be contrasted with the social rigidity characteristic of societies such as the United States, that are composed of narrowly based interest organizations. In fact, the criteria selected by Katzenstein for evaluating the performance of a political economic system and determining the superiority of corporatism conform closely to the conditions for sustained economic growth cited by theorists such as Mancur Olson (1982):

the extent to which social coalitions, political institutions, and public policies facilitate or impede *shifts in the factors of production that increase economic efficiency* with due regard to the requirements of political legitimacy. (Katzenstein 1985:29; emphasis added)

Olson's theory of economic decline is based on the rigidity and inflexibility in the factors of production that result when self-interested organizations seek to defend the narrow interests of their members. Under corporatism interest groups are often described as "peak associations" that are "broadly based and organize a very large proportion of producers and workers" (Katzenstein 1985: 33). According to Olson's thesis, this system of association would give rise to one of the distinguishing traits of corporatism identified by Katzenstein: an ideology of social partnership that "mitigates class conflict" and facilitates "notions of public interest." Representatives of peak associations meet to bargain over and set broad parameters on wages, investment strategies, employment targets, social spending, economic regulations, and so on. Once a certain set of national economic policies has been established, the members of each association are expected to abide by the agreement in the name of the general collective good, with compliance enforced on members from the top down within each encompassing organization.

It should be clear that corporatism is, for all practical purposes, a political mechanism designed to elicit consent and maintain social order in the name of economic growth and prosperity. It differs from the more authoritarian forms of political control in that social order and compliance are based not on terror and coercion but on negotiation and legitimacy.

One of the central questions, of course, is who benefits most from this arrangement? The capitalist class? The working class? Political authorities? There is considerable debate over this issue. Some observers believe corporatism is a means to restrain and control the working class and strengthen the position of the capitalist class and the capitalist system (Panitch 1979; 1980). While it is true that corporatism is most often employed in the context of a capitalist economy, and is therefore "structurally constrained" to support the imperative of private capital accumulation, it is equally true that many of the economic policies stemming from corporatist negotiation allocate resources on a nonmarket basis. In this sense the economic policies often involve considerable government intervention and therefore convert the system away from a pure market capitalist model.

A number of empirical studies of the macro-economic effects of corporatist practice suggest that this political arrangement supports higher levels of employment and lower levels of inflation (Cameron 1978; Schmidt 1982; Kenworthy 1995). Corporatism also may appear attractive in the face of alternative capitalist policies designed to stimulate capital accumulation, such as the anti-inflationary monetarist policies that, as a condition for subsequent economic expansion, subject the economy to a recessionary phase that clearly cripples the working class and undermines wage levels. Such policies have been the recent experience of the United States and Great Britain. There remains widespread skepticism over the long-term efficacy of such policies and a general recognition that some form of social contract and state planning is inevitable. Some version of corporatism, taking into account national differences, is a frequently mentioned strategy aimed at alleviating the political-economic stalemate and market uncertainty.

Free Market versus State-Directed Development

It should be emphasized that there is no consensus over which particular form of capitalism is best suited for dynamic socio-economic development. The development policy debate rages on. In fact, there is considerable debate over the very question of whether a nation's ability to produce for, and successfully compete in, international markets, has any appreciable impact on the health of the domestic economy (see Krugman 1994a; 1996; Kuttner 1997). Many arguments for a particular type of capitalist strategy (e.g., Thurow 1992b) assume this is the primary objective of development policy. Nonetheless, there are some clearly defined cleavages. One of the most obvious, which also overlaps with the individualistic (or competitive) versus communitarian (or cooperative) capitalism dichotomy, centers on the relative advantage of a free market versus state-directed strategy. The United States is associated with the former, Japan and Germany the latter.

Arguments for or against a market or state development strategy tend to select particular countries as either showcases for a particular strategy or examples of a wrong-headed development approach. East Asia is often held up as a region that has not only experienced rapid economic growth but has also moved into a highly competitive position in the world economy. The realization of both of these objectives may be responsible for the association of these two factors in much of the development literature. What is especially interesting about the East Asian nations is their selection as exemplary models of development by both market-oriented and state-oriented theorists.

Much of the current enthusiasm for what has been described as an *export-oriented industrialization strategy* is based on the recent experience of a handful of less-developed nations, most notably Hong Kong, Singapore, South Korea, and Taiwan. Since about 1960 each of these nations has pursued a concerted trade strategy that emphasizes the industrial production of goods for export markets. This represents a departure from the alternative strategy—import-substitution industrialization (ISI)—which emphasizes the internal production of manufactured products for domestic markets.

The comparative economic performance of the inward- versus outward-oriented nations supports arguments for an export-led industrialization strategy. Examining a variety of macro-economic indicators, from the growth in GNP to the share of the labor force in industry, a World Bank (1987:85) report concludes: "The figures suggest that the economic performance of the outward-oriented economies has been broadly superior to that of the inward-oriented economies in almost all respects."

The World Bank is by no means a totally unbiased, nonpartisan agency. It tends to associate the outward-oriented export strategy with its preference for an "open economy." The outward-oriented economy is regarded as more "open" to the extent that it "does not discriminate between production for the domestic market and exports, nor between purchases of domestic goods and foreign goods" (World Bank 1987:78). Again, this is contrasted with inward-oriented policies that presumably discourage production for export and place restrictions on the importation of foreign goods. In short, at least in theory, the outward-oriented strategy is more in line with the tenets of free trade and liberal economic policy that allow the free flow of goods and foreign capital investment across national borders. This free market philosophy tends to be favored by the World Bank and the International Monetary Fund not only for the economic benefits presumably accruing to the less-developed nations that follow the outward-oriented strategy, but also for the opportunities this policy affords financial and industrial capital in the developed industrial nations. In reality, however, the terms "open," "free," and "unrestricted" are not wholly applicable to the regimes that exercise the outward-oriented strategy.

One of the most systematic analyses of the relationship between competing theoretical arguments and the actual development policies implemented in East Asia can be found in the work of Robert Wade (1988; 1990). In his book *Governing the Market*, Wade addresses the arguments of the free market neo-classical theorists regarding the optimal recipe for development and attempts to determine whether the success of East Asian industrialization vindicates or refutes this perspective. As noted, the recent economic performance of these nations has been used as evidence to support both the free market and state-directed development models. Among the free market theorists the emphasis is placed upon the actions of entrepreneurs and the private sector, the free markets for commodities and labor, the absence of "central planning" by government, and the export-oriented approach to foreign trade. Free markets and free trade are the terms that are most often associated with East Asian industrialization. This free market, *neo-classical*, or what has come to be known as the *neo-liberal*, approach, assumes that economic growth and efficiency are maximized when capital investment and the exchange of goods and services are conducted by private capitalists with a minimum of government intervention, regulation, taxation, or redistribution. Market outcomes, in this view, are optimal outcomes, and any efforts by government to adjust or intervene are distortions that will only produce a less optimal outcome. It is widely assumed, among these theorists, that the poor economic performance of Latin American nations is due to the excessive role of the state while the East Asian nations have practiced a much more open, unregulated, free market approach.

Wade reviews the evidence that is typically garnered in support of the neo-classical thesis and identifies a critical point of confusion among these theorists—the assumption that an outward-oriented export development strategy is synonymous with free trade and free markets. The neo-classical or neo-liberal theorists have a preference for economies that develop industries that export and compete in international markets versus industries that are designed to produce for the domestic market, and that are protected from competition with foreign firms. This preference seems to have translated into a corollary belief that export-oriented industrialization strategies, commonly associated with East Asian nations, involve adherence to free market/free trade principles.

Wade advances an alternative explanation for East Asian, and in particular Taiwanese, economic development that he calls the *governed market theory*. According to Wade (1990:26–27) East Asian industrialization is a product of:

1. very high levels of productive investment, making for fast transfer of newer techniques into actual production;

2. more investment than would have occurred in the absence of government intervention; and

3. exposure of many industries to international competition, in foreign markets if not at home. . . . These are the proximate causes. At a second level of causation, they are themselves the result of a set of government economic policies. Using incentives, controls, and mechanisms to spread risk, these policies enabled the government to guide—or govern—market processes of resource allocation so as to produce different production and investment outcomes than would have occurred with either free market or simulated free market policies.

More specifically, in the case of Taiwan, the government "guided the market" through the following general policies (Wade 1990:27–28):

1. redistributing agricultural land in the early post-war period;

2. taking control over the financial system and ensuring that financial capital meets the needs of the industrial sector;

3. regulating the impact of foreign competition and controlling the distribution of foreign exchange used to import goods;

4. export promotion schemes;

5. maintaining the stability of financial variables that influences long-term investment (e.g., interest and exchange rates);

6. promoting technology acquisition from multinational corporations and building a national technology infrastructure;

7. providing direct assistance to strategic industries and export firms.

Together, these various policies point to governmental involvement in (a) land reform, which had the impact of weakening the landowning class in relation to the domestic capitalist class; (b) the finance capital sector, which provides the necessary financial resources to domestic industries; (c) both the export and import sides of foreign trade; (d) the establishment of technological infrastructure that supports the research and development needs of the economy; and (e) support for particular firms and industries deemed critical for the long-term economic development of the nation. This pattern of government involvement in Taiwan is a clear departure from the free market scenario advanced by the neo-classical and neo-liberal policy advisors. And yet, Taiwan has experienced some of the most dramatic economic advances of any East Asian nation in terms of GNP per capita, manufactured exports to the United States, the development of producer good industries, and level of capital formation.[3]

Another element of the state role that is also ignored by those advocating free market liberalism involves the political arrangements in East Asia. Not only does the economic sphere fail to correspond to the liberal ideal; the political apparatus is also characterized by a heavy-handed state. The terms used to describe the South Korean political-economic model include *bureaucratic authoritarian corporatism* (Deyo 1981) and *bureaucratic authoritarian industrializing regime* (Cumings 1984). As was noted in the earlier discussion of bureaucratic authoritarianism, such a system tends to be instituted as a means to control and deactivate the population in the name of modernization and economic growth. The term *neo-fascist* has also been applied to the South Korean regime.

The important implication of these various caricatures is that the export-oriented strategy is accompanied by a political arrangement that involves tight controls over the actions of labor and the working classes. The purpose is to discourage unionization, collective bargaining, and higher wages for industrial workers. These political actions are a direct product of a strategy that hinges on attracting foreign capital investment and producing competitive world-market commodities.

The ability of other nations to employ this accumulation strategy is contingent on the ability to control the domestic labor force, coordinate economic enterprises, and attract foreign investment. These factors strike at a variety of levels of analysis and, ultimately, given the ''open'' nature of this development policy, international-level opportunities and constraints must also be considered.

SOCIALIST TRANSITION TO MARKET-BASED ECONOMIES

An analysis of comparative economic systems would be incomplete without some consideration of the demise of socialism and the transition to market-based economies. Diagnoses of the economic ills of socialism are now widely available (e.g., Denitch 1990; Kornai 1986). An early analysis, provided prior to the collapse of Eastern and Central European socialism, was contained in Alec Nove's *The Economics of Feasible Socialism* (1983). Nove advanced a variety of compelling explanations for the economic failure of Soviet-style socialism and raised many issues of central importance for development economics.

While Nove believed that efforts to implement socialism were worthwhile, he also emphasized that a reliance on the writings of Marx for this purpose was futile and self-defeating. According to Nove, Marx made numerous assumptions about socialist society that, unfortunately, either trivialized the economic difficulties facing socialist regimes or encouraged the view that economic problems would automatically disappear the moment the capitalist class had been overthrown. The most damaging assumption among these, for Nove, was that socialism would emerge in an economic context of post-scarcity material abundance. If a society actually possesses unlimited resources and, therefore, transcends scarcity, then economic decisions are significantly simplified, tradeoffs are a thing of the past, and basic conflicts and choices concerning resource allocation are transcended.

In place of the assumption of material abundance, Nove preferred the more sobering concept of *opportunity cost*, which refers to the fact that allocating resources to one area means that other, possibly more profitable, avenues of activity are forgone. This is one version of the *zero-sum game*. Resources are finite, and thus each and every need cannot be satisfied simultaneously—some gain and some lose.

One of the basic problems faced by socialist states was the effective coordination of production and distribution through a centralized planning mechanism. Eliminating the capitalist market meant that the state had to assume responsibility for ensuring that what is needed is produced, that what is needed to produce is produced, that goods are allocated and distributed where they are required, that human energy is expended in sufficient quantities, and so on. Nove repeatedly emphasized the point that the task of state socialism is immense and complex. It requires information, motivation, and means. The use of bureaucratic organizations with multilevel hierarchies was the unavoidable mechanism for the provision of these essential elements of economic production under a planned economy. Resources, orders, authority, incentives, and decisions were distributed through hierarchical structures. These basic organizational problems were, for Nove, never adequately confronted by most socialists, and it is on this count that he was most critical of Marx, who, he states:

never considered the organisational implications of his ideas. By this I do not mean a blueprint or an organisational diagram, but basic principles such as: the necessary coexistence of centralisation and decentralisation, the need to reconcile the inevitable differences of view about what needs to be done; the importance of responsibility and of implementation of decisions taken, including the provision of the means of implementation. (1983:59)

Nove also devoted a great deal of space to outlining some of the practical problems that inevitably arise in a centralized planned economy and how certain reforms may be required in order to attain the desired results. He clearly favored, instead of a totally planned system, the introduction of some level of market competition for the production and sale of consumer goods. He noted that all economies are interested in matching the quantity of the production of commodities with a corresponding level of demand—that what is produced will be consumed. One of the greatest economic uncertainties is predicting at time A what consumers will need and want at time B. In a planned economy the costs of this uncertainty can be handled, such that all that is produced is consumed, by letting the *producers determine consumption.*

This highlights the importance of *choice.* The more choice there is, the less predictability for obvious reasons. It is therefore tempting for planners to limit or even eliminate choice, in the interests of good forecasting and the avoidance of the waste which is the inevitable consequence of getting a forecast wrong. . . . An aspect of choice is competition . . . if customers are free to seek their sources of supply, then the converse is that producers will seek customers. (1983:41)

Nove was well aware that competition for consumers and the inevitable mismatch in ex ante production and ex post consumption results in a waste of resources. In response to this obvious drawback of competition, he made a very simple argument, repeated throughout his book, that is often unappreciated by the tireless partisans of socialism and capitalism:

no perfect system exists or can exist, that in general all institutional arrangements carry with them advantages *and* disadvantages. One can seldom get something for nothing. . . . The best solution is bound to be a compromise. (1983:42)

Many economic problems presumably inherent to one system or the other tend to emerge in different ways in both systems. A case in point is the negative externality or diseconomy. As indicated in our discussion of capitalism, private rationality does not always yield socially rational outcomes. It is often assumed that in a socialist economy all externalities are internalized in a single state bureaucracy. Yet, as Nove demonstrates, diseconomies are not necessarily the result of private ownership of productive property but, rather, of the *separation of decision-making units.* Under state socialism many different departments and agencies are evaluated on their ability to fulfill parts of the larger plan. Successful fulfillment of the plan requires both a realistic production target and access to the supplies required to produce the particular good or service. Thus, there is a built-in incentive for enterprise managers to desire and set planning targets that can easily be met, to overapply for inputs, and to hoard labor and materials. This is rational from the standpoint of the manager who is driven by the plan fulfillment (rather than the profit) motive. But collectively the effect is to create shortages and bottlenecks, and reduce the potential surplus that would be generated if managers were willing to take greater risks and required to pay for redundant labor and supplies. Thus, external diseconomies arise out of the organization of state socialism just as they do under systems of private capitalism.

The strength of planned socialist economies has involved the ability to mobilize and direct resources toward large-scale measurable economic objectives. The Soviet Union was able to collectivize agriculture, build a modern industrial infrastructure, and maintain a military industrial complex. As has been the case with many less-developed nations, the active intervention of the state has been a major strategy in "catching up" with the more advanced industrial societies as Gerschenkron's thesis has pointed out. However, once the heavy industrial infrastructure stage of development was established, and the economy required a shift toward the production of consumer goods and high-technology components with an increasing emphasis on quality rather than quantity, the limits of the socialist model begin to emerge. The problems related to coordination of production processes, realistic pricing of goods, and firm level incentives to innovate and compete produced a highly inefficient and uncompetitive economic condition.

Because the economy was explicitly directed and planned by state managers, rather than hidden behind the mystifying veil of market forces, economic failure became political failure and the pressures for change mounted at all levels of the society. These developments have produced some interesting assessments regarding the role of socialism as a development strategy. Dahrendorf (1990) views state socialism as a temporary strategy designed to move less-developed nations forward that must ultimately be replaced by capitalism. "In this sense, capitalism succeeds socialism" (1990:46). Similarly, Lukes (1990:573–574) concludes that "socialism can no longer be considered an alternative socioeconomic system that is viable or superior to capitalism."

While the problems with the centrally planned and bureaucratically centralized socialist economies have been widely identified and have clearly contributed to the decline of socialism, there is much less certainty about the strategy and model for rebuilding these economies. There is no historical precedent for such a transformation. There has also been a tendency to commit the comparative analytical fallacy outlined above which contrasts the real failure of centrally planned economies with a utopianized version of market capitalism. More specifically, it is highly misleading to view the relative success of capitalist economies as the product of neo-classical free market economic practices. This produces the equally problematic policy prescriptions for economic transition that are based on the direct application of neo-classical economic principles (Murrell 1991).

Almost all observers believe that the socialist states must decentralize economic decision-making and allow a greater role for market forces. The primary failure of the centrally planned economies lies in the inability to adjust, innovate, and compete in a rapidly changing and increasingly complex global economy. Two terms most often used to describe the necessary reforms are *privatization* and *liberalization*. Privatization refers to the shift of economic resources from state or public ownership to individual, corporate, or private ownership. Liberalization involves the deregulation of economic processes and decision-making and allowing market forces to determine the value and allocation of goods, services, and property. More specifically, in addition to the general shift toward privatization and liberalization, the transition to a market-based economy involves the following policy components (Fisher and Gelb 1991; Lairson and Skidmore 1993):

1. elimination of budget deficits that fuel inflation
2. elimination of price controls and other government subsidies
3. creation of a currency that can exchange with other nations' currency in real prices
4. elimination of barriers to trade and the free flow of goods and services
5. establishment of market prices for goods and property
6. reform of economic enterprises through privatization and exposure to market (profit-based) discipline
7. establish institutions that can provide finance capital, protect private property, encourage entrepreneurial activity, collect taxes, and cushion the economic impact on disadvantaged groups.

While each of these components suggests a policy direction for various sectors of the economy, the actual course of the transition has varied across the nations of Central and Eastern Europe. It is important to emphasize that the ability to institute these economic reforms is heavily dependent upon the institutional apparatus that developed and existed under the socialist system (Fischer and Gelb 1991; Stark 1994). Fischer and Gelb analyze two initial conditions for the reform process—the level of macro-economic imbalance and the degree of centralization. Countries with higher levels of macro-economic imbalance, such as Poland, began the reform process with budget deficits, supply and demand imbalances, inflationary pressures and considerable external debt. For countries faced with these macro-economic difficulties, the reform process involves not just restructuring the ownership of assets but also stabilizing government accounting and establishing a stable currency. In short, macro-economic stabilization is one of the initial tasks required for reform. The second dimension—degree of economic decentralization—involves the extent to which economic enterprises have been exposed to market incentives and allowed discretion over economic decision-making (versus tight centralized control by the state and the economic plan). All things being equal, it is assumed that the transition to a market-based economy will be smoother and easier where the prior socialist regime allowed greater enterprise-level latitude and exposed enterprises to international market forces. The analytical framework would suggest that the reform process may take a particular and more lengthy path for countries with high preexisting levels of macro-economic imbalance and economic centralization (such as the former U.S.S.R. and Bulgaria). In contrast, countries with greater macro-economic balance and economic decentralization, such as Hungary, may be better situated for the transition to a market-based economy.

A related but more sophisticated analysis is provided by Stark (1994), who examines the privatization strategies of different Central and Eastern European nations noting that "these privatization programs are not derived from master blueprints but are shaped by the specific institutional resources that are legacies of the path of exit from state socialism. Seen from this vantage point, transformation processes taking place in contemporary East–Central Europe resemble less architectural design than bricolage, construction by whatever comes to hand" (1994:170).

Stark (1994:171) utilizes three dimensions, posed as questions, to outline the privatization strategies of the various economies. "(1) How are the state's assets evaluated? (2) Who can acquire these assets? and (3) With what resources are ownership rights acquired?" Assets can be evaluated and valued by the central authority of the state or by competitive market bidding. Assets can be made available to private citizens or they can only be offered to existing and emerging corporate units. Assets can be distributed on the basis of monetary resources or political resources. The direction of the privatization strategy is determined by these decisions which, in turn, are the product of the economic structure and institutionalized practices of the various socialist states. Several examples should serve to clarify the possible strategic choices.

In Germany, assets have been assessed by a trust agency, or *Treuhandanstalt*, that is a public privatization agency with the responsibility for privatizing, reorganizing, liquidating, and ultimately finding investors that will assume control of the state assets. Thus, in the German case we find the administrative valuation of assets, targeted for acquisition by corporate units (including management and employee buyouts), on the basis of financial rather than political positional resources.

In Czechoslovakia the valuation of assets has been based on market-determined demand through the use of a voucher-auction system. The vouchers are used, along with financial resources, to provide all citizens the opportunity to buy equity shares in privatized enterprises. Thus, like Germany, financial resources are a primary factor in determining the acquisition of property but, in contrast to Germany, valuation is determined by the market (rather than a trust agency) and individuals (rather than corporate units) are the intended recipients of privatized assets.

Examples of other configurations are: (a) Hungary, combining a bargaining valuation of assets between the state and investors, corporate units as the recipient of assets, and the use of political-economic positional resources under the socialist regime to obtain assets; and (b) Poland, which has combined bargaining, citizen grants, and allocation of resources based on positional rather than strictly financial resources.

While the privatization processes have a long way to go in all four of these countries, the variations in strategy can be linked more specifically to "their distinctive paths of extrication from state socialism" that have "had the consequence that the current political institutions and forms of interest intermediation between state and society differ significantly across the four cases . . . it is the relationship between different types of democracy and different types of capitalism, rather than the abstractions of democracy and capitalism, that holds the clue to explaining differences in contemporary eastern Europe" (Stark 1994: 188).

As the work of Stark might suggest, the experience of transition will vary greatly across the different countries. Thus far, a wide variety of problems and conflicts have emerged in the implementation of market reforms. One of the central debates has been over the speed at which such reform should be instituted. Some have argued that a gradual reform process is required in order to avoid the "compatibility problem" involving the coexistence of socialist and capitalist, and thus mutually incompatible, institutional arrangements. Others, among them those who have seen the failure and inadequacy of past reform efforts, advocate a radical and swift transformation toward a market economy (Sachs 1993). Ericson (1991:25–26), representing the latter view, writes:

any reform must be disruptive on a historically unprecedented scale. An entire world must be discarded including all of its economic and most of its social and political institutions, and concluding with its physical structure of production capital and technology . . . the economic space must be cleared to allow new institutions to arise from and support the autonomous, self-interested interaction of economic agents.

Poland represents one of the more extreme applications of this position and is indicative of the potential consequences of a strategy that shows little sensitivity to the institutional complexity of the social change process. In Poland a program of "shock therapy" was instituted as a means to promote rapid transition to a market economy. The principles of privatization and liberalization strictly guided the economic plan. The immediate result was recession, a sharp decline in the standard of living, rising unemployment, inflation, and increasing income inequality. These consequences of market reform, typical of almost all East Central European nations undergoing the transition to capitalism, have obviously called into question the original enthusiasm for a market economy. These outcomes have also produced a high level of political opposition and conflict which, in the case of Poland, has resulted in a return to power of parties associated with the former Communist Party. The political backlash against the market reforms, fueled by high expectations and then widespread economic misery, has been a major element in the story of the transition to market capitalism. In a recent book by the architect of the Polish economic transformation, Leszek

Balcerowicz (1995), some of these problems are acknowledged, particularly the problems associated with insufficient institutional supports for a market economy—political, social, legal, cultural—and the difficulty in sustaining the "political capital" necessary to institute drastic economic reforms.

While it is far too early to evaluate such an unprecedented and monumental economic transformation, it is unlikely that the former socialist states will return to a centralized command economic system. Rather, the challenge appears to be that of developing the complementary institutions that will both support a market-based economy and also provide sufficient state intervention to guide and direct economic activity and protect segments of the population from the negative by-products of unbridled market reform.

NOTES

1. The relationship between socio-economic systems and development is part of the larger field of comparative economics. Useful texts in this area are Zimbalist and Sherman (1984), Kohler (1989), and Eliott (1973).

2. Other analyses of comparative capitalist institutions include Piore and Sabel 1984; Porter 1990; Whitley 1994; Williamson 1975; Henderson 1996.

3. For an alternative view of the vitality and sustainability of the East Asian economies, see Bello and Rosenfeld (1992); Krugman (1994a); and Young (1994).

6

The International System and the World Economy

> The modern world comprises a single capitalist world-economy . . . nation-states are *not* societies that have separate, parallel histories, but parts of a whole reflecting that whole. To be sure, since different parts of the world play and have played differing roles in the capitalist world-economy, they have dramatically different internal socio-economic profiles and hence distinctive politics. But to understand the internal class contradictions and political struggles of a particular state, we must first situate it in the world-economy. (Wallerstein 1984: 122–123)

In this chapter we turn to the broadest macro level of analysis, the international level. Theories of development operating at the international level view nations as part of a global system. The features and dynamics of this global system—imperialism, colonialism, the world market, foreign trade, flows of capital investment, MNC investment—are viewed as forces influencing the socio-economic development of nations. The international system shapes and constrains national development strategies and has a major impact upon the organizational and individual levels of analysis. Theoretical and empirical work at the international level has expanded greatly over the past decade as a consequence of globalizing trends in economic activity.

DEPENDENCY/WORLD-ECONOMY THEORY

A consideration of the international level of analysis brings us to one of the most influential paradigms in the contemporary study of social change—dependency/world-economy theory. As we shall see, this theory (and there is some debate over whether it can be called a theory, see Lall 1975) contains a wide assortment of hypotheses and propositions advanced by a variety of theorists.

There are, however, three basic premises that inform all versions of dependency/world-economy theory. First, the socio-economic structure and development of less-developed nations are best understood by examining the historical pattern of integration into, and interaction with, the capitalist world economy. Second, as the first premise implies, the theoretical framework must extend beyond the societal level of analysis and consider the role of broader world-economic structures and forces in shaping national development. Dependency/world-economy theory emerged in reaction, and as an alternative, to sociological modernization and economic growth models that emphasized internal national, rather than external international, effects on development. Third, the global system, highly interconnected and interdependent, is characterized by an unequal distribution of power and influence. This results in some nations being more vulnerable, more dependent, and subjected to greater exploitation than others. Unequal and asymmetric interaction between rich and poor nations is a central theme in this model. The emphasis is on international relations within a world-economic system. The major explanatory variables in this model of social change are those that define the nature of international exchange and interaction.

This chapter will review the arguments of some of the major theorists associated with dependency/world-economy theory. This is followed by a consideration of the emerging and mounting attacks on this thesis and some recent revisions.

Dependency Theory: Some Early Arguments[1]

International-level models tend to focus on the interaction between nation-states and the political-economic forces that regulate these interactions. Trade relations lie at the center of these models because the exchange of goods raises questions about international specialization, different methods of production, export vulnerability, the balance of payments, and the terms of trade. Positions in the international trade network also influence rates of socio-economic development and growth.

In the late 1940s standard models of international trade and economic development were beginning to come under attack. The most concerted effort came from the United Nations' Economic Commission for Latin America (ECLA), headed by Raul Prebisch (1950). Up to this point theories of international trade were heavily influenced by the work of David Ricardo (1933) and his "law of comparative advantage." This so-called law stipulated that each nation should specialize in the production of goods it could produce most cheaply in comparison with other goods. In his example, if Portugal could produce wine more cheaply than textiles, and England could produce textiles more cheaply than wine, Portugal should specialize in the production of wine, and England in the production of textiles. In turn, England's demand for wine and Portugal's demand for textiles could be met through trade. Under this system it was claimed that nations would use their resources most efficiently and the net cost of producing various goods would be minimized. If followed faithfully, a logical outcome of this law (and one advocated by numerous development agencies) would be *specialization* in the production and export of a narrow range of goods. One of the major tasks of Prebisch and his ECLA colleagues was to examine the impact of specialization on economic development.

One of the questions raised by the ECLA group was whether the "terms of trade" were equitable for nations specializing in the production of different commodities. The *terms of trade* refers to the relationship between the world-market price of a nation's imports and exports. Optimally, a nation wants the world-market price of its exports to exceed the world-market price of its imports. If less-developed nations specialize in the production and export of primary agro-mineral products, such as coffee, bananas, and copper, given their comparative advantage in this line of goods, how does this affect the terms of trade and, ultimately, growth and development? Under the comparative advantage arrangement, specialization in the production of agro-mineral primary products would obviously necessitate the importation of manufactured and industrial goods. The terms of trade between these different commodities therefore emerges as a significant issue.

A major contention of the ECLA group was that a serious bias existed against primary agro-mineral product exporters because the world-market price of most primary products had experienced a steady decline, while manufactured products had become more expensive. Under the system of international specialization, less-developed nations experience a decline in their per unit export revenue, while the cost of imported manufactured products remains stable or increases. This trend had created, according to ECLA, a chronic balance of payments crisis for Latin American nations. The *balance of payments*—the relationship between the total cost of imports and the total income derived from exports—would be in a state of chronic deficit so long as less-developed nations pursued a primary product specialization strategy. It was further contended that this specialization strategy, instead of being mutually beneficial to all parties involved, worked to the advantage of the industrial nations and to the detriment of less-developed nations.

The work of the ECLA group on the issue of international trade laid the groundwork for a critical and global analysis of development problems. One important implication of their work was that the international trade structure, based on specialization and a division of labor between nations, contributed to economic decline and stagnation among less-developed nations. This shifted the level of analysis from internal national characteristics to the mechanisms of world-market exchange.

Second, the claim that the terms of trade worked to the benefit of the industrialized nations of the "center" at the expense of the less-developed "periphery'' suggested unequal and exploitative political economic relations between regions of the world. This came to be a basic tenet of dependency theory.

The divergent payoffs from international specialization raised a third critical point about the *source* of comparative advantage. Why does one nation have a comparative advantage in producing nutmeg, while another nation has a comparative advantage in the production of automobiles? The conventional response was that nations possessed different "factor endowments"—that is, different quantities and qualities of natural resources, labor, and capital. These factor endowments were taken as given, as a part of the natural order rather than something that required explanation. The ECLA school called into question the origin of comparative advantage and economic specialization. They pointed to the historical legacy of colonialism, and the external implantation of primary product export systems by the colonial powers as the source of contemporary specialization patterns.

Finally, the ECLA arguments raised the question of whether *imbalanced growth models* were a viable basis for sustained economic expansion. Imbalanced growth models argue that rather than developing a broad number of industries simultaneously, a nation should develop or specialize in a single line of production. Through international trade other necessary products can be imported. It is assumed that, over time, other industries and sectors will emerge to produce products for, and consume the output of, the original sector. The relationship of this model to the arguments of comparative advantage should be apparent. In response and opposition to the logic of this model ECLA prescribed a national policy of *import substitution industrialization* (ISI) that would facilitate the domestic production of previously imported industrial goods. This strategy was proposed in order to create a more balanced economic structure and reduce dependence on external sources.

Shortly after ECLA made its recommendations, reservations were raised about the ability of import substitution to resolve the developmental difficulties of Latin American nations. One of the major figures in this revision, Celso Furtado, was a member of ECLA and heavily involved in development policy in Brazil. Furtado's work (1965; 1970; 1973) is significant in its emphasis on the inherent limits of import substitution, formulations on the role of colonialism and multinational capital, the discussion of consumption patterns and the distribution of income, and the use of the concept "peripheral capitalism."

Furtado was less sanguine about the prospects for long-term development under import substitution. Like Prebisch, he felt that the international division of labor based on the law of comparative advantage had served to concentrate the benefits of technical progress among the advanced industrial societies. Obviously, some effort had to be made to shift into other areas of production. However, Furtado regarded the ISI strategy as unsatisfactory. Initial stages of import substitution would inevitably involve domestic production for existing and dynamic internal markets. In Latin America many of the most dynamic markets were those for Western-style luxury goods demanded by a narrow elite segment of landowners and capitalists. For Furtado, the application of the import substitution principle to an already distorted social structure meant extending the discontinuities imposed by Western culture to the domestic economy. That is, the traditional pattern of elite importation of luxury consumer goods would simply be replaced by the domestic production of these same types of products. Furtado believed this strategy would only reinforce the concentration of income in the hands of a small elite and restrict the prospects for long-term, balanced industrial growth.

Furtado introduced the concept of *peripheral capitalism* to describe the unique pattern of Third World development characterized by import substitution based on Western consumption patterns, an inability to generate productive innovations, and phases of socio-economic development shaped by the decisions of outsiders. This latter feature of peripheral capitalism, labeled "external dependence," remains a central part of contemporary dependency theory. The outside forces to which he referred were the industrialized nations of Europe and North America and their multinational corporate appendages. According to Furtado, multinational corporations extend the cultural domination of the West, introduce inappropriate consumption patterns, and distort the economic structures of less-developed nations. The vilification of the multinational corporation is another component of Furtado's analysis that is echoed in almost every subsequent rendition of dependency theory. The idea of external dependence also stands as a defining characteristic of the dependency condition and has been incorporated into what is one of the most widely used definitions of dependence:

By dependence we mean a situation in which the economy of certain countries is conditioned by the development and expansion of another economy to which the former is subjected. The relation . . . assumes the form of dependence when some countries (the dominant ones) can expand and be self sustaining, while other countries (the dependent ones) can do this only as a reflection of that expansion. (Dos Santos 1970:231)

A third major influence on dependency theory comes from the writings of Paul Baran. In Baran's seminal work, *The Political Economy of Growth* (1957), he formulated a model of underdevelopment that pointed to the distinct developmental condition of less-developed nations arising out of colonialism and imperialism. As discussed in Chapter 4, the concept of surplus played a major role in Baran's theory of economic growth. Baran tried to identify the reasons why nations did not realize their potential surplus, which was much larger than the actual surplus. As it relates to the international level of analysis Baran pointed to the forces of colonialism, imperialist penetration, and the extraction of surplus from the less-developed periphery to the advanced center states.

It is interesting to note that in contrast to some later dependency theorists, Baran regarded competitive capitalism as a relatively progressive force (in the sense of moving societies toward socialism) that had not completely penetrated the Third World (see especially his article in 1952). He implied that the problem in backward nations was the partial or incomplete incorporation of capitalism, and its combination with feudal patterns of organization and social relations. The external imposition of capitalism into precapitalist societies created a distinct socio-economic structure that contained many obstacles to sustained economic growth. According to Baran, the international spread of capitalism was instigated by the needs and demands of monopoly capitalism in the advanced countries for new sources of profit. Thus, capitalism did not emerge organically in the Third World, it was imposed from the outside; and the capitalism that was introduced was of a monopoly rather than competitive form. Baran regarded these two factors—capitalism from without and its monopoly form—as largely responsible for the retrogressive effects of capitalism on underdeveloped nations.

Baran's elaboration of the relationship between underdeveloped societies and the imperialist forces of the world economy has also had an enormous influence on contemporary versions of dependency theory. According to Baran, the crisis of monopoly capitalism among the advanced Western nations—fully elaborated in Baran and Sweezy's *Monopoly Capital* (1966)—resulted not only in the expansion of government spending within advanced capitalist states but also the international expansion of multinational corporations. The monopoly stage of capitalism further required new locations and sources for investment, production, and raw materials.

Baran cited two major flow mechanisms of imperialist expansion and exploitation. First, like the ECLA group, Baran pointed to the *trade flows* between developed and underdeveloped states. Multinational corporations extracted required primary products from less-developed nations at low cost. Less-developed economies imported more expensive industrial goods from the advanced capitalist states. This exchange of primary products for manufactured goods is still regarded as a defining characteristic of the dependent and unequal relations between rich and poor nations.

Second, and equally critical from Baran's perspective, was the *flow of surplus* from the underdeveloped to advanced nations. Profits from multinational enterprises located in less-developed nations tended to be sent abroad rather than reinvested, thus undermining the prospects for sustained economic expansion. As we shall see, the international exploitation of underdeveloped nations by developed states, through the mechanisms of unequal trade and "surplus drainage," remain consistent themes in the arguments of contemporary dependency theorists.

Metropolis and Satellite: Andre Gunder Frank

The single most important figure in the development of dependency theory is Andre Gunder Frank. His writings in the mid- and late 1960s, based on his study of Latin America, date the beginning of an explicit dependency theory. Although the theory has been modified since these initial formulations, there are numerous elements that have been retained.

One of these central elements is the rejection of economic and sociological models of development based on the experience of Western Europe and North America. For Frank, the issue is whether what now constitutes the Third World is, or ever was, in a comparable position to preindustrial Europe and North America. If one believes that there is only one single path to socio-economic development, then conventional theories and prescriptions based on Western historical experience might be relevant for understanding the currently under-developed nations and their economic problems. However, according to Frank, the historical experiences are so different as to make the Western-based models obsolete and useless.

> The now developed countries were never *under*developed, though they may have been *un*developed. It is also widely believed that the contemporary underdevelopment of a country can be understood as the product or reflection solely of its own economic, po-litical, social, and cultural characteristics or structure. Yet historical research demonstrates that contemporary underdevelopment is in large part the historical product of past and continuing economic and other relations between the satellite underdeveloped and the now developed metropolitan countries. (1969:54)

In pointing to the distinct socio-economic histories of developed and underde-veloped societies, Frank is also reiterating a number of basic dependency prem-ises. First, that contemporary underdevelopment is the product of external rather than simply internal structures and forces. Second, that the legacy of colonial relations between developed and underdeveloped nations places the underde-veloped world in a qualitatively different position than was the case for prein-dustrial Europe and North America.

Describing the nature and the effect of the relationship between what Frank calls the *satellite* and *metropolitan* nations is a central analytic focus of de-pendency theory. This international perspective points to an often overlooked aspect of the development of the West—involving superordinate and exploita-tive relations with Asia, Africa, and Latin America—as well as the influence of these historical forces on the socio-economic structures of the now underdevel-oped countries. In short, Frank argues that the development of Western Europe and North America was enhanced by the exploitation and underdevelopment of the world's hinterlands—the now underdeveloped nations. In this model, de-velopment and underdevelopment are two sides of the same coin in an inter-national capitalist economy.

A second integral component of the dependency model involves the rejection of the *dual society thesis*. This thesis posits the existence of a dual economic structure in less-developed economies containing a modern dynamic capitalist sector and a backward feudal subsistence sector. The model attributes under-development to the fact that a large part of the economy remains under the sway of feudal practices. The solution is to expose the presumably isolated feudal sectors to the forces of capitalism existing in modern sectors and industrialized nations. In sharp contrast to this view, Frank (as well as most other dependency and world-economy theorists) argues that all territories of the world have been penetrated by the forces of world capitalism and that *the diffusion of world capitalism is responsible for the contemporary underdevelopment of Third World regions and nations.*

Therefore, the economic, political, social, and cultural institutions and relations we now observe there are the products of the historical development of the capitalist system no less than are the seemingly more modern or capitalist features of the national metropoles of these underdeveloped countries. (1969:5)

The two general themes reviewed above—the historical development of underdevelopment and the rejection of dual society logic—lay the groundwork for a set of dependency propositions or "hypotheses" regarding the development process. Frank's first hypothesis states "that in contrast to the development of the world metropolis which is no one's satellite, the development of the national and other subordinate metropolises is limited by their satellite status" (1969:9). Again, Frank emphasizes the distinct historical position of the contemporary underdeveloped world. Further, the status of satellite implies weakness, vulnerability, and subordination. Nations in this position may produce a significant economic surplus but a large portion is said to be drained off by the metropolitan nations that control production, trade, and exchange in satellite nations. This economic surplus is then used to advance the fortunes and interests of the capitalist class in the metropolis.

The second hypothesis advanced by Frank is in direct contrast to the assertions of the dual society thesis: "satellites experience their greatest economic development and especially their most classically capitalist industrial development if and when their ties to their metropolis are weakest" (1969:9–10). According to dual society theory, we would expect contact with the capitalist nations of the metropolis to break down feudal barriers and to stimulate capitalist expansion. However, if, as Frank contends, satellite–metropolis relations are exploitative and asymmetrical, then the greatest potential exists when these ties are broken and nations can engage in autonomous, indigenous-based development programs.

A notable historical period is often used in support of this thesis—the period between World War I and World War II during which the metropolitan nations were preoccupied with the two wars and economic depression and, therefore, unable to maintain their presence in and domination over the less-developed satellite states. A number of Latin American nations, previously bound by the ties of dependency, experienced a significant phase of industrial development during this period. In Brazil in the early 1930s a political alliance hostile to the feudal oligarchy, and led by the domestic industrial capitalist class, came to power and established the Estado Novo under the Vargas regime. Policies were instituted to advance national industry, to include the political participation of the working class, to create a rational state bureaucracy, and to usher in some form of democracy.

Similar developments occurred in Argentina during the same period where a policy of import substitution industrialization was initiated. This process involved the extensive internal production of formerly imported goods. In many ways this policy was necessitated by the depression in Europe and North America which curtailed trade and capital flows. However, out of this transformation emerged a strengthened national industrial capitalist class and a politically active working class which laid the basis for the populist Peronist movement in the mid-1940s. Neither of these movements, however, led to sustained, long-term, autonomous industrial development due to the reestablishment after World War II of metropolitan expansion, especially by the United States, that renewed the structure of dependence. The temporary phase, however, is often used as evidence in support of Frank's thesis.

The transitory nature of the autonomous development phase leads us to Frank's corollary of the second hypothesis, ''when the metropolis recovers from its crisis and reestablishes the trade and investment ties which fully reincorporate the satellites into the system, or when the metropolis expands to incorporate previously isolated regions into the world-wide system, the previous development and industrialization of these regions is choked off or channelled into directions which are not self-perpetuating and promising'' (1969:11).

Frank's third hypothesis argues that ''the regions which are the most underdeveloped and feudal-seeming today are the ones which had the closest ties to the metropolis in the past'' (1969:13). Frank uses as examples to support this claim those regions that historically served as a major source of agro-mineral primary products for the industrial development of the metropolis. Because the wealth and surplus derived from this primary product sector accrued to the world metropolis, and as demand for the products or the mineral wealth eventually evaporated, these areas were abandoned to become some of the most destitute regions in the world. This argument stands as a further challenge to the view that poor regions and countries are those which have not benefited from the diffusion of world capitalist forces.

Stephen Bunker's (1984) research on the historical experience of the Brazilian Amazon provides a relevant case study lending support and much greater detail to this general thesis. Advancing what he describes as a ''commodity-based model of underdevelopment,'' Bunker points to the ''extractive commodities'' that are exported to the metropolis where they are refined, finished, and processed. These can include petroleum, minerals, lumber and nuts from natural forests and undomesticated trees, fish, and so on. Bunker traces the historical role of the Amazon Basin in providing commodities to Europe and America from the sixteenth to the twentieth centuries. This region exported spices, animal oils, rubber, and light metals, yet ''despite its long history of supplying valued commodities for world trade, the Amazon Basin is one of the poorest areas in the world, and the economic and social systems on which many of its inhabitants depend are seriously threatened by disruption or extinction" (Bunker 1984: 1022).

The reason for this result is that particular demographic, organizational, and environmental structures that were created for the purpose of exporting a particular extractive commodity—and eventually abandoned when the demand for the product waned or was replaced by a synthetic substitute—restricted subsequent forms of economic production and expansion. In the specific case of the Brazilian Amazon the intense colonial extraction of native spices slowly destroyed the fragile human settlements and ecosystem on which the productive system depended. In the second nineteenth-century expansionary phase rubber was the export commodity extracted and the extraction process required a large labor force. Due to the prior destruction of the human population, local labor was scarce and had to be recruited through the migration of peasant populations from other regions, who then developed a relationship of debt servitude with the commercial landowners. The Brazilian rubber boom ended when Asian rubber plantations outcompeted the Amazon producers. Thus, "the rubber boom repeated the pattern of original colonization—rapid enrichment of a small group followed by a sudden collapse and enduring poverty" (Bunker 1984:1032).

Frank advances two final and related hypotheses that elaborate further a general and very important point. The fourth and fifth hypotheses are directed to the issue of the development of the latifundia—the large-scale commercial agricultural enterprise.[2] For Frank, the common distinction made between hacienda and plantation agriculture—that they represent systems of feudalism and capitalism, respectively—is false. Instead, the latifundia—often characterized by feudal social relationships (the hacienda) and described as a precapitalist system—has historically been an agricultural enterprise heavily penetrated by the forces of international capitalism. However, in contrast to the expectations of the dual society thesis, the seemingly feudal institutions employed for the production of export crops do not disappear, but rather intensify under the influence of commercial agriculture. Again, Frank is rejecting the dual society contention that feudal contact with capitalist markets transforms the relations and forces of economic production toward rational efficient capitalism.

This paradox—market forces reinforcing rather than transforming feudal institutions—is explained by Chilcote and Edelstein (1986:24) who note that:

commerce provides an incentive for the lord to extract a greater surplus from his serfs so that he can sell it to purchase luxury goods. But this change can be accomplished *within* the manorial system, using the position accorded the lord in the feudal society to make possible the increased demands on the serf. Ironically, instead of breaking feudal bonds in favor of a system of free labor, traditional relationships and agricultural methods are preserved, and the only change is a greater extraction of surplus from the serfs. (emphasis in original)

The reference to commerce raises an important issue that is central to much of the debate among dependency and Marxist theorists. This involves the distinction between merchant and industrial capitalism. *Merchant capitalism* refers to the process by which commodities are bought for one price and sold for another or, as the saying goes, "buying cheap and selling dear." When Frank (and, as we shall see, Wallerstein) refers to the worldwide expansion of capitalism, or the global dominance of market forces as early as the sixteenth century, he is referring to mercantile or merchant capitalism. Merchants were interested in gaining low-cost access to agricultural and mineral commodities in the less-developed world that could then be sold for a profit in European markets. Feudal landowners, in turn, were interested in selling these agricultural commodities to merchants and using the proceeds for the purchase of luxury goods produced primarily in Europe. Both parties were able to satisfy their needs under the feudal arrangements.

What is significant in the merchant form of capitalism is that the merchants did not have any interest in reorganizing the methods and system of agricultural production. As long as the primary commodities could be acquired cheaply, merchants were indifferent to the means used by the landowners to extract labor and a surplus from peasants. This leads Frank to reject the dual society argument that feudal structures persist because of a lack of contact with market forces, or that the hacienda is a feudal remnant and the plantation a capitalist institution. It should also be noted, at this point, that Frank defines capitalist institutions as *those that have contact with and produce for a market.* In this way Frank can contend that the international expansion of capitalism interacted with, supported, and reinforced these backward, feudal productive structures and, therefore, contributed to the underdevelopment of the Third World.

In contrast to merchant capital, which primarily involves the *exchange* of commodities, *industrial capitalism* involves the *production* of commodities under a particular set of conditions. In this system, a capitalist or entrepreneur who owns productive property brings together wage labor, capital, and raw materials for the purpose of producing a commodity at the lowest possible cost in order to secure a profit through sale in the market. The critical part of this process, however, is the use of labor in as productive a way as possible so that goods can be produced cheaply and efficiently. Some of the methods for organizing the labor process have already been discussed. This form of capitalist profit obviously differs from that obtained under merchant capitalism in that these capitalists have a direct interest in the methods, organization, and social relations of production.

The Capitalist World Economy: Immanuel Wallerstein

The world-economy theory developed by Wallerstein is often associated with dependency theory. Both approaches reject the view that national development can be explained by examining the internal characteristics of nation-states. Instead, nations are seen as open systems that are heavily influenced by economic forces and patterns of exchange at the international level. Like Frank, Waller-

stein also dismisses the dual society thesis that attributes economic backwardness to feudal conditions of production and lack of exposure to market forces.
In fact, for Wallerstein, the whole notion of stages of development or socio-
economic systems, such as feudalism and capitalism, is misleading since, in his
view, there is only world development and a world system. In order to understand Wallerstein's argument one must grasp his definition of a social system:

> We take as the defining characteristic of a social system to be the existence within it
> of a division of labor, such that the various sectors or areas within it are dependent upon
> economic exchange with others for the smooth and continuous provisioning of the needs
> of the area. (1979:5)

Wallerstein is clearly working at a *world level of analysis* where nation-states
are the interacting parts of a larger system. The parts carry out particular functions dictated by an international division of labor. The essence of this world
social system is the "production for sale in a market in which the object is to
realize the maximum profit" (1974:398). Where this defines the purpose of
national production and exchange the international system can be described as
a capitalist world economy. Thus, Wallerstein regards the sixteenth-century international economy as a capitalist world economy and, for the same period,
any agricultural production for the world market as capitalist agriculture. In
short, Wallerstein does not believe there is any useful purpose in distinguishing
between various systems of agriculture nor forms of capitalism. There is one
social system—the capitalist world economy—and those nations that participate
in this system (i.e., produce and exchange commodities) are capitalist.

The somewhat extreme and unorthodox nature of Wallerstein's position with
respect to the universal categorization of all forms of national production as
capitalist is difficult to sustain. This contention is qualified to a considerable
extent with the concept of *modes of labor control* (Wallerstein 1974). Modes
of labor control refers to those socio-economic relations and political structures
that are instituted in order to ensure effective control over workers for the purpose of profitable world-economic production. There is a great deal of value in
this concept. It provides a useful way to link the myriad societal and industrial
organizational arrangements throughout the world with the requirement for cost-
effective world-market production. All nations are under pressure to produce
competitively for international trade and this influences the national organizational strategies of labor control. In Wallerstein's model these different modes
of labor control are the *effects* of world-market pressures. Regardless of their
specific socio-political nature (e.g., slave, feudal, fascist, socialist), they are considered parts of a larger capitalist world system and, therefore, capitalist.

Another element of Wallerstein's model involves describing the international
system as a type of social-class system. The language and imagery of social
stratification and class relations is pervasive in Wallerstein's description of
world-system dynamics. Like individuals in a stratified society who occupy so-

cial-class positions, nations occupy class-like structural positions in the world economy. The three major positions are the *core*, the *semiperiphery*, and the *periphery*.

The *core* is composed of the advanced capitalist states of North America and Western Europe. Core states are politically and militarily powerful, have a high per capita GNP, and specialize in the production of manufactured and high-tech commodities. At the bottom of the international division of labor are the nations of the *periphery*. Peripheral nations are militarily weak, have a low per capita GNP, and tend to specialize in the export of agro-mineral primary products. The *semiperiphery* are those nations somewhere between the core and periphery. Semiperipheral states have relatively strong governmental structures, moderate levels of GNP, and are moving toward greater levels of industrial production. They are sometimes referred to as the "newly industrialized countries" or NICs.

The relationship between the core and the periphery in Wallerstein's account is very similar to Frank's description of the interaction between metropolis and satellite, but the social-class analogy to unequal resources, power, and exploitation is much more apparent in the writing of Wallerstein. While his critics may accuse him of ignoring social-class relations within nations, Wallerstein does not ignore this dynamic at the international level. For example, he states that "capitalism involves not only appropriation of the surplus value by an owner from a laborer, but an appropriation of surplus of the whole world economy by core areas" (1979:401). The core, in this view, is equivalent to a world-level capitalist class, the periphery is the highly exploited working class, the semiperiphery is the middle class.

The function of the semiperiphery is also conceptualized in class-structure terms. As Wallerstein remarks, "the world economy as an economy would function every bit as well without a semi-periphery. But it would be far less politically stable for it would mean a polarized world-system. . . . The middle strata is both exploited and exploiter" (1979:405). As with a national middle class, the semiperiphery serves as the buffer zone between the antagonistic nations of core and periphery. It is a co-opted stratum that is supportive of world capitalism because it is made up of nations that have experienced some upward mobility. That experience also serves as a concrete example for peripheral nations—that international mobility is possible within the existing structure of the capitalist world economy. With the appropriate mode of labor control the periphery also can achieve international status and power.

Wallerstein points to the competitive strategies that are employed by peripheral and semiperipheral nations for the purpose of international upward mobility. Most notable is the emergence of "statist" and "mercantile" political structures. Consistent with his larger model, Wallerstein does not regard these kinds of state systems as anything but capitalist. "The fact that all enterprises are nationalized in these countries does not make the participation of these enterprises in the world economy one that does not conform to the mode of operation of a capitalist market system: seeking increased efficiency of production in order to realize a maximum price on sales, thus achieving more favorable allocation of the surplus of the world economy'' (1974:413).

Wallerstein's position on this matter leads him to characterize socialist and/ or communist states as capitalist because they too are parts of a capitalist whole that participates in world-market production and trade. Not surprisingly this argument has generated some heated debate. It has also raised some intriguing theoretical issues.[3]

In spite of the many critical assessments that have been made in recent years there are many important lessons that can be learned from this world-system perspective. One of the most important is that all nations, be they capitalist or socialist, are structurally constrained by their need to produce and exchange products in a world market. What this means is that nations often pursue foreign and trade policies that seem to contradict the public pronouncements of official state ideology. In short, the imperative of economic accumulation may override political ideology. Andre Gunder Frank (1980) has aptly described this arrangement as ''transideological enterprise.'' Requirements for modern technology, finance capital, and export markets—all for the purpose of capital accumulation and growth—bind nations with vastly different socio-political systems and ideologies. This suggests something akin to a ''convergence theory,'' but through the logic of participation in international production and exchange. All nations that seek to modernize through world-market exchange must ''toe the line,'' conform to the macro logic of world capitalism, and repress ideological instincts.

The issue of structural convergence in world-system theory has become a major theme in the current literature on globalization. What links these perspectives is the level of analysis at which they operate—the world-systemic level. J. David Singer (1961), in an influential essay on the level-of-analysis problem in the study of international relations, identifies a number of difficulties that result from the choice of a *systemic* framework. First, ''it tends to lead the observer into a position which exaggerates the impact of the system upon the national actors and, conversely, discounts the impact of the actors on the system'' (1961:80). This is clearly true of world-system theory. In this view, it is the systemic logic of world capitalism that determines the behavior of nation-states, and their motives for action. Nation-states do not and cannot transform or influence the operation of the system; rather, they conform to its requirements and logic.

Second, according to Singer, the systemic level of analysis ''almost inevitably requires that we postulate a high degree of uniformity . . . we allow little room for divergence in the behavior of our parts when we focus on the whole'' (1961: 81). As already noted, in world-system theory the nature of the whole determines the substance of the parts. This ensures a uniformity such that all the parts of the system are capitalist regardless of internal national, social, and economic relations. The seemingly significant variations in socio-economic forms of organization and ideology are regarded as secondary epiphenomena of the broader logic of world capitalism. The bottom line motive of all world-system participants is the maximization of profit through the exchange of commodities in the world market.

Singer's final point is that "though the systemic model does not necessarily preclude comparison and contrast among the national subsystems, it usually eventuates in rather gross comparisons based on relatively crude dimensions and characteristics" (1961:83). The broad division of nations into core, periphery, and semiperiphery is indicative of this tendency. These broad structural categories, used to define the classes and relationships at the world-system level, often serve to obscure the significant variation among nations occupying common positions.

Variations on a Dependency Theme: Samir Amin

The work of Samir Amin represents a systematic attempt to combine and integrate the various insights of dependency and world-system theory. He raises many critical issues and introduces a number of valuable concepts that contribute to a clearer understanding of global capitalism and underdevelopment in the periphery.

One of the key issues for Amin (1976) is the way in which the laws of the capitalist economic system contribute to the tendency toward worldwide expansion and imperialism. In order to demonstrate that the capitalist system is characterized by a tendency toward international expansion—that this is an integral part of the process of capital accumulation—Amin must differentiate capitalism as it exists in the imperialist center states (advanced capitalist societies) from that which exists in the periphery (the underdeveloped world).

He describes capitalism in the center states as *autocentric capitalism*. Autocentric capitalism requires the existence of a "capacity to produce" and a "capacity to consume." These terms, used frequently by Amin, refer to the more familiar concepts of supply (produce) and demand (consume). For capital accumulation to take place, conditions must exist that encourage private investment by capitalists in the production and supply of commodities. This is what is meant by the capacity to produce—the existence of a certain set of conditions that encourage private investment. Capitalists are more likely to invest and produce where production costs are low enough so that each commodity produced can be sold for a reasonable profit. The ability to realize a profit requires that the second condition also be met—the capacity to consume. This refers to the existence of adequate levels of effective demand for the product. If products are produced cheaply, but cannot be sold, profit is not realized. For these reasons capital accumulation requires a combination of favorable supply-side (capacity to produce) and demand-side (capacity to consume) conditions. These are the dual requirements for capitalist expansion.

One of the fundamental contradictions of a capitalist economy can be found in the relationship between these two requirements. An example of this contradiction can be seen if one considers wage levels. On the one hand, low wage levels support the capacity to produce as they contribute to low production costs and thus the potential for enlarged profits. On the other hand, low wages will restrict the size of the market and, therefore, the capacity to consume. The opposite case—high wage levels that enhance the capacity to consume commodities—discourages the capacity to produce. Attempts to resolve this contradiction, and the associated economic crises, result in the global expansion of capitalism. For Amin, imperialism and the emergence of monopolies are responses to the crises of autocentric accumulation. Peripheral nations are used as a base for low-cost production as well as an outlet or market for certain commodities. Thus, the international mobility of productive capital and commodities is seen as an inevitable outcome of the laws of autocentric capitalism. These efforts, aimed at resolving crises in the center, shape the nature of capitalist development in the periphery.

In contrast to autocentric accumulation, peripheral capitalist economies are characterized by *extraverted accumulation*. This term is meant to describe the export-oriented or ''outward-looking'' nature of underdeveloped economies. Extraversion is the product of the historical legacy of exploitation by external forces. As with Frank and Wallerstein, these external forces originate in the center states (or metropolis or core). From the early stages of colonial expansion, where colonies provided agro-mineral products to the center states, to the contemporary incursion of foreign investment, the socio-economic structure of the periphery has been shaped by export activities. According to Amin, extraverted accumulation creates a number of structural distortions that prevent sustained and autonomous economic expansion.

The concept of *disarticulation* plays a central role in Amin's theory of peripheral capitalism and underdevelopment. Disarticulation refers to missing or nonexistent links between segments of the economy. DeJanvry (1981) makes a useful distinction, implied by Amin, between *social disarticulation* and *sectoral disarticulation*. Sectoral disarticulation refers to an economic structure that lacks forward and backward linkages between productive sectors. As an example, take the case of an economy that is involved in the extraction of a mineral resource. Under the system of sectoral disarticulation the machines used to extract the minerals are imported from industrialized nations. Therefore, there is no national or internal *backward linkage* from the mineral sector to a capital goods sector that provides machines and equipment for mineral extraction. Suppose also that the mineral resource is exported in its raw form and processed or refined in the industrialized nations. Thus, there is also no internal *forward linkage* from the mineral extractive sector to a mineral processing sector that would manufacture the raw material into some other commodity within the peripheral nation. This type of disarticulation has negative economic consequences because the relatively dynamic economic activity in the mineral sector does not spill over and stimulate economic activity in other domestic sectors. This is due to the fact that the other sectors that supply the inputs and receive the output from the extractive sector do not exist within the peripheral economy but, rather, in the industrialized center states.

Social disarticulation refers to the situation where the relationship between the capacity to produce and the capacity to consume is weak and tenuous— commodities can be produced and sold profitably in spite of the absence of a capacity to consume in the national economy. This form of disarticulation is best illustrated if we consider a consumer goods industry. Where an economy is characterized by social *articulation* the profitability of this industry depends on the buying power of the national working classes. Under an extraverted economy, where the consumer goods are exported to working-class consumers in the industrialized nations, *profitability is maintained independent of the wage levels of the domestic population.* Thus, extraverted accumulation and development can proceed where wages are extremely low because productive sectors of extraverted peripheral economies are not dependent on the internal market. As Amin notes: "Wages appear not as both a cost and an income that creates a demand essential for the working of the model, but merely as a cost, with demand originating elsewhere—either externally, or in the income of the privileged categories of society" (Amin 1976:194).

The concept of social disarticulation is a useful tool for understanding the relationship between the world-economic orientation and the political practices carried out in peripheral nations. Where wages are a pure cost there is little incentive by elites to promote redistributive income policies, tolerate union organization, or allow wages to rise. Instead, there is pressure against redistribution of income, unions are often outlawed or repressed, and the standard of living in many vibrant export economies can experience significant decline. The prevalence of authoritarianism and mass repression in peripheral nations can be understood as a partial product of the fact that internal demand is not the driving force for capital accumulation. Further, in order for exports to remain competitive, and for nations to attract foreign investment, supply-side (capacity to produce) conditions tend to take precedence over the demand-side (capacity to consume) in extraverted economies.

The condition of disarticulation in peripheral economies results, according to Amin, in crises that can be distinguished from those that emerge in center states. Most notable is the manifestation of economic crisis at the level of the balance of payments. Because of sectoral disarticulation, the capacity to produce in peripheral economies depends on the foreign exchange revenue derived from export trade. This foreign exchange is used to purchase capital inputs needed for production. Because of social disarticulation, foreign exchange levels depend on the level of demand in the world economy. When, for whatever reason, export revenues decline, this affects the balance of payments and the ability to import required capital goods. The balance-of-payments crisis, then, signals a larger economic crisis. Extraverted economies feel economic hard times when the trade ledger falls into disequilibrium—import costs exceed export receipts. As Amin continually emphasizes, "Since the underdeveloped economies are extraverted, all their problems emerge in the balance of payments. Every considerable economic change that occurs in the course of development has an effect on the various elements in the balance of payments." (1976:252).

These problems are aggravated further if we consider what Amin calls the *balance of real payments*. By this he means the balance between exports and the inflow of capital investment (the credit side) versus imports and the backflow of profits (the debit side). Amin's basic argument is that, historically, nations first penetrated by colonial expansion experienced a period of surplus in their balance of payments. This began to slowly deteriorate as unfavorable terms of trade evolved to the advantage of manufactured goods and to the detriment of peripheral exports. Amin cites Prebisch on this issue but he also points to an additional factor that can serve either to offset or accentuate the unfavorable terms of trade—the movement of foreign capital investment. With foreign investment there is the inflow of capital and, inevitably, the backflow of profits:

> It is the backflow of profits, growing bigger and bigger, that in the end becomes responsible, together with the movement of the trade balance already analyzed, for the chronic deficit in the balance of the underdeveloped countries in our time. During the nineteenth century the increasing flow of capital, exceeding the backflow of profits, made up for the progressive worsening in the trade balance. In the twentieth century the increasing backflow of profits, exceeding the inflow of new capital, is added to the progressive worsening of the trade balance, and so makes the overall balance of payments even less favorable. (Amin 1976:257)

Under the system of extraverted and disarticulated accumulation we also find that the potentially dynamic "multiplier" and "accelerator" effects are severely restricted. Conventional economic theory posits a certain number of economic forces that contribute to sustained economic expansion. The *multiplier effect* refers to the expansion of total income that results from changes in investment. Investment spending initiates a chain reaction that produces proportionately greater increases in the total income. This distributes income throughout the economy, which gives rise to the accelerator effect. The *accelerator effect* refers to the impact of a rise in consumer demand which, in turn, creates a proportionately greater demand for producer goods (equipment, machines, etc.). Both concepts describe the momentum and cumulative effects that are created by expansion in different segments of the economy. In order for these effects to operate, it is assumed that national economic sectors are connected and articulated so that changes in one sphere are felt in other spheres. The peripheral condition of disarticulation described above weakens or removes the effects of these economic forces.

INTERNATIONAL-LEVEL MECHANISMS: INVESTMENT DEPENDENCE AND THE DEBT CRISIS

This section provides an elaboration of two international-level mechanisms that have a significant effect on the socio-economic development of nations. Among those who emphasize international-level forces, investment and debt are two of the major external factors shaping the internal developmental trajectory of nation-states.

Investment Dependence

One form of dependence most often emphasized by dependency theorists and represented in cross-national studies claiming to test dependency theory is investment dependence. The international flow of capital is seen as a central mechanism by which the advanced capitalist states dominate, exploit, and retard the development of less-developed nations. In this section we consider the arguments that have been made regarding the impact of direct foreign investment on economic development.

The interest in investment dependence stems from the pivotal role of multinational corporations in dependency formulations. Multinational corporations are the organizational embodiment of imperialism, the metropolis, monopoly capital, and the core of the world system. Their investment behavior in the periphery is regarded by dependency theorists as largely exploitative. In many dependency formulations multinational corporate investment is said to promote underdevelopment, stagnation, and economic backwardness.

It is worth noting that this view of multinational corporations, as having a retrogressive effect on the development of regions and nations, runs counter to the standard neo-classical interpretation found in dual society theories (see Singer 1979) as well as the orthodox Marxist position that the expansion of capitalism is ultimately a progressive force (Warren 1980). How is it that multinational corporations retard the development of less-developed nations or reinforce backward economic structures? The most common argument about the direct effects of foreign investment is that multinational corporations actually drain surplus from the less-developed nations. This *surplus drainage thesis* is based on data that indicate, consistent with the claims of Amin, a net outflow of corporate profits from a number of less-developed nations. Multinational corporations, through direct foreign investment, own and control enterprises and industries in other nations. The profits derived from these ventures do not remain as a capital resource for these countries nor are they used to expand production in other sectors. Rather, profits are typically exported back to the core and/or placed in more profitable investment outlets. This is referred to as the *repatriation of profits* and is a standard operating procedure of international capital. It retards development because the surplus, produced in the less-developed economy, is unavailable to fuel further economic expansion and other spinoffs. It is through this mechanism that the analogy to class exploitation is most apparent, as value produced by the natural, human, and capital resources in less-developed nations is appropriated by MNCs. In Frank's words, "the satellites remain underdeveloped for lack of access to their own surplus" (1969:15).

A second reason that multinational investment is considered a negative force is its impact on the autonomy of less-developed nations. If multinational corporations control and decide upon the major investments in the countries they penetrate, to what extent does this undermine the ability of nations to direct their own development? Is the pace of growth and distribution of investment determined by the host nations or have they lost control of the process to multinational capital? It is clearly implied by dependency theorists that the resources possessed by multinational corporations permit them to dominate the economies and governments of less-developed nations. Further, this means that the development process is shaped by the interests of external forces and may run counter to national goals. For example, it is often argued that MNCs introduce inappropriate technology for production in less-developed economies. MNCs may utilize highly capital-intensive productive techniques even though the nation is plagued by high rates of unemployment and a labor surplus. These techniques may be profitable from the perspective of the investing MNC but they do not address the economic and employment needs of the nation.

A third dependency-related claim about the negative role of MNC foreign investment concerns its effects on the structure of the economy. It is often argued that foreign investment distorts the allocation of the labor force and the distribution of economic activity. The first form of distortion created by foreign investment is the *enclave economy* (Cardoso and Faletto 1979). Enclave economies are isolated economic sectors that employ relatively modern and efficient methods for the purpose of export production. These economies emerge as foreign capital, attracted to certain regions that possess agricultural and mineral resources demanded by markets in the core, gains access to natural resources and invests heavily in the capital and technology required to extract the resource. Enclave economies are typically the most dynamic sectors of the national economy and they can generate considerable foreign exchange through their export-oriented activities.

The distortions that result from enclave economies can best be understood using Amin's concepts of "extraversion" and "sectoral disarticulation." Enclave sectors are a basic component of the broader system of extraversion given the export-oriented nature of enclave production. Because production is dictated by and oriented toward external markets the enclave sector is poorly articulated with the rest of the national economy. Capital inputs tend to be imported, and the extracted primary products exported; thus few internal backward and forward linkages or spinoffs are generated. This enclave sector, then, is very much an appendage of the advanced capitalist economy from which the capital investment originates.

As Cardoso and Faletto (1979:71) note for Latin America:

Incorporation of the Latin American export system into the world market through the creation of enclaves required Latin American countries to form a "modern sector" that was a kind of technological and financial extension of central economies. Thus, the relative success of the export system was based on a highly specialized enclave economy with large surpluses. Growth of the export sector did not always create an internal market. It led to concentration of income in the enclave sector.

The latter point suggests, again as indicated by Amin, that accelerator effects tend to be negligible where production is sectorally concentrated and disarticulated.

The effects of foreign investment on the productive structure of less-developed economies also serve to shape the class structure and distribution of income. Dependency theorists tend to emphasize the close links between foreign capital and certain elite segments. The native *comprador elite* aligns itself with foreign capital and tends to support free trade and other policies that facilitate the import and export requirements of MNCs. The comprador class bases its privilege on and benefits from service to these external interests and is usually involved in some export- or import-related activity. This native, but subservient, elite often opposes efforts by domestic capitalists to establish indigenous industries or policies that raise working-class wages.

For the above reasons, and there are many more that have been advanced (see Bornschier, Volker, and Chase-Dunn 1985), a dependency proposition has emerged suggesting that those nations most extensively penetrated by multinational capital will be the most exploited and distorted and will, therefore, have the lowest rates of economic growth. The number of studies that have investigated this hypothesis are far too numerous to review. The one word that best describes the accumulated results is "mixed." A large number of cross-national studies have supported the dependency proposition and an equally significant number have rejected it. As with many empirical ventures in social science, the data did not speak for themselves nor did they have the final word. Instead, the positive or negative effect of foreign investment has depended upon the sample, the type of foreign investment measure, the years analyzed, the number and type of control variables, the estimation procedure, and so on.

Apart from the actual statistical results, it is surprising that so much effort has gone (and continues to go) into examining the effect of foreign investment on economic growth. What is even more perplexing is the belief that these statistical exercises somehow "test," "prove," or "disprove" dependency or world-economy theory. It is absurd to argue that the empirical validity of the historically rich and theoretically complex dependency world-economy literature hinges on the strength and statistical significance of the relationship between imperfect measures of foreign capital penetration and the change in gross national product.

Some of the blame for the reduction of sophisticated theoretical relationships into statistical equations lies with dependency theorists themselves who have frequently advanced an oversimplified *stagnation thesis*—that foreign capital has a universally retrogressive impact on the growth rates of less-developed economies. Although, as noted, there is an abundance of empirical literature reporting negative effects of foreign investment on the economic growth of peripheral nations, its effects on economic production and international inequality are much more complex. It is not enough to say that the current world system benefits the core at the expense of the periphery and, therefore, the central mechanism of imperialism—foreign investment—serves to reinforce this stratified system. This static conception belies the accumulated evidence on the changing international division of labor (Froebel et al. 1980), and the critical role played by capital from the advanced core states in facilitating this worldwide transformation.

The general dependency/world-economy model is sound in its emphasis on the internationalization of capital, and its structuring influence on production in the periphery. The problem is the expected net effect of foreign capital penetration. Although it is not unreasonable to hypothesize a general economic effect for the presence of foreign capital, many of the dependency/world-economy theories suggest effects that are likely contingent on the sector in which the capital is invested (see Jaffee and Stokes 1986). In terms of the effects on trade dependence, foreign investment is not placed exclusively into productive sectors that reinforce traditional patterns of Third World production, such as agro-mining sectors. A significant portion is also placed in manufacturing and heavy industrial sectors, and thus, in this way, can be seen as a critical factor responsible for *modifying* traditional patterns of specialization and serving as a potential source of growth and dynamism, albeit uneven and imbalanced.

Such a trend does not undermine the validity of dependency/world-economy theory. To make such a claim only points to a second and rather striking deficiency with many of the empirical tests of the theory—the exclusive use of economic growth to measure the effects of dependence. It is a methodologically irresistible variable because of its metric properties and cross-national availability; yet as an indicator of the consequences of dependency relations it obscures the many structural effects of dependent world-market participation that are outlined in the vast number of theoretical works on dependence. It is paradoxical that the same theorists and researchers who point to the inability of growth in GNP to lay the foundation for sustained, balanced, and equitable economic expansion often rely on this very same measure for the purpose of assessing the empirical validity of dependency theory. A careful reading of the literature should make it abundantly clear that dependency does not preclude growth, nor vice versa.

This fact is acknowledged by the concept of "dependent development," associated with Cardoso and Faletto (1979:xxiii–xxiv), which defines a particular form of growth and underdevelopment that is simultaneously economically dynamic and structurally distorting:

By development, in this context, we mean "capitalist development." This form of development, in the periphery as well as in the center, produces as it evolves, in a cyclical way, wealth and poverty, accumulation and shortage of capital, employment for some and unemployment for others. So we do not mean by the notion of "development" the achievement of a more egalitarian or more just society. These are not consequences expected from capitalist development, especially in peripheral economies.

By pointing to the existence of a process of capitalistic expansion in the periphery, we make a double criticism. We criticize those who expect permanent stagnation in underdeveloped dependent countries because of a constant decline in the rate of profit or the "narrowness of internal markets," which supposedly function as an unsurpassable obstacle to capitalistic advancement. But we also criticize those who expect capitalistic development of peripheral economies to solve problems such as distribution of property, full employment, better income distribution, and better living conditions for people. . . . Development, in this context, means the progress of productive forces, mainly through the import of technology, capital accumulation, penetration of local economies by foreign enterprises, increasing numbers of wage-earning groups, and intensification of social division of labor.

Support for the basic arguments of the "dependent development" position is provided both by case studies (Evans 1979) and time-series analyses of single countries (Bradshaw 1988). The findings of this research point to the important role of the state as an ally of foreign capital in directing the process of economic growth. It appears that foreign investment can facilitate growth in less-developed economies, particularly in the modern manufacturing sectors and often at the expense of agriculture (Bradshaw 1988). The net results may be highly uneven growth, increasing income inequality, and balance-of-payment crises. The fact that such counterproductive patterns accompany economic growth should be sufficient to indicate the problem with evaluating the efficacy of development theories using only economic growth measures.

The Debt Crisis

A second powerful example of the impact of international forces on the developmental trajectory of nation-states is provided by the extended Third World debt crisis of the 1970s and 1980s. (This section draws heavily from the following sources: Frieden 1981; Loxley 1986; Biersteker 1990; Walton and Ragin 1990.) One of the most significant and persistent problems that has faced less-developed nations has been the balance-of-payments deficit when the cost of the import of goods and services exceeds the revenue derived from export receipts for goods and services sold abroad. As noted, a good part of the deficit is the product of declining or deteriorating terms of trade, where the average price of a nation's exports is progressively less than the cost of its imports. While this deterioration of the terms of trade can be linked to the particular forms of export specialization, a number of factors contributed to a worsening of the situation in the 1970s. First, the rising price of oil as a result of the action of the OPEC oil cartel put a major strain on oil importing countries. Second, the mid-1970s found the core capitalist nations suffering from economic crises and recession that severely reduced the demand for exports from less-developed nations. Third, as the economic crisis worsened in the core, and unemployment increased, there was a move to impose various trade restrictions on the import of goods from other developed and less-developed nations. Taken together, these three factors resulted in rising import costs, declining export receipts, and widespread balance of payments deficits.

While export revenues were declining for many nations, and the balance-of-payments deficit was increasing, there was also an expansion in state involvement in the economy. As discussed in Chapter 5, the absence of a strong capitalist class to launch significant industrial development projects, and the concern over excessive reliance and dependence on foreign investment, prompted state managers, particularly in Latin American nations, to initiate public sector involvement in industrial projects. This was supported by borrowed funds from commercial banks. The 1970s also saw a significant increase in the role of private commercial bank lending to less-developed nations. Commercial banks in the core were anxious to find borrowers for the increasing sums of money flowing into their coffers from OPEC ''petrodollars'' as well as shifts of investment capital from industrial production and stocks into bonds and money market accounts. However, balance-of-payments problems persisted and this created an even more severe bind for less-developed nations—a combination of debt obligations and insufficient export revenues.

As countries were threatening to default on their loan obligations, many turned to the International Monetary Fund (IMF). The IMF is an international agency created at the end of World War II for the purpose of regulating the international economy and ensuring that nations do not resort to protectionist policies or measures designed to restrict the flow of capital and commodities, as had occurred in the 1930s. If a nation is experiencing economic difficulty it can apply for credit from the IMF. However, the IMF imposes conditions on nations in exchange for the loan. ''Stabilization'' or ''austerity'' programs are usually required in order to secure an IMF loan and receive the certification that is often desired by commercial banks willing to renegotiate the terms of their loans. These stabilization programs are the most controversial aspect of the IMF role and there has been a great deal of debate and conflict revolving around the impact of these programs. The programs usually require or include the following (Loxley 1986; Biersteker 1990):

1. *Currency devaluations.* This is done to make exports cheaper and more competitive and imports more expensive with the hope of stimulating demand for exports and discouraging the purchase of imported goods.

2. *General reduction in government spending and intervention.* This is consistent with the ideological bias of the IMF against public sector intervention and in favor of laissez-faire market solutions.

3. *Anti-inflationary policies.* This usually requires higher interest rates and a tight money policy which usually brings on recessionary economic conditions.

4. *Privatization of publicly owned enterprises.* This is both consistent with the anti-statist orientation of the IMF and viewed as a means to generate some needed revenue through the sale of public assets.

5. *Elimination of barriers to the free flow of goods and foreign investment.* This is designed to open the economy to greater levels of international competition and investment by foreign MNCs.

6. *Implement wage controls and restraints.* This is another element of the anti-inflationary policy as well as a potential means to attract foreign investment.

7. *Elimination of subsidies on food, transportation, and housing.* This is a way to reduce the government role and government spending.

The implementation of these policies has clear and unequal distributional consequences (Onimode 1989). Most generally, the urban poor and working classes pay the highest price. More specifically, public employees may be laid off, the prices for consumer goods may rise, real wages decline, firms that import products or that depend upon the domestic market see rising costs and a reduction in demand. The beneficiaries tend to be businesses-oriented toward export markets, foreign investors, multinational corporations, and the agricultural sector that produces cash crops for export.

Given the severe impact that these policies have on the economy and the general welfare of the population, it is not surprising that they also bring political consequences. Governments must often resort to bureaucratic authoritarian measures as a way to handle the opposition and resistance generated by these economic policies. Mass political demonstrations, strikes, and riots are the typical responses to the IMF-imposed economic measures. From 1976 to 1989, a period of widespread balance-of-payments crises among LDCs, eighty-five protest incidents were reported in twenty-six countries. The following report from the *New York Times* (March 1, 1989) provides a typical example of the IMF impact:

Venezuela's President said today that dozens of people had been killed and hundreds wounded in rioting over economic measures imposed by the government to satisfy its creditors.

President Perez responded to the unrest by suspending basic constitutional guarantees and imposing a nationwide curfew. Hundreds of arrests were reported.

The violence in Venezuela, an oil producer whose prosperity in the 1970s has given way to a $33 billion foreign debt, is the worst since the early 1960s. . . . President Perez has sought to persuade the International Monetary Fund and the World Bank to continue lending to Venezuela. Prices for a wide range of consumer goods and services have risen sharply as the government has moved to phase out price controls.

It is now worth summarizing the chain of causation, involving a variety of levels of analysis, that ultimately creates a political crisis in less-developed nations. It begins with a balance-of-payments deficit that is heavily influenced by a nation's world-economic position and foreign trade profile. As nations search for sources of external capital to launch industrial projects they often turn to commercial banks. As the private debt burden increases, the nations turn to the IMF for assistance in closing the trade deficit gap and securing certification for loan renegotiations.

IMF support and certification is contingent upon the implementation of an economic policy package or "stabilization" program. The impact of this program on the population fuels protests and riots. The government responds with the suspension of constitutional and democratic political processes and, often, the installation of authoritarian forms of social control. It is important to emphasize that much of the national-level decision-making and policy implementation is shaped by external international forces.

An appreciation of this level-of-analysis issue is largely absent, however, if one examines the IMF stabilization program which rests upon the assumption that the economic difficulties of LDCs are the product of inadequate domestic economic policy. In fact, internal economic difficulties stem, to a large extent, from international-level dynamics that are largely beyond the control of national governments. For this reason, the stabilization programs have had a dismal record in promoting the sustained socio-economic development of less-developed nations (Bradshaw and Wahl 1991).

CRITIQUES OF DEPENDENCY/WORLD-ECONOMY THEORY

The accumulated critiques of dependency/world-economy theory are too numerous to review here.[4] There are, however, a number of early statements that identify the basic problems and raise the fundamental issues. Robert Brenner's (1977) essay on the "origins of capitalist development" is the most notable of the Marxist critiques. Brenner views the underdevelopment theories of Frank and others as a logical reaction to the inadequacies of orthodox Marxist theory predicting that the international expansion of capitalism would stimulate industrial capitalist development in all nations of the world. Given the existing disparities between rich and poor nations, some revision was obviously required.

According to Brenner, dependency theorists have come to accept only half of the Marxist proposition—that capitalism has expanded worldwide. However, since this has not had a universally progressive impact, dependency theorists develop a theory of international capitalist development that assumes the impoverishment and exploitation of some regions as a condition for the enrichment and affluence of others. Thus, we have the metropolis exploiting the satellites and the core exploiting the periphery. For Brenner, the assumption that capitalism has expanded worldwide and penetrated all societies is problematic because it is not based on the existence of what he sees as the defining characteristic of capitalism—the emergence of a particular set of social-class relationships.

Brenner emphasizes repeatedly the concepts of "wage labor" and "relative surplus value." His point is that a system of wage labor signifies *capitalist social relations*—where laborers are hired by capitalists for a wage and brought together with capital goods and raw materials for the purpose of commodity production. Under these social relations, in comparison to precapitalist or feudal arrangements, owners are compelled to utilize productive techniques that allow them to produce the greatest amount of output in a given amount of labor time. The wage labor "constraint" and the forces of competition drive capitalists to increase the productivity of labor. *Relative surplus value* is created using superior organizational and productive techniques that reduce the per unit cost of production. Higher levels of output are achieved with constant inputs of labor. This is compared with *absolute surplus value* which rises because of greater inputs of labor or an extended working day. The essence of capitalism, for Brenner, is the wage labor–social relationship and the production of relative as opposed to absolute surplus value.

As noted, Wallerstein defines capitalism as production for profit in a market. Brenner rejects this view because production for profit in a market can and did take place without the wage labor relationship, and without the production of relative surplus value. Merchant capitalism and production for trade represent only one form of capitalism and, at least for Brenner, an insufficient one.

It is important to emphasize that the debate between Wallerstein and other Marxists, such as Brenner, is basically an argument over the appropriate level of analysis (see Denemark and Thomas 1988). As Wallerstein's inclusion in this chapter indicates, he is operating at a world-systemic level of analysis. The properties and laws of the system determine the nature of and developmental trajectory of the parts. For Brenner and other Marxist critics, the appropriate level of analysis is the nation-state and the focal unit is class relations and class struggle. Again we see a fundamental division in the explanation of socio-economic development hinging on the dispute over the appropriate level of analysis. What is particularly ironic in this case is that the various theorists on both sides of the debate regard themselves as Marxists. Further, the early neo-Marxist arguments, in reaction to conventional neo-classical and modernization models, advocated expanding the level of analysis to include the role of imperialist exploitation and the pernicious effects of world-market forces. This is now regarded by those like Brenner as antithetical to orthodox Marxist doctrine. A return to internal social-class processes is urged as the more correct way to understand underdevelopment. Class relations need to be brought back into the analysis.

A second Marxist critique of dependency theory comes from a diverse group of scholars who advocate a *modes of production approach* to the study of development (see Ruccio and Simon 1988, for an outstanding and in-depth review of this and other radical perspectives). The modes of production approach, like Brenner's critique, rejects the dependency/world-economy claim that there is a single economic system and that all nations and forms of social organization participating in and producing for this system are capitalist. Instead, it is contended that the international economy and national economies can contain different modes of production simultaneously, and that the relationship between different modes should lie at the center of any analysis of development and underdevelopment. The critical implication is that not all societies and forms of production are entirely capitalist and that the absence of the capitalist mode of production may be the cause of underdevelopment.

Some of the key concepts and definitions used in the modes of production perspective were first elaborated by Ernesto Laclau (1977). Most central is the *mode of production* which Laclau defined as "an integrated complex of social productive forces and relations linked to a determinate type of ownership of the means of production" (1977:34). More specifically, different modes of production are determined by the forms of labor control responsible for the production of surplus, the system of surplus appropriation, and the ownership/control of productive resources. Thus, a capitalist mode of production is characterized by a wage labor system of control, appropriation of the surplus by the nonproducing class (capitalists), and ownership and control of the means of production by this same nonproducer class. As with Brenner, it is the conditions under which commodities are produced, not exchanged, which determines the mode of production as capitalist, feudal, and so on.

Laclau introduced a second distinct concept, *economic system*, which he defined as "the mutual relations between the different sectors of the economy, or between different production units, whether on a regional, national, or world scale" (1977:35). An economic system can contain more than one mode of production. The economic system does not, in this model, determine the nature of the parts of that system. The coexistence of different modes of production within an economic system has implications for the socio-economic development of the larger society. In this sense, as described by dual society theory, two modes of production may exist side by side, but the important difference is that in the mode of production approach they interact. The coexistence of different modes is usually assumed to be a temporary transitional phase on the road to the dominance of a single mode of production.

The mode of production theorists attempt to show the ways in which different modes of production coexist, reinforce each other, and/or stand as obstacles to development. In most of the formulations on underdevelopment and backwardness, capitalist and noncapitalist modes of production coexist within a single national economy. The persistence of the noncapitalist mode in less-developed nations, even in the face of world capitalist expansion, is attributed to its functional relationship with merchant capitalism or the capitalist mode of production. These possibilities were illustrated in the earlier discussion of the commercial hacienda and the systems of "functional dualism." It is usually argued that noncapitalist modes of production stand as obstacles to sustained capitalist development. In short, only with the complete victory of the capitalist mode of production, and the elimination of noncapitalist modes, can full-scale capitalist industrialization occur.

In response to these critical assessments Christopher Chase-Dunn has provided a reconceptualization of world-economy theory in his book *Global Formation* (1989). This work represents an effort to "formulate a structural theory of the capitalist world-economy" that addresses some of the issues that have been raised regarding the viability of the Wallersteinian model. One of Chase-Dunn's first tasks is to reconceptualize and redefine the meaning of capitalism. As Chase-Dunn candidly acknowledges, Wallerstein's totalizing definition of capitalism is a metatheoretical claim fraught with difficulties. Most notably, arguing that all national units of a capitalist world economy are themselves capitalist produces a static conception of the global system that has difficulty accounting for the changes, tensions, and contradictions that arise from resistance and opposition to the logic of capitalism. As Chase-Dunn (1989:27) argues:

It is more useful to conceptualize modes of production in terms of *logical boundaries* rather than spatial boundaries. This allows for the articulation between different modes, and for the competition between modes within a single socio-economic system . . . if we eliminate the possibility of the coexistence of modes, we cannot discuss situations in which modes of production may be vying with each other for domination, and thus our ability to analyze transformation is accordingly limited.

While all nations in the world economy may be *spatially* subsumed within a capitalist world system, there are *logical* boundaries that delineate different forms or modes of economic production. Borrowing from Althusser and Balibar's (1970) distinction between a mode of production and a "social formation," Chase-Dunn categorizes the world system as a social formation and thus the title of the book (*Global Formation*) is indicative of a less deterministic notion of the international level of analysis. Within the global formation there can exist a variety of modes of production that may complement or contradict one another. These articulations between and among modes (such as socialist and capitalist) are the raw material generating tension and transformation both nationally and globally. The capitalist mode of production, or what Chase-Dunn (1989:43) describes as "real capitalism," involves (a) generalized commodity production; (b) private ownership and control of the means of production; (c) accumulation of capital based primarily upon the competitive production of commodities; (d) the exploitation of free commodified labor; and (e) a combination of social-class exploitation with core-periphery exploitation with the former more important, quantitatively, than the latter.

Note that this new specification pays greater attention to the social relations and the "commodified" nature of production inputs (a and d). It also retains some of the Wallersteinian features such as state ownership of the means of production, political-military power, and core-periphery forms of exploitation. According to Chase-Dunn this redefinition of capitalism allows one to "drop Wallerstein's totality assumption" and to "separately analyze the logical boundaries of modes of production and the spatial boundaries of world-systems."

This corrective to prior world-economy formulations can be interpreted as an effort to incorporate variations in societal-level characteristics into the large model of international development. This can also be seen in Chase-Dunn's elaboration of core-periphery, and semiperiphery dynamics as well as discussions of the role of the state in promoting world-economic mobility and competitiveness.

A final Marxist-based attack on dependency theory is represented by the work of Bill Warren in his book *Imperialism: Pioneer of Capitalism* (1980). Warren returns to what might be regarded as the orthodox Marxist position—that the world expansion of capitalism is a progressive force that serves to initiate capitalist industrialization, revolutionize the forces of production, and lay the groundwork for world capitalism and, ultimately, world socialism. He believes that this fundamental Marxist tenet regarding the expansion of capital was subverted by Lenin's (1948) writings on the role of imperialism as a stage of core capitalist development that involved the rise of monopoly enterprises, the export of capital to less-developed regions, and the "parasitic" and "retrogressive" effect of this "monopoly capital" stage. Warren rejects all of these characterizations of imperialism as presented by Lenin, and later incorporated into dependency theory. He goes on to argue that:

Direct colonialism, far from having retarded or distorted indigenous capitalist development that might otherwise have occurred, acted as a powerful engine of progressive social change, advancing capitalist development far more rapidly than was conceivable in any other way, both by its destructive effects on pre-capitalist social systems and by its implantation of elements of capitalism. Indeed, although introduced into the Third World externally, capitalism has struck deep roots there and developed its own increasingly vigorous internal dynamic. . . . Within a context of growing economic interdependence, the ties of "dependence" (or subordination) binding the Third World and the imperialist world have been and are being markedly loosened with the rise of indigenous capitalisms; the distribution of political-economic power within the capitalist world is thereby growing less uneven. Consequently, although one dimension of imperialism is the domination and exploitation of the non-communist world by a handful of major advanced capitalist countries (the United States, West Germany, Britain, France, Japan, etc.), we are nevertheless in an era of declining imperialism and advancing capitalism. (Warren 1980:9–10)

Warren's position on the role of colonialism and imperialism stands in sharp contrast to the claims of dependency and world-economy theory (see Amin 1984 for a response to Warren's thesis). For Warren, colonialism and imperialism are mechanisms that serve to destroy inefficient and backward precapitalist modes of production and form the basis for the establishment of industrial capitalism and indigenous development.

A similar thesis is advanced in the various case studies of African nations by Sender and Smith (1986). In their theoretical and empirical account they attempt to show how the period of colonialism promoted the beginnings of a wage labor system and the potential for dynamic capitalist development. During the post-independence period there have been significant variations in the economic performance of African nations which they attribute not to the exploitative forces of the world economy nor multinational corporations, but rather to the internal macro-economic policies pursued by African elites. In this sense their analysis reinterprets the historical role of capitalist expansion and proposes a return to an examination of internal, societal-level economic policies as the appropriate explanatory framework for the study of socio-economic development.

While many of the Marxist-based critiques of dependency/world-economy theory centered on the assumptions of the theoretical model and the conceptualization of capitalism, a second wave of critique centered on the empirical validity of the theoretical expectations in the face of genuine industrial development in peripheral nations. One of the initial and perhaps most influential challenges was launched by Alice Amsden (1979) in her economic and historical analysis of Taiwan. Addressing dependency theory, she writes (1979:342):

The major thesis of dependency theory is that the rise of foreign trade and the arrival of foreign capital from the "core" lie at the heart of underdevelopment in the "periphery." Taiwan, however, presents dependency theory with a paradox. It is both more integrated in world capitalism than other poor market economics and more developed. ... That is, capital accumulation proceeds on the basis of technological innovation and greater efficiency rather than on the basis of longer hours of work and more intensive effort *alone*. This is what we mean by "developed."

Amsden goes on to argue that the analysis of socio-economic development cannot focus exclusively on imperialism as the causal factor but must also consider, as equally primary, internal (societal- or national-level) production and social relations. When these are included, an analysis of Taiwan indicates that land reform and the state have been critical factors responsible for industrial development. More generally, Amsden seems to concur with the more orthodox Marxist-based critics in concluding that "the roots of underdevelopment may be seen to lie not so much in surplus extraction through unequal exchange and the repatriation of profits, but rather in local class relationships" (1979:372).

As a growing number of peripheral and semiperipheral (or newly industrializing countries or NICs) nations have experienced significant industrial development and economic growth, there has been a parallel revision of international-level arguments.

For the most part, theorists have presented the global capitalist apparatus as primarily a *constraint* on the development prospects of noncore nations. If we consider structures such as the world economy as posing not only constraints but also *opportunities*, we can better understand some of the more recent developments involving the world-economic ascent of peripheral and semiperipheral nations and regions.

The opportunities-as-well-as-constraint approach informs much of the recent international-level theorizing on socio-economic development. One of the clearest examples of this shift is found in the work of Gereffi (1994), who both points to a number of fallacies embedded in the formerly dominant approaches to development and offers a revised conceptualization of global interactions and dependency/world-economy formulations, as well as the new international division of labor (NIDL) model of Froebel et al. (1980), that contained a number of assumptions and expectations that have been proven empirically incorrect. Most generally, these models seriously underestimated the ability of peripheral and semiperipheral nations, particularly in East Asia, to launch significant industrial and technologically sophisticated development projects. It was generally assumed that most of the industrial production was of the labor-intensive, export-platform, simple assembly variety. Further, where the relocation and dispersion of economic activity from the core has occurred, it was assumed that all phases of production would be controlled and dominated by core-based transnational corporations. Finally, little distinction was made between the various forms of world-economic participation by semiperipheral or newly industrializing countries, and, accordingly, the differential developmental prospects and trajectories.

Gereffi attempts to correct these inadequacies in previous theorizing through the introduction of the concept of transnational economic linkages (TNELs). It is important to note that this concept is operationalized with reference to what were previously referred to as forms of dependency (e.g., debt dependence, trade dependence, investment dependence, etc.). However, the negative connotation associated with the term *dependency*, and the implicit assumption that forms of dependency are primarily constraints on, rather than facilitators of, development has led to a reconceptualization that begins with the very term used to describe the phenomenon. TNELs is a neutral, descriptive term that suggests neither necessarily negative nor positive effects on socio-economic development. Gereffi identifies four main TNELs—foreign aid, foreign trade, direct foreign investment, and foreign loans (private and public). He describes the economic linkages as "resources that may be used, singly or in diverse combinations and sequences, to finance development" (1994:40). Gereffi further notes that the availability of these resources is determined and mediated by both international-level and societal-level factors and conditions. TNELs also have an impact on the relative power of domestic economic sectors and social classes. Gereffi's elaboration of the various TNELs and their differential role in shaping the developmental trajectories of Latin America and East Asia have a number of implications for the theoretical revision of dependency/world-economy theory.

First, as already suggested, the reference to TNELs as "resources" signals an acknowledgement that world-economic interactions between the core and other regions can have potentially positive effects on national socio-economic development. Further, as the economic performance of several East Asian nations indicates, these linkages can also stimulate forms of socio-economic development that extend well beyond the TNC-dominated, low-wage, export-platform variety. Second, the timing of and sequence in which nations utilize the different TNELs have a major effect on the developmental impact of the TNEL. This is clearest in the case of foreign trade and the difference between Latin America and East Asia in terms of when certain trade strategies were implemented. Gereffi makes a convincing case that the earlier initiation in East Asia of an export-oriented strategy has contributed to the industrial success of this region. This suggests the importance of not only identifying the particular form of world-economic integration, in this case foreign trade, but also the timing and sequence of these economic linkages. Third, these global economic linkages are not simply imposed upon powerless, impotent peripheral and semiperipheral nations. Rather, states have the capacity to pursue policies that can either make the resources available or mediate their impact on domestic actors and the development process. This represents a shift back to the societal level of analysis in identifying factors, in this case the role of the state, that can determine the global-level prospects of a nation (see Evans 1995).

GLOBALIZATION AS A QUALITATIVELY NEW PHENOMENON

Dependency/world-economy theory shifted the focus from the national to international level of analysis, and pointed to the importance of capital flows and the international division of labor. The 1990s have seen a further explosion in the field of international political economy. This has served as a partial vindication of the arguments made by dependency/world-economy theorists.

It is now widely recognized by all development theorists that capitalism is an international system that influences all nations through the diffusion of culture, the exchange of products, and the flow of capital. A growing number of development theorists take the analysis one step further and argue that the contemporary world economy has shifted to a new mode that is qualitatively distinct from the past. Dicken (1992:1), for example, makes a distinction between internationalization and globalization:

economic activity is becoming not only more *internationalized* but . . . it is becoming increasingly globalized. . . . "Internationalization" refers simply to the increasing geographical spread of economic activities across national boundaries—as such it is not a new phenomenon. "Globalization" of economic activity is qualitatively different. It is a more advanced and complex form of internationalization which implies a degree of *functional integration between internationally dispersed economic activities*. (emphasis added)

Dicken goes on to further distinguish this emerging economic system from that identified by world-economy theorists. "The straightforward exchange between core and peripheral areas, based upon a broad division of labour, is being transformed into a highly complex, kaleidoscopic structure involving the *fragmentation* of many production processes and their *geographical relocation* on a global scale in ways which slice through national boundaries" (1992:4).

Hirst and Thompson (1996:8) also outline the distinction between an international and globalized economy. "An *international economy* is one in which the principle entities are national economies. Trade and investment produce growing interconnections between these still national economies. Such a process involves the increasing integration of more and more nations and economic actors into world market relationships. . . . A *globalized economy* is an ideal type distinct from that of the international economy and can be developed by contrast with it. In such a system distinct national economies are subsumed and rearticulated into the system by international processes and transactions.'' In this version of the globalized economy, as many observers have argued, national economies lose their primacy as actors shaping and influencing the international system. The determinant level of analysis becomes the global level.

Similarly, from different quarters, Lester Thurow has argued that the economic world is undergoing a profound transformation. He borrows some conceptual tools from the physical sciences—"plate tectonics" and "punctuated equilibrium''—to analyze these cataclysmic changes. Just as there are geological plates that slowly shift and alter the landscape of continents, so there are also economic plates that have been slowly shifting and reshaping the economic landscape. These shifting plates give rise to "punctuated equilibrium" (a term used in the biological sciences) that involves a sudden change in the environment and, accordingly, the rules and strategies required for success and survival. Thurow (1996:8–9) argues that

Shifts in technology, transportation, and communication are creating a world where anything can be made anywhere on the face of the earth. National economies fade away. A substantial disconnect arises between global business firms with a worldview and national governments that focus on the welfare of "their" voters. Countries splinter, regional trading blocs grow, the global economy becomes even more interconnected. (1996:9)

Another variant of the globalization thesis is advanced by McMichael (1996), who distinguishes the contemporary global production system from prior world-economic arrangements.

The global production system depends on a technological division of labor *within* industrial subsectors rather than a social division between economic sectors like industry and agriculture. . . . Instead of countries specializing in an export sector (manufacturing or agriculture), production sites in countries specialize in a constituent part of a production process spread across several countries. (McMichael 1996:90–91)

This global production system signals, for McMichael, a much broader transformation in the logic of national social change. He describes the post–World War I period up until the 1970s as one dominated by the *developmentalist* project—an organized strategy of national economic growth, including an international system of alliances and assistance established within the competitive and militarized terms of the cold war'' (1996:296). Today the development project is no longer the hegemonic doctrine driving social change. It has been superseded by the *globalization project* which refers to "an emerging vision of the world and its resources as a globally organized and managed free world/free enterprise economy pursued by a largely unaccountable political and economic elite" (1996:300).

The shift from developmentalism to globalism has several implications for the levels of analysis that lie below the international system. McMichael cites the impact on labor markets, labor processes, and the nation-state. The global organization of production has created greater instability in employment due to organizational efforts to develop lean and competitive corporate structures. As a result, employment is not only unstable but there is a steady increase in the size of the surplus labor pool throughout the world. This, in turn, has given rise to an expansion in informal labor processes by the displaced labor force. As noted in Chapter 3, the informal sector consists of a wide variety of unregulated economic activities. These kinds of activities expand where formal employment opportunities become increasingly unstable or scarce in relation to the supply of labor. The third major implication of the globalization project is the decreasing autonomy and legitimacy of the nation-state. As national boundaries become more permeable, and economic activities extend beyond national borders and across the globe, the ability of the nation-state to regulate economic activity, or pursue coherent development policies, is severely reduced.

Another illustration is provided by the work of Ross and Trachte (1990) who describe *global capitalism* as a new capitalist social formation. Just as "competitive capitalism" (late nineteenth and early twentieth centuries) was superseded by "monopoly capitalism" (post–World War II), the latter is being replaced by distinct global production relations that involve the "disaggregation of stages of production across national boundaries under the organizational structures of individual firms and enterprises." More systematically, Ross and Trachte analyze each capitalist social formation in terms of three "central strategic relationships"—the capital-to-labor relationship, the capital-to-capital relationship, and the capital-to-state relationship.

Just as competitive and monopoly capitalism could be defined by the distinctive nature of these three relationships, global capitalism signifies a new and distinct social formation by virtue of also redefining these relationships. Under global capitalism the capital-to-labor relationship, which refers to the levers or mechanisms that allow capital to extract surplus from the working class, takes on a *spatial character*. "The use or threatened use of capital mobility provides this capacity and becomes the primary lever of exploitation in sectors where the global variant emerges as dominant. More concretely, monopoly sector and other firms become global by locating parts or phases of their production processes in regions where low-wage and/or politically repressed working classes are located. In a direct manner, this lowers labor costs, and indirectly the *threat* of further relocations provides the leverage needed to extract concessions from the work force still employed at older production sites" (Ross and Trachte 1990: 65).

With regard to the capital-to-capital relationship, Ross and Trachte emphasize the heightened levels of international competition between firms and the constant effort to secure sources of cost advantage through outsourcing and mechanisms for ensuring steady profit flows through conglomeration.

The relationship between capital and the state also takes on a new form due to the enhanced ability of capital to locate production facilities any place in the world. This severely weakens the ability of the state, at all levels, to regulate and tax businesses. In a similar fashion to the capital-to-labor relation, capital is able to extract concessions from the state by using the capital mobility threat. Furthermore, the intense levels of international competition and challenge to domestic enterprises contributes to state economic policies that are much more sympathetic to the needs of private industry. The net result is a dominance of supply-side economic logic that encourages policies aimed at lowering the production costs of capital.

A number of points should be noted about Ross and Trachte's arguments regarding global capitalism. First, a central element in their analysis is the "spatial character" or enhanced mobility of capital under global capitalism. This is a fundamental component of most theories advancing the argument that capitalism is entering a qualitatively new phase. It has also contributed to the important role of geography and geographers in the analysis of contemporary capitalism. Due to technological advances in transportation, communication, and financial capital deployment, geographic space is regarded as a less formidable obstacle or constraint. Thus, capital is able to either shift productive facilities or enter into arrangements with other firms, anywhere in the world. Ironically, as Harvey (1980) and others have noted, as firms become less tied to a particular location, and more able to shift facilities elsewhere, perceptions about geographic location become *more* important as regions seek to attract the increasingly footloose enterprises. A greater number of regions and locations become viable destinations for private capital and there is increased pressure on state, local, and regional governments to "create" an attractive business climate that can attract mobile capital.

A second and related issue concerns Ross and Trachte's argument that the capital-to-capital relationship involves an intensification of competition. While it may be the case that the global economy is characterized by high levels of turbulence and flux, there is also a clear movement, as outlined in Chapter 3, for firms to enter into alliances, partnerships, and other network arrangements that require cooperation and coordination rather than cutthroat market competition.

Third, all of the various renditions of the globalization thesis emphasize the dispersal of productive facilities throughout the globe. This suggests a process of de-agglomeration and de-territorialization of production and a highly spatially disintegrated system of economic activity. However, there are some recently emerging patterns (see Chapter 3) that suggest both a theoretical and strategic rationale for, and structural and geographic reintegration of, spatially linked productive activities.

Finally, just as it is assumed that a highly dispersed system of production is necessarily more profitable than a spatially integrated arrangement, it is also assumed that the single most important factor in determining production cost, and location decision, is labor cost. However, the productivity of labor is also a critical factor affecting costs and one which can compensate for relatively high wages. According to Golub's (1995) comparative analysis of wage rates and productivity levels for the United States and East Asian newly industrializing countries (NICs), much of the cost advantage derived from lower labor costs is offset by lower productivity rates. If one looks at *unit labor costs*, which are affected by both the average hourly rate of pay as well as the number of units of a product that can be produced in an hour (the productivity element), cost differences between the United States and East Asian countries narrow significantly. One must also consider the quality of infrastructure and transportation services in determining the relative cost advantage of particular locations. Many studies of the globalization phenomenon ignore all of these factors in arriving at conclusions about the likely long-term consequences of capital mobility. On the other hand, it is equally important to note that the transfer of technology to less-developed nations, coupled with the reduced reliance on labor-intensive forms of production, can (and has) result(ed) in a rapidly closing productivity gap between advanced capitalist and less-developed nations.

Commodity Chains

All renditions of the globalization thesis make reference to "disaggregated stages of production" or the "functional integration between internationally dispersed economic activities." This feature of global capitalism has been analyzed more systematically using the concept of *commodity chains* (Hopkins and Wallerstein 1986). A commodity chain is a "network of labor and production processes whose end result is a finished commodity" (Hopkins and Wallerstein 1986:159). Under the regime of globalization these commodity chains, which are production processes that extend across geographic space and between independent firms, are increasingly complex and dispersed. They are often characterized by a network alliance, or partnership structure among firms.

Gereffi divides the commodity chains into four major segments that include raw material supply, production, exporting, and distribution and marketing. One might also add research and development and product design to this list. With regard to the global or international level of analysis, a critical issue concerns the geographic distribution of these various activities and the relative benefits derived from each.

Gereffi and Korzeniewicz's (1990) analysis of commodity chains of the international footwear industry provides a clear example of kinds of activities, geographic sites, and organizational processes that contribute to the commodity chain process. The primary raw material inputs for footwear are cattle and crude oil. These are converted or processed into rawhide/leather and synthetic rubber, respectively. The use of these materials differs by global region. A second distinction among the semiperipheral nations participating in the footwear industry can be found in the relative size of the organizational units of production. Taiwan relies on a large number of small firms, Brazil on a combination of small and medium-sized firms, and South Korea on large enterprises. The size of these organizational units has some impact on the particular footwear export niche that the nation occupies. Taiwan's smaller firms are able to produce for and respond to smaller, specialized markets and shifting fashion demands. At the other end of the spectrum, South Korea's industrial structure favors mass production and, accordingly, this nation has specialized in production for the huge and expanding markets in athletic footwear.

As a labor-intensive activity, the production site for footwear is heavily influenced by relative wage costs and heavily dependent on female labor. Clearly, wages in the footwear industry are lower in Latin America and East Asia than in the United States and other core countries. This represents a part of the comparative advantage that permits these nations to participate in this particular commodity chain. On the other hand, it does not entirely explain the location of production facilities since there are many nations with much lower wage costs, and wage rates in East Asia, the largest production site, now exceed those in Latin America. There are other productivity and competitiveness enhancing factors, such as the quality of infrastructure, interfirm network structures, and the range and size of domestic producers and subcontractors, that determine commodity chain involvement.

The third component of the commodity chain, the export network, addresses the process by which the footwear products are transferred from the production site to the distributors in the core consumer markets. Again, the form of export network utilized is closely related to the size of the production units. The small-to medium-sized producers in Brazil and Taiwan rely upon small export traders for distribution to consumer markets. This results in a decentralized system of securing buyers for a wide range of footwear styles and designs. South Korea, on the other hand, has a smaller number of large-size producers which, in turn, rely on a smaller number of export traders and trade companies to distribute the product. The production of a single line of athletic footwear for a mass market also entails a less decentralized system of distribution.

As we move to the final phase of the commodity chain, the marketing and sale of the product, we find the most intensive involvement of core-based capital and, not surprisingly, the most profitable activity. As noted, one of the key questions explored by commodity chain analysts is the relative value-added and profitability derived from these far-flung economic activities. It is a general contention of world-economy theorists that the chains are organized to channel the lion's share of profit into the coffers of core capitalist firms. Gereffi and

Korzeniewicz's (1990:65–66) analysis of the footwear industry supports this general thesis:

> The amount of economic surplus in the industry varies by sector. The core's activities with the highest economic surplus overall are at the marketing and retail end of the commodity chain, where American and European shoe companies and retailers are able to reap the profits generated by footwear brand names, control over retail chains of department stores and specialized shoe outlets, and the steady growth in U.S. consumer demand for a wide range of shoes. . . . The bulk of the profits in the footwear industry thus is concentrated in the core countries.

While this was the conclusion for the analysis of footwear, the commodity chain framework suggests that there are possibilities and prospects for upward mobility through participation in commodity chains. World-economic upward mobility depends upon the movement from traditional peripheral economic activities to those that involve a higher value-added process and production for growing and specialized markets. Gereffi and Korzeniewicz's analysis also shows that the involvement of Latin American and East Asian nations in the footwear commodity chains has resulted in the capturing of a large and expanding market, production for this market carried out primarily by local private capital, and increasing unit value-added in footwear exports over time. Furthermore, these same nations, particularly Taiwan and South Korea, participate in other industry commodity chains that involve technology-intensive products and control the marketing and distribution network for these products.

Technology and Globalization

Technology is another key element in discussions about the emerging global economy. Nations with the greatest comparative advantage in international production and trade have always tended to be those that possessed the most advanced and sophisticated production technology. Today, however, there is a clear sense that we are witnessing a technological revolution, particularly in the area of information technologies. These new direct and indirect means of production range from automated production to robotics to telecommunications, and they have facilitated the dispersal of production across the globe. Castells (1993: 19–20) in particular, has focused upon this continually emerging factor:

> [E]conomic and organizational transformations in the world economy take place (and not by accident) in the midst of one of the most significant technological revolutions of human history. The core of that revolution is in information technologies. . . . This technological revolution has been stimulated in its applications by a demand generated by the economic and organizational transformations. . . . In turn, the new technologies constitute the indispensable material base for such transformations. . . .

the various features of structural economic transformation that we have identified relate closely to each other. In fact, they join together to form a new type of economy that I ...call the "informational economy" because, at its core, the fundamental source of wealth generation lies in the ability to create new knowledge and apply it to every realm of human activity by means of enhanced technological and organizational procedures of information processing. The informational economy tends to be, in its essence, a global economy, and its structure and logic define, within the emerging world order, a new international division of labor.

Castells believes that the new informational technologies have been stimulated by the transnational organizational desire for a more spatially dispersed production system and they now stand as the single most important means, or material base, for both the further transformation of the world economy and the stimulation of socio-economic growth and development. He cites several key factors in determining the prospects and relative position of nations in this new international division of labor (1993:21–23). These include the technological capacity of the national economy, access to a large, integrated and expanding market, sizable differences between costs at the points of production and prices at the points of consumption for these goods, and the capacity of the state to implement developmental policies and strategies.

The increasing importance of technological capacity has given rise to new international economic constraints and forms of economic dependency. Castells and Laserna (1994) cite *technological dependence* as an international force responsible for the relative rise and decline of nations and regions in the 1980s. With particular focus on Latin America, Castells and Laserna cite the low technological level of production and exports which has placed this region in a weak position vis-à-vis East Asian nations. The inability to establish a technological infrastructure has its source, according to Castells and Laserna, in the poor export performance in the area of industrial products. In the absence of a sufficient flow of foreign exchange, Latin American nations have been handicapped in their ability to import the requisite technological components. In this respect, something of a "vicious circle" operates. Latin American economies "cannot import high technology because they do not export enough industrial products, and they cannot export manufactured goods because their industrial base is obsolete without high-technology imports" (Castells and Laserna 1994:61). Contributing to the inadequate infrastructure in technology has been a continued reliance on agriculture commodity and raw material exports, low levels of technology transfer from transnational corporations (especially as compared with East Asian nations) and a state sector weakened by heavy external debt obligations, IMF-imposed stabilization programs and, accordingly, inadequate public investment in technology-enhancing infrastructure. As a result of all these factors, Castells and Laserna conclude that Latin America has become a relatively technologically backward region and, as a consequence, it has experienced downward mobility in the world economy.

The Rise of Regional Trading Blocs

Regional trading blocs have an ambiguous relationship to the larger process of globalization. On the one hand these blocs are designed to eliminate national obstacles, and tariff and nontariff barriers, to the free flow of capital and goods. In this sense they operate at a supranational level and are consistent with the economic globalization trend. On the other hand, the trading blocs are regional rather than global and thus only include and integrate selected regional trading partners within the free trade agreement. They are included as an element of the larger globalization phenomenon given their relationship to the international level of analysis and their presumed impact on socio-economic development.

Various free trade agreements operating at the global level have been instituted and enforced during the post-war period. Most significant is the General Agreement on Tariffs and Trade (GATT), an agreement among over 100 countries that stipulates the rules and procedures governing international trade relations. The primary purpose of GATT has been to establish some uniform standards and procedures for the predictable exchange of goods and, more generally, to discourage tariffs and trade barriers and encourage free trade. Since the inception of GATT there have been periodic meetings, or "rounds" designed to revise and update the agreement to consider current needs and changing global situations. The most recent "Uruguay round," for example, addressed issues related to the perennial problem of trade barriers, service sector trade, intellectual ownership and property rights, foreign investment, and the one area that GATT has had the greatest difficulty regulating—agricultural trade. The proliferation of regional free trade blocs can be seen as a response to the difficulties entailed in establishing an international agreement among 100 or more nations. As we noted in the discussion of dependency theory, free international trade is not viewed as mutually beneficial for all nations, and the structural disadvantage related to differences in economic power and resources inevitably produces conflict over the rules governing exchange. Even among those nations that would seem to benefit the most from free trade agreements, there are internal divisions based on social-class and economic sectoral interests. A consideration of the NAFTA debate and economic impact will serve to illustrate some of the problems related to this free trade trend.

The North American Free Trade Agreement (NAFTA) has established a free trade zone between the United States, Canada, and Mexico. While the agreement with Canada generated very little media coverage or controversy, the agreement with Mexico produced a major political debate over the wisdom of free trade agreements generally and with less-developed nations in particular. There are two central issues involved in the debate over such free trade agreements. The first is the general question of whether a nation will be better off or worse off as a result of the free trade agreement. The second and related issue concerns the different social and environmental standards in the different countries and the implications of these differences for the parties involved.

On the question of whether the nation will gain or lose, the advocates of the treaty view free trade agreements as mutually beneficial to all parties. Thus, both Mexico and the United States will experience a net economic gain from the arrangement. It was argued that U.S. investment in Mexico would improve the standard of living in Mexico, result in a demand for machines and production goods from U.S. producers, and generate a rising demand for U.S. consumer goods as Mexican workers used their higher wages to purchase U.S. products. Opponents of the treaty believed that it would stimulate a shift of manufacturing resources into Mexico to exploit the cheap labor and lax environmental regulations, that it would have a depressing effect on wages in the United States, as American workers must compete with the low-wage Mexican workforce, and that the Mexican workforce would receive insufficient wage levels to stimulate any demand for U.S. consumer products. Instead of optimistic scenarios presented by proponents, opponents believed the net effect would be further job loss in basic manufacturing, a growing trade deficit with Mexico, and pressures to lower wages and labor and environmental standards in order for the United States to compete with Mexico. Much of the opposition to NAFTA was based upon the second issue—the different social and economic conditions and standards prevailing in Mexico. The objections to NAFTA capture many of the concerns voiced about the larger process of globalization.

The arguments for and against NAFTA can now be evaluated. Most of the evidence thus far refutes the claims advanced by supporters of the trade pact. The expectations and projections of expanded U.S. exports to the open market of Mexico have not come to pass. Since 1993 the trade surplus with Mexico ($1.7 billion) has turned into a $16 billion deficit. A large portion of the deficit is accounted for by cars, trucks, auto parts, furniture, and apparel.

It was also claimed that NAFTA would improve the Mexican economy and increase Mexican wages thus slowing the growth of U.S. maquiladora firms. *Maquiladoras* are foreign-owned firms located along the Mexican side of the U.S.–Mexican border that engage in primarily labor-intensive manufacturing. Under the maquiladora system, foreign companies can ship tools, raw materials, and components duty-free to Mexico. The manufactured and assembled goods are then typically exported back to the United States or other core nations. Since the inception of NAFTA, a long list of U.S. firms have shifted part or all of their operations to the Mexican side of the border and one Mexican economist predicts the maquiladora sector will add close to 400 new plants by the year 2000 and increase the maquiladora workforce from 579,000 in 1994 to 943,000 (*Business Week, Economic Trends*, June 26, 1995).

In terms of the job loss due to increased competition from Mexico and Canada, the U.S. Department of Labor has certified the loss of around 128,000 jobs. Most observers believe the job loss numbers are much greater than those officially certified by the Department of Labor. On almost every count, the data on the impact of NAFTA refutes the inflated claims made by its supporters. It is important to indicate that much of the failure can be linked to the Mexican "peso crisis" in 1994 and the subsequent sharp devaluation of the Mexican currency. This had the effect of sharply reducing the cost of Mexican exports while increasing the cost of U.S. imports to Mexico. This not only contributed to the trade deficit but also stimulated the relocation of facilities to Mexico as the fallen peso has reduced Mexican wage rates by at least 30%. Thus, the standard of living in Mexico has declined and the prospect of Mexican workers using their wage gains to purchase U.S.-made products is virtually nil. While the devaluation of the Mexican peso is responsible for much of the negative repercussions of NAFTA, many observers contend that the NAFTA agreement required a devaluation of the overvalued Mexican currency in order for Mexico to retain a competitive position with the United States (Dornbusch and Werner 1994; Warner 1995).

NAFTA has also enhanced the ability of employers to use the relocation threat against workers seeking higher wages or union representation. A study by Kate Bronfenbrenner reports an increase in management threats to close factories in the face of union organizing efforts since the inception of NAFTA (*Business Week*, July 7, 1997).

One of the few NAFTA bright spots thus far is in the increasing demand by Mexican factories for U.S. components and capital goods. Companies locating in Mexico are turning to U.S. suppliers of machinery and components, rather than Asian sources, given the NAFTA arrangements and geographic proximity.

ASSESSING THE GLOBALIZATION THESIS

Globalization—as a set of forces and an economic logic that operates at a supranational level subsuming all those national units and levels of analysis within its domain—obviously has major implications for the levels-of-analysis scheme outlined throughout this book. Many theorists and observers speak of a qualitatively new phase of capitalism that entails the demise of state and national autonomy. Overall, the vast literature, both academic and popular, on the globalization phenomenon suggests the decreasing importance of national institutional structures in determining economic activity and outcomes and/or some new form of convergence among nation-states as they are subjected to common global forces. According to Robert Reich, the former Secretary of Labor, "There will be no national products or technologies, no national corporations, no national industries. There will no longer be national economies, at least as we have come to understand that concept" (1991:3). This scenario—the dawning of a new global age that will render national political and economic institutions impotent—is not shared by all observers, theorists, and policy-makers. In fact, there is now a growing literature that challenges and rejects some of the more extreme versions of the globalization thesis. A key question is the extent to which national economies remain relevant units for the analysis of economic activity, capital accumulation, and corporate organizational behavior.

Robert Wade (1996) contends that national economic borders continue to

define distinctive modes of capital accumulation and economic activity. Support
for his argument revolves around the fact that most production and economic
activity remains intimately wedded to a national base. Around 90% of production in industrialized economies is directed toward the domestic market. Consumption is also largely satisfied, again up to 90%, by domestic producers.
Similarly, the bulk of capital investment by national firms is devoted to domestic
investment. Corporations, even those that are defined as multinational and transnational, retain their home base for strategic decision-making and research and
development activities. Finally, national differences in the rate and pattern of
technological development suggest the persistence of variations in national institutional forms of economic technological and entrepreneurial capacity. Each
of these observations contradicts the globalization thesis that national boundaries
are blurring, that firms are no longer tied to their nation of origin, or that national
institutional differences become increasingly meaningless as the logic of global
capitalism dictates corporate strategy and structure.

Pauly and Reich (1997) advance an equally strident critique of the globalization argument that multinational corporate behavior has lost its national character. In order to determine whether a convergence has occurred among the
MNCs in the United States, Germany, and Japan, they suggest an examination
of corporate governance structures, research and development patterns, and investment and intrafirm trade flows. Rather than viewing these corporate behavior
patterns as a response to global market forces, Pauly and Reich believe that
firms remain embedded in national ideological and institutional foundations that
shape and influence corporate behavior.

Corporate governance structures are defined as ''the rules and norms that
guide the internal relationships among various 'stakeholders' in a business enterprise, including owners, directors, managers, creditors, suppliers, employees,
and customers.'' These rules and norms vary by nation and have a major impact
on the incentive structure shaping corporate behavior. The question is whether
there is a global logic that reduces the significance of these institutional norms
and produces a convergence in corporate behavior. One of the most significant
and widely cited corporate governance distinctions exists between Anglo-
American and Japanese systems. The Anglo-American system places the greatest
emphasis on protecting shareholders against potential managerial abuse through
capital market pressure for short-term financial performance; the Japanese system entails higher levels of cross-shareholding among related and affiliated
firms, which produces a more long-term and patient investment approach with
less regard for individual shareholders. This is one example of a national institutional difference that translates into significant variations in the behavior of
firms (see Kester 1996; Roe 1994). These cross-national differences remain and
persist in spite of the increasing international scope of corporate operations.
Pauly and Reich (1997:12) report ''that we did not find evidence for, or credible
expectations of, substantive convergence in core strictures of corporate governance and basic financing across Germany, Japan and the United States.'' Na-

tional institutional capabilities, rather, seem to constrain or prohibit the employment of alternative governance structures.

While technology may be viewed as a leading mechanism advancing the globalization of production and finance, it too is closely connected to national institutions and economic trends. The evidence does not suggest the rise of a "technoglobalism" that transcends national boundaries. Pauly and Reich report that MNCs in the major industrial societies tend to maintain their basic research and development operations within their home nations. Furthermore, the data indicate significant variations in MNC research and development strategies and spending patterns that can largely be explained by the national systems of innovation. Patel and Povitts' (1991) analysis of eleven industrialized nations concludes that:

the production of technology remains far from globalized. Its heavy concentration in the industrialised—as compared to the developing countries—has been recognised for a long time . . . country-specific factors create both the general conditions that determine the volume of technological activities, and the specific inducement mechanisms that determine their direction.

Thus, national governments can establish technological infrastructures that advance the objectives of competitiveness (see Porter 1990) and implement fiscal incentives that facilitate organizational-level investments in research and development. These national-level policies, in turn, can have a significant impact on the international competitive prowess of transnational corporations as well as the ability of nations to deploy efficiently their stocks of human capital resources.

Investment and intrafirm trade patterns also exhibit a distinct national flavor. In comparing Japanese and German MNCs, Pauly and Reich find a greater willingness among U.S. firms to outsource production and rely on unaffiliated foreign firms for inputs and components. In contrast, Japanese and German MNCs establish and retain intrafirm trade networks with national affiliated firms as the primary suppliers of inputs and components even when facilities are located on foreign soil. This differential pattern has a significant impact on trade flows. As Pauly and Reich (1997:17) emphasize,

the external investment operations of German and Japanese firms tend to enhance the prospects for overall exports from their home base, while comparable American operations tend to substitute for U.S. exports. . . . Foreign investments undertaken by U.S. firms tend to be—"trade-displacing." Their Japanese and, to a lesser extent, their German analogs tend to be "trade creating."

These national differences in firm behavior carry their own advantages and disadvantages and it is difficult to argue that there should be a convergence toward one practice or the other. The outsourcing strategy practiced by U.S. firms may be viewed as a best practice on primarily cost-cutting grounds while intrafirm or intra-affiliate patterns of exchange might produce a tighter and more dependable relationship between producers and suppliers. The latter strategy has the further advantage of producing the positive externality for the larger national economy through the promotion of exports to foreign facilities.

A further piece of evidence bearing upon the question of corporate divergence or convergence in the face of globalization is provided by a comparative study of corporate restructuring practices. Usui and Colignon (1996) examine the corporate restructuring response to prolonged worldwide recession among U.S., Japanese, and German international firms. Some observers who advance a strong globalization thesis argue that the response of firms should be similar or converging due to the common global market pressures that determine corporate behavior. As an alternative, Usui and Colignon advance a "social embeddedness" argument that assumes "economic activity is shaped and modified by networks of interorganizational relations and the configuration of institutional relations of society" (1996: 553). Looking specifically at cross-national patterns of adjustment and human resource deployment, Usui and Colignon find that common global recessionary pressures produce different organizational restructuring responses. In the United States restructuring is more likely to take the form of layoffs, permanent downsizing of personnel, and cuts in investment in research and development. Japanese firms, in contrast, employ adjustment strategies that are designed to reduce the impact on employees and avoid layoffs and terminations. The ability to implement these different strategies is contingent upon what Usui and Colignon refer to as the "institutional configuration" that includes the corporate governance structure (discussed previously), the industrial organizational structure, government policies, and broader patterns of public opinion regarding appropriate and inappropriate corporate behavior. National variations on each of these institutional dimensions mediate and modify the impact of global market forces on corporate policy and strategy. Rather than viewing convergence as a shift toward "best practices," Usui and Calignon not only observe no pattern of convergence but also argue that "the success of Japanese world corporations may depend on maintaining their Japanese uniqueness in the fact of global pressure to conform to market-efficiency logic" (1996: 571).

Finally, systematic analysis of the globalization thesis by Hirst and Thompson (1996:2) leads to the conclusion that "globalization as conceived by the more extreme globalizers, is largely a myth." This pointed assessment is based upon several critical points that reinforce and complement the literature cited above. Quoted in full, they are as follows:

1. The present highly internationalized economy is not unprecedented: it is one of a number of distinct conjunctures or states of the international economy that have existed since an economy based on modern industrial technology began to be generalized

from the 1860s. In some respects, the current international economy is *less* open and integrated than the regime that prevailed from 1870 to 1914.

2. Genuinely transnational companies (TNCs) appear to be relatively rare. Most companies are nationally based and trade multinationally on the strength of a major national location of production and sales, and there seems to be no major tendency towards the growth of truly international companies.

3. Capital mobility is not producing a massive shift of investment and employment from the advanced to the developing countries. Rather, foreign direct investment (FDI) is highly concentrated among the advanced industrial economies and the Third World remains marginal in both investment and trade, a small minority of newly industrializing countries apart.

4. As some of the extreme advocates of globalization recognize, the world economy is far from being genuinely ''global.'' Rather, trade, investment and financial flows are concentrated in the Triad of Europe, Japan, and North America and this dominance seems set to continue.

5. These major economic powers, the G3, thus have the capacity, especially if they coordinate policy, to exert powerful governance pressures over financial markets and other economic tendencies. Global markets are thus by no means beyond regulation and control, even though the current scope and objectives of economic governance are limited by the divergent interests of the great powers and the economic doctrines prevalent among their elites.

NOTES

1. For an extensive review of the origins of, and theorists associated with, the dependency/world-economy perspective see Chilcote (1984) and, for a more critical assessment, Brewer (1980).

2. The fourth and fifth hypotheses are, specifically: ''One is that the latifundium, irrespective of whether it appears as a plantation or a hacienda today, was typically born as a commercial enterprise which created for itself the institutions which permitted it to respond to increased demand in the world or national market by expanding the amount of its land, capital, and labor and to increase the supply of its products. The fifth hypothesis is that the latifundia which appear isolated, subsistence-based, and semi-feudal today saw the demand for their products or their productive capacity decline and that they are to be found principally in the above-named former agricultural and mining export regions whose economic activity declined in general.''

3. See the lucid review and critique of Wallerstein by Gorin (1985).

4. Critical appraisals of dependency/world-economy theory are offered by Lall (1975), Brewer (1980), Cypher (1979), Palma (1978), and Warren (1980).

7

Conclusion

This book has reviewed theories of socio-economic development and their relationship to the different levels of analysis. Explanations for socio-economic development center on the individual, work organizations, the prevailing social institutions, and the dynamics of the international system. Each of these focal points has its own built-in strengths and weaknesses. Ultimately, different levels of analysis must be integrated in order to gain a complete picture of the opportunities for and constraints on development. One must avoid a psychological or structural determinism that takes cultural beliefs or structural arrangements as independent forces beyond the influence of other levels of analysis.

This chapter summarizes some of the observations and arguments advanced in previous chapters about the explanatory logic of the different levels of analysis and associated theories. It concludes with some practical suggestions for studying socio-economic development.

1. *Individual-level* theories of development place the greatest emphasis on the causal role of individual characteristics. Particular cultural beliefs, attitudes, motives, and forms of human capital are believed to be required in quantities sufficient for industrial development to take place.

One of the difficulties with this model is the tendency to engage in simple forms of psychological reductionism. The cultural values and beliefs of a nation's population are inferred from the level of economic development. It is assumed that modernization requires a certain psycho-cultural mind-set. If a nation is poor, then the population is assumed to lack the necessary set of values and beliefs. Rich nations, conversely, are assumed to possess a population with the ''appropriate'' consciousness.

A second shortcoming of the individual-level model is the tendency to view individuals in isolation from social, economic, and political structures. An important question concerning subjective sentiments and individual attributes is the origin of these characteristics and their possible effect on the larger society. Neither question can be answered without extending the theoretical framework to include other levels of analysis. Individual motives, behavior, and consciousness are a direct result of the organization of property and power in a society. The developmental effect of human capital expansion or achievement motivation will be contingent on the level of industrial/technological development and existing opportunity structures. It is purely asociological to view these individual-level characteristics, and their effects, in isolation from organizational and institutional structures.

2. *Organizational-level* theories of development focus on the structure of work organizations. A consideration of the organizational level is necessary in order to understand the economic behavior and incentives of individual actors. The "backward," "traditional," and "irrational" economic beliefs and behaviors, assumed to be the cause of underdevelopment in individual-level theses, often find their sources in the organizational arrangements of production. These arrangements also affect the level of productivity and efficiency and, in turn, contribute to or restrict the level of a nation's potential economic output. In this sense the organizational level of analysis provides a theoretical basis for explaining individual-level sentiments and behavior as well as the broader process of national development.

Political movements and revolts frequently stem from the reaction to particular forms of work organization and the associated patterns of economic distribution. An important component of development is the transition from agricultural to industrial forms of organization. Labor process studies of industrial capitalist economies link the evolution of organizational arrangements to the pace and rate of capital accumulation and growth. More recently, the emphasis has been placed on emerging organizational forms revolving around interorganizational networks and alliances as the keys to socio-economic development.

3. The *societal level* of analysis gives rise to the widest assortment of explanations for development. Generally, societal-level theories emphasize the role of national institutions in promoting development. As noted, much of this literature—the structural modernization and political development variants—is influenced by structural functionalism. This results in institutional prescriptions for developmental success that advocate abstract operating principles related to an ideal-type bureaucratic model. The political and sociological modernization literature has also been permeated by a distinct pro-order bias that produces a defensive and politically conservative model of development.

Conventional economic theories of development also operate at the societal level and attempt to determine the mechanisms promoting economic growth. Growth models assume that development stems from a set of macro-economic conditions subject to manipulation by national governments. It is important to recognize the social and political implications of these growth models and the fact that the conditions presumed necessary for growth exact greater costs on certain segments of the population, particularly workers. The inegalitarian results of standard economic growth policies have fueled the proliferation of alternative models that emphasize equity over growth and alternative measures that include the human side of development.

The comparative analysis of socio-economic systems also falls within the societal level of analysis. Models of capitalism and socialism contain arguments about the relative superiority of economic institutions as engines of growth and development. One must always be aware of the divergence between theory and practice in every type of economic system, and the fact that all economic arangements contain their own irrationalities and contradictions. There are inevitably trade-offs when choosing any kind of development strategy, and these usually raise issues that fall beyond the realm of economic calculation: equality, justice, freedom, autonomy, quality of life, fairness, public welfare, and the collective good.

At present, most nations of the world are attempting to devise some variant of a market-based development strategy in order to participate and compete in the world capitalist economy. These strategies typically involve some combination of state economic policy and intervention—industrial policy, managed trade, neo-mercantilism, or a governed market—alongside fewer restrictions and regulations on the private sector. The relative role of state and market, or public and private sector influence, remains the most significant issue when examining societal-level development strategies.

4. *International-level* theories have dominated the study of development since the mid-1970s. The most influential approach has been the dependency/world-economy perspective. Its popularity is associated with the trend in social science toward structural explanations that emphasize the environment, external forces, and structural constraints. Ultimately, this requires including broader levels of analysis. In the case of dependency/world-economy theory this means that nations are not "free to choose" or autonomous, self-determined units but parts of a global system whose logic affects national outcomes and determines national policies. This is an invaluable contribution to development theory, and there are few scholars today who confine their study of national development exclusively to internal national factors.

More recent assessments of dependency/world-economy theory have criticized its tendency toward structural determinism. These critiques have come from Marxists and non-Marxists alike, and essentially advocate a less deterministic and more dialectical approach toward national/world-economy interaction. In short, social-class relations, national policies, and internal national struggles have significant effects on development that cannot be reduced to epiphenomena of the logic of world capitalism. The currently popular globalization perspective raises many of the same issues related to the the determinant impact of world-economic forces.

The work by MacEwan and Tabb (1989) is representative of an effort to integrate and synthesize national and international levels of analysis. They use the concept of *combined and uneven development* to describe the dynamic relationship between the national/societal and international levels of analysis.[1] They go on to explain that:

> While developments in many regions of the international economy are unified or "combined" by the international operation of capitalism, they nonetheless proceed in an "uneven" manner because of multiple national foundations of capitalist activity. Distinct national foundations embody separate social structures, styles of political organization, and historical experiences, and these yield different responses to economic interdependence. The difference [*sic*] between the unevenly developing parts of the system matter, but those differences always exist within the interconnections of the entire system. (1989: 69)

MacEwan and Tabb offer a useful theoretical strategy for the analysis of socio-economic development. The notion of combined and uneven development is an explicit recognition of two fundamental facts: (1) that capitalism is a global system of economic organization affecting all nations that participate in the world economy, and (2) that there are important national variations within the global system related to internal class relations and the political-economic policies of national governments. MacEwan and Tabb argue that the current era of international instability is the product of the interaction between these two levels of analysis.[2] Thus, they reject a deterministic, one-way analysis in favor of an integrative approach:

> In the current periods of crisis, economic affairs would appear to be moving us toward a global system. . . . In short, it would appear that the international economy is becoming more and more "combined."
>
> Yet the extreme globalist interpretation of these occurrences can be sustained only by a thorough separation of economics and politics, a separation which would be damaging to reality. . . . Politics, and other aspects of national-specific social organization, maintain capitalism's "unevenness." (1989:69–70)

Students of development are well-advised to follow the type of analytic scheme advanced by MacEwan and Tabb. Their arguments reflect the emerging theoretical effort to bring class, politics, and national policy back into the development equation while retaining a global perspective. In addition to the national and international factors emphasized in MacEwan and Tabb's analysis, one should not lose sight of the lower levels of analysis involving the pitfalls of global determinism and national voluntarism. By grasping the multiple levels of socio-economic development theory and social reality, it is hoped that readers will approach the literature with a more critical eye and construct an explanatory theoretical framework that is integrative rather than exclusionary.

Finally, a concrete example, which captures some of the complex interrelationships among the four theoretical levels, is found in Robert Wade's (1990) recent analysis of the economic development of Taiwan. While Wade's case study focuses primarily on the role of the Taiwanese government in directing private sector activity, there are important links forged between cultural historical factors, patterns of industrial organization, and global dynamics.

In Taiwan, the ideological belief system combines historically traditional values supporting nation, family, and obedience to authority with a strong nationalist flavor emphasizing competition with and struggle against the mainland Chinese government and economic system. These nationalist values play a significant role in the mobilization of human energy and labor, and provide legitimacy for government policies designed to advance Taiwan's international economic position. In this example, *individual-level cultural values* are understood in the broader context of historical Chinese traditions and the more recent division between Taiwan and mainland China. Their impact on the development process is mediated and garnered through organizational-level production processes and state economic policy and planning.

The *organizational-level production system* is another component mentioned in Wade's analysis. Taiwan's industrial organizational structure is, unlike Japan and Korea, made up of a larger number of smaller-sized firms and smaller business groups. A large portion of Taiwan's exports come from the small and medium-sized firms that depend on the larger firms as suppliers for material and chemical inputs. The smaller firm size has resulted in a labor force that is more difficult to organize given its dispersed status, and more easy to control through the paternalistic management practices typical in small enterprises (Deyo 1982). The smaller firms have also proven to be quite flexible and opportunistic as well as responsive to the efforts by the state to promote export production.

The *societal level of analysis*, the primary focus of Wade's study, centers on government policy vis-à-vis the private sector (and the configuration of small and large firms) and the international economy. The state both ''governs the market,'' through various policies, plans, and fiscal incentives, and promotes and protects firms at the global level.

The *international level of analysis* is particularly important for understanding the economic success of Taiwan. The state may have directed and encouraged particular forms of production and investment but the ability to translate these efforts into export-oriented development required an international market for the goods produced. Much of the government strategy has been based on changing international conditions and the rapid emergence of subcontracting relations and commodity-chain-like configurations across the globe. These forces both shape government policy and provide real opportunities for a select group of developing countries.

This simple example provides one approach to the analysis of socio-economic development. Identifying the four levels of analysis, and integrating the social, economic, and political forces operating at each level, allows for a more complete analytical framework than is possible if one chooses only a single factor or level of explanation. Increasingly, social scientists are constructing multilevel theoretical models and designing multilevel research strategies. This indicates a greater sensitivity to the various levels of social action and process and signals the possibility for greater theoretical integration across disparate levels of analysis.

NOTES

1. This term was first used by Leon Trotsky (1959) to describe the different paths to socialism in the world economy. It has also been used by dependency theorists (e.g., Sunken and Paz 1970).

2. See MacEwan and Tabb (1989b) for a collection of essays that applies the "combined and uneven development" model to specific contemporary development issues.

Bibliography

Abercrombie, Nicholas, Stephen Hill, and Bryan Turner. 1986. *Sovereign Individuals of Capitalism*. London: Allen and Unwin.

Adelman, Irma, and Cynthia Morris. 1973. *Economic Growth and Social Equity in Developing Countries*. Stanford, CA: Stanford University Press.

Aglietta, Michel. 1979. *A Theory of Capitalist Regulation: The US Experience*. London: NLB.

Alexander, Jeffrey C., and Bernhard Giesen. 1987. "From Reduction to Linkage: The Long View of the Micro-Macro Link." Pp. 1–42 in Jeffrey Alexander et al. (eds.), *The Micro-Macro Link*. Berkeley: University of California Press.

Alford, Robert, and Roger Friedland. 1985. *Powers of Theory: Capitalism, the State and Democracy*. New York: Cambridge University Press.

Almond, Gabriel. 1960. "Introduction." Pp. 1–15 in Gabriel Almond (ed.), *The Politics of Developing Areas*. Princeton, NJ: Princeton University Press.

———. 1965. "A Developmental Approach to Political Systems." *World Politics* 17: 183–214.

Almond, Gabriel, and G. Bingham Powell. 1978. *Comparative Politics: System, Process and Policy*. 2nd ed. Boston: Little, Brown and Company.

Althusser, L., and E. Balibar. 1970. *Reading Capital*. London: New Left Books.

Amin, Samir. 1976. *Unequal Development*. New York: Monthly Review Press.

———. 1984. "Expansion or Crisis of Capitalism?" *Contemporary Marxism* (Fall):3–17.

Amsden, Alice. 1979. "Taiwan's Economic History: A Case of *Etatisme* and a Challenge to Dependency Theory." *Modern China* 5:341–380.

Andrisani, Paul L., and Herbert S. Parnes. 1983. "Commitment to the Work Ethic and Success in the Labor Market: A Review of Research Findings." Pp. 101–120 in Jack Barbash, Robert Lampman, Sar A. Levitan, and Gus Tyler (eds.), *The Work Ethic: A Critical Analysis*. Madison, WI: Industrial Relations Research Association.

Arato, Andrew. 1978. "Understanding Bureaucratic Centralism." *Telos* 35:73–87.

Archer, Margaret. 1988. *Culture and Agency: The Place of Culture in Social Theory.* Cambridge: Cambridge University Press.

Aronowitz, Stanley, and William DiFazio. 1994. *The Jobless Future.* Minneapolis: University of Minnesota Press.

Badaracco, Joseph J., Jr. 1991. *The Knowledge Link.* Boston: Harvard Business School Press.

Baden, S., A. M. Goetz, C. Green, and M. Guhathakurta. 1994. *Background to Gender Issues in Bangladesh.* Bridge Report, Number 26. Brighton, United Kingdom: Institute of Development Studies.

Balcerowicz, Leszek. 1995. *Socialism, Capitalism, Transformation.* Ithaca, NY: Cornell University Press.

Baran, Paul. 1952. "On the Political Economy of Backwardness." *The Manchester School* (January):66–84.

———. 1957. *The Political Economy of Growth.* New York: Monthly Review Press.

Baran, Paul, and E. J. Hobsbawm. 1961. "The Stages of Growth." *Kyklos* 14:234–242.

Baran, Paul, and Paul Sweezy. 1966. *Monopoly Capital.* New York: Monthly Review Press.

Barbash, Jack, Robert J. Lampman, Sar A. Levitan, and Gus Tyler (eds.). 1983. *The Work Ethic—A Critical Analysis.* Madison, WI: Industrial Relations Research Association.

Baster, Nancy. 1972. *Measuring Development: The Role and Adequacy of Development Indicators.* London: Frank Cass.

Becker, Gary. 1964. *Human Capital.* New York: National Bureau of Economic Research.

Bellah, Robert N., Richard Madsen, William M. Sullivan, Ann Swidler, and Steven M. Tipton. 1985. *Habits of the Heart: Individualism and Commitment in American Life.* Berkeley: University of California Press.

Bello, Walden, and Stephanie Rosenfeld. 1992. *Dragons in Distress: Asia's Miracle Economies in Crisis.* San Francisco: The Institute for Food and Development Policy.

Biersteker, Thomas J. 1990. "Reducing the Role of the State in the Economy: A Conceptual Exploration of IMF and World Bank Prescriptions." *International Studies Quarterly* 34:477–492.

Block, Fred. 1977. "The Ruling Class Does Not Rule: Notes on the Marxist Theory of the State." *Socialist Revolution* 333:6–28.

Bornschier, Volker, and Christopher Chase-Dunn. 1985. *Transnational Corporations and Underdevelopment.* New York: Praeger.

Boswell, Terry. 1987. "Accumulation Innovations in the American Economy: The Affinity for Japanese Solutions to the Current Crisis." Pp. 95–126 in T. Boswell and A. Bergesen (eds.), *America's Changing Role in the World System.* New York: Praeger.

Bowles, Samuel, and Richard Edwards. 1985. *Understanding Capitalism: Competition, Command, and Change in the U.S. Economy.* New York: Harper and Row.

Bowles, Samuel, and Herb Gintis. 1982. "The Crisis of Liberal Democratic Capitalism: The Case of the United States." *Politics and Society* 11(1).

Bradshaw, York, and Ana-Marie Wahl. 1991. "Foreign Debt Expansion, the International Monetary Fund, and Regional Variation in Third World Poverty." *International Studies Quarterly* 35:251–272.

Bradshaw, York W. 1988. "Reassessing Economic Dependency and Uneven Development: The Kenyan Experience." *American Sociological Review* 59:693–708.

Braidotti, R., E. Charkiewicz, S. Hausler, and S. Weiringa. 1994. *Women, the Environmental and Sustainable Development: Towards a Theoretical Synthesis*. London: Zed Books.

Braverman, Harry. 1974. *Labor and Monopoly Capital*. New York: Monthly Review Press.

Brenner, Robert. 1977. "The Origins of Capitalist Development: A Critique of Neo-Smithian Marxism." *New Left Review* 104:25–92.

Brewer, Anthony. 1980. *Marxist Theories of Imperialism: A Critical Survey*. London: Routledge and Kegan Paul.

Brus, Wlodzimierz. 1975. *Socialist Ownership and Political Systems*. London: Routledge and Kegan Paul.

Bunker, Stephen. 1984. "Modes of Extraction, Unequal Exchange, and the Progressive Underdevelopment of an Extreme Periphery: The Brazilian Amazon, 1600–1980." *American Journal of Sociology* 84:651–683.

Burawoy, Michael, and James Lukacs. 1985. "Mythologies of Work: A Comparison of Firms in State Socialism and Advanced Capitalism." *American Sociological Review* 50:723–737.

Business Week. 1990. "Mighty Mitsubishi Is on the Move." September 24:98–107.

———. 1996a. "Has Outsourcing Gone Too Far?" April 1:26–28.

———. 1996b. "Keiretsu Connections." July 22:52–54.

———. 1996c. "The Triumph of the New Economy." December 30:24–29.

———. 1997. "The Border." May 12:64–74.

Buvinic, M., and Geeta Rao Gupta. 1994. *Targeting Poor Women-headed Households and Women-maintained Families in Developing Countries: Views on a Policy Dilemma*. Washington, DC: International Center for Research on Women.

Cameron, David. 1978. "The Expansion of the Public Economy: A Comparative Analysis." *American Political Science Review* 72:1243–1261.

Campbell, Tom. 1981. *Seven Theories of Human Society*. Oxford: Clarendon Press.

Cardoso, Fernando Henrique, and Enzo Faletto. 1979. *Dependency and Development in Latin America*. Berkeley: University of California Press.

Castells, Manuel. 1993. "The Informational Economy and the New International Division of Labor." Pp. 15–43 in Martin Carnoy, Manuel Cartels, Stephen S. Cohen, and Fernando Henrique Cardoso (eds.), *The New Global Economy in the Information Age*. University Park: Pennsylvania State University Press.

Castells, Manuel, and Roberto Laserna. 1994. "The New Dependency: Technical Change and Socioeconomic Restructuring in Latin America." Pp. 57–83 in A. Douglas Kincaid and Alejandro Portes (eds.), *Comparative National Development: Society and Economy in the New Global Order*. Chapel Hill: University of North Carolina Press.

Chase-Dunn, Christopher. 1982. "Socialist States in the Capitalist World-Economy." Pp. 21–56 in Christopher Chase-Dunn (ed.), *Socialist States in the World-System*. Beverly Hills, CA: Sage.

———. 1987. "Cycles, Trends, or Transformation? The World-System Since 1945." Pp. 57–83 in Terry Boswell and Albert Bergesen (eds.), *America's Changing Role in the World-System*. New York: Praeger.

————. 1989. *Global Formation: Structures of the World-Economy*. Cambridge, MA: Blackwell.

Chilcote, Ronald H. 1984. *Theories of Development and Underdevelopment*. Boulder, CO: Westview.

Chilcote, Ronald H., and Joel Edelstein. 1986. *Latin America: Capitalist and Socialist Perspectives of Development and Underdevelopment*. Boulder, CO: Westview.

Chirot, Daniel. 1986. *Social Change in the Modern Era*. New York: Harcourt Brace Jovanovich.

Clark, Gordon. 1981. "The Employment Relation and Spatial Division of Labor." *Annals of the Association of American Geographers* 71:412–424.

Clawson, Dan. 1980. *Bureaucracy and the Labor Process: The Transformation of U.S. Industry, 1860–1920*. New York: Monthly Review Press.

Clegg, Stewart, Paul Boreham, and Geoff Dow. 1986. *Class, Politics and the Economy*. Boston: Routledge and Kegan Paul.

Clegg, Stewart R. 1990. *Modern Organizations: Organizational Studies in the Postmodern World*. Newbury Park, CA: Sage.

Cochran, Thomas Childs. 1985. *Challenge to American Values*. New York: Oxford University Press.

Coleman, James S. 1986. "Social Theory, Social Research and a Theory of Action." *American Journal of Sociology* 91:1309–1335.

————. 1988. "Free Riders and Zealots: The Role of Social Networks." *Sociological Theory* 6:52–57.

Collins, Randall. 1981. "On the Microfoundations of Macrosociology." *American Journal of Sociology* 86:984–1014.

Converse, Phillip. 1964. "The Nature of Belief Systems in Mass Publics." Pp. 206–261 in David Apter (ed.), *Ideology and Discontent*. New York: The Free Press.

Cornelius, Wayne. 1975. *Politics and the Migrant Poor in Mexico City*. Stanford, CA: Stanford University Press.

Cumings, Bruce. 1984. "The Origins and Development of the Northeast Asian Political Economy: Industrial Sectors, Product Cycles, and Political Consequences." *International Organizations* 38:1–40.

Cypher, James M. 1979. "The Internationalization of Capital and the Transformation of Social Formations: A Critique of the Monthly Review School." *The Review of Radical Political Economics* (Winter):33–49.

Dahrendorf, Ralf. 1990. *Reflections on the Revolution in Europe*. London: Chatto and Windus.

Daly, Herman E. 1996. *Beyond Growth: The Economics of Sustainable Development*. Boston: Beacon.

deJanvry, Alain. 1981. *The Agrarian Question and Reformism in Latin America*. Baltimore: Johns Hopkins University Press.

Denemark, Robert, A., and Kenneth Thomas. 1988. "The Brenner–Wallerstein Debate." *International Studies Quarterly* 32:47–65.

Denitch, Bogdan. 1990. *Limits and Possibilities: The Crisis of Yugoslav Socialism and State Socialist Systems*. Minneapolis: University of Minnesota Press.

Deutsch, Karl. 1966. "Social Mobilization and Political Development." Pp. 205–226 in Jason L. Gable and Richard W. Finkle (eds.), *Political Development and Social Change*. New York: John Wiley.

Deyo, Frederic C. 1981. *Dependent Development and Industrial Order: An Asian Case Study*. New York: Praeger.

———. 1982. "State Labor Regimes and the New Asian Industrialism." Paper presented at the American Sociological Association meetings, San Francisco.

Dicken, Peter. 1992. *Global Shift: The Internationalization of Economic Activity*. New York: Guilford Press.

Dohse, Knuth, Ulrich Jurgens, and Thomas Malsch. 1985. "From 'Fordism' to 'Toyotaism'? The Social Organization of the Labor Process in the Japanese Automobile Industry." *Politics and Society* 14:115–146.

Domar, Evsey. 1946. "Capital Expansion, Rate of Growth, and Employment." *Econometrica* X:137–147.

Domhoff, William. 1971. *Higher Circles: The Governing Class in America*. New York: Random House.

Dore, Ronald. 1973. *British Factory, Japanese Factory: The Origins of National Diversity in Industrial Relations*. Berkeley: University of California Press.

———. 1990. "Reflections on Culture and Social Change." Pp. 353–367 in Gary Gereffi and Donald L. Wyman (eds.), *Manufacturing Miracles: Paths of Industrialization in Latin America and East Asia*. Princeton, NJ: Princeton University Press.

Dornbusch, Rudiger, and Alejandro Werner. 1994. "Mexico: Stabilization, Reform, and No Growth." *Brookings Paper on Economic Activity* (Spring), no. 1.

Dos Santos, Theotonio. 1970. "The Structure of Dependence." *American Economic Review* 60:231–236.

Dumont, Rene. 1973. *Socialisms and Development*. New York: Praeger.

Durkheim, Emile. 1966. *On the Division of Labor in Society*. Translated by George Simpson. New York: The Free Press.

Duvall, Raymond, and John A. Freeman. 1981. "The State and Dependent Capitalism." *International Studies Quarterly* 25:99–118.

Edel, Abraham. 1979. *Analyzing Concepts in Social Science: Science, Ideology, and Value*. New Brunswick, NJ: Transaction Books.

Edwards, Richard. 1979. *Contested Terrain*. New York: Basic Books.

Eisenstadt, S. N. 1968a. *The Protestant Ethic and Modernization: A Comparative View*. New York: Basic Books.

———. 1968b. "The Protestant Ethic Thesis in an Analytical and Comparative Framework." Pp. 3–45 in S. N. Eisenstadt (ed.), *The Protestant Ethic and Modernization: A Comparative View*. New York: Basic Books.

Eliott, John E. 1973. *Comparative Economic Systems*. Englewood Cliffs, NJ: Prentice-Hall.

Ericson, Richard, E. 1991. "The Classical Soviet-Type Economy: Nature of the System and Implications for Reform." *Journal of Economic Perspectives* 5(4):11–27.

Esping-Andersen, Gosta. 1984. *Politics versus Markets: The Social Democratic Road to Power*. Princeton, NJ: Princeton University Press.

Etzioni, Amitai. 1988. *The Moral Dimension: Toward a New Economics*. New York: The Free Press.

Evans, Peter. 1979. *Dependent Development: the Alliance of Multinational, State, and Local Capital in Brazil*. Princeton, NJ: Princeton University Press.

———. 1982. "Reinventing the Bourgeoisie: State Entrepreneurship and Class Formation in Dependent Capitalist Development." *American Journal of Sociology* (supplement) 88:S210–S247.

———. 1995. *Embedded Autonomy: States and Industrial Transformation*. Princeton, NJ: Princeton University Press.

Evans, Peter B., Dietrich Rueschemeyer, and Theda Skocpol. 1985. *Bringing the State Back In*. Cambridge: Cambridge University Press.

Fischer, Stanley, and Alan Gelb. 1991. "The Process of Socialist Economic Transformation." *Journal of Economic Perspectives* 5(4):91–105.

Florida, Richard, and Martin Kenney. 1990. "High-Technology Restructuring in the USA and Japan." *Environment and Planning* 22:233–252.

Form, William, and Kyuttan Bae. 1988. "Convergence Theory and the Korean Connection." *Social Forces* 66:618–644.

Frank, Andre Gunder. 1969. *Latin America: Underdevelopment or Revolution*. New York: Monthly Review Press.

———. 1980. "Long Live Transideological Enterprise! The Socialist Economics in the Capitalist International Division of Labor and West-East-South Political Economic Relations." Pp. 178–262 in Andre Gunder Frank, *Crisis: In the World Economy*. New York: Holmes and Meier.

Frieden, Jeff. 1981. "Third World Indebted Industrialization: International Finance in Mexico, Brazil, Algeria and South Korea." *International Organization* 35: 407–431.

Froebel, V., J. Heinrichs, and O. Kreye. 1980. *The New International Division of Labor*. Cambridge: Cambridge University Press.

Fukao, Mitsuhiro. 1995. *Financial Integration, Corporate Governance, and the Performance of Multinational Companies*. Washington, DC: Brookings Institution.

Fukuyama, Francis. 1992. *The End of History and the Last Man*. New York: Free Press.

Furtado, Celso. 1965. *Diagnosis of the Brazilian Crisis*. Berkeley: University of California Press.

———. 1970. *Economic Development of Latin America: Historical Background and Contemporary Problems*. Cambridge: Cambridge University Press.

———. 1973. "The Concept of External Dependence in the Study of Underdevelopment." Pp. 42–61 in Charles Wilber (ed.), *The Political Economy of Development and Underdevelopment*. New York: Random House.

Gereffi, Gary. 1994. "Rethinking Development Theory: Insights from East Asia and Latin America." Pp. 26–56 in A. Douglas Kincaid and Alejandro Portes (eds.), *Comparative National Development: Society and Economy in the New Global Order*. Chapel Hill: University of North Carolina Press.

Gereffi, Gary, and Gary G. Hamilton. 1996. "Commodity Chains and Embedded Networks: The Economic Organization of Global Capitalism." Paper presented at the annual meetings of the American Sociological Association, New York, 1996.

Gereffi, Gary, and Miguel Korzeniewicz. 1990. "Commodity Chains and Footwear Exports in the Semiperiphery." Pp. 45–68 in William G. Martin (ed.), *Semiperipheral States in the World Economy*. Westport, CT: Greenwood Press.

———. 1994. *Commodity Chains and Global Capitalism*. Westport, CT: Greenwood Press.

Gereffi, Gary, and Donald L. Wyman. 1990. *Manufacturing Miracles: Paths of Industrialization in Latin America and East Asia*. Princeton, NJ: Princeton University Press.

Gerlach, Michael. 1992. *Alliance Capitalism*. New York: Oxford University Press.

Gerschenkron, Alexander. 1962. *Economic Backwardness in Historical Perspective*. Cambridge, MA: Harvard University Press.

Giddens, Anthony. 1984. *The Constitution of Society: Outline of the Theory of Structuration*. Berkeley: University of California Press.

Gillis, Malcolm, Dwight Perkins, Michael Roemer, and Donald Snodgrass. 1987. *Economics of Development*. 2nd ed. New York: W. W. Norton.

Gold, David A., Clarence Y. Lo, and Erik Olin Wright. 1975. "Recent Developments in Marx's Theories of the Capitalist State." *Monthly Review* (October):29–51.

Golub, Stephen. 1995. "Productivity and Labor Costs in Newly Industrializing Countries." *Federal Reserve Bank of San Francisco Weekly Letter*, No. 95–27.

Gordon, David. 1996. *Fat and Mean: The Corporate Squeeze of Working Americans and the Myth of Managerial "Downsizing."* New York: The Free Press.

Gorham, Lucy. 1987. *No Longer Leading: A Scorecard on U.S. Economic Performance*. Washington, DC: Economic Policy Institute.

Gorin, Zeev. 1985. "Socialist Societies and World System Theory." *Science and Society* 59:332–366.

Gouldner, Alvin. 1970. *The Coming Crisis of Western Sociology*. New York: Basic Books.

Grant, Wyn. 1985. "Introduction." Pp. 1–31 in Wyn Grant (ed.), *The Political Economy of Corporatism*. New York: St. Martin's Press.

Haddad, L., L. R. Brown, A. Richter, and L. Smith. 1995. "The Gender Dimensions of Economic Adjustment Policies: Potential Interactions and Evidence to Date." *World Development* 23(6).

Hage, Jerald, and Kurt Finsterbusch. 1987. *Organizational Change as a Development Strategy: Models and Tactics for Improving Third World Organizations*. Boulder, CO: Lynne Rienner.

Hage, Jerald, Maurice A. Garnier, and Bruce Fuller. 1988. "The Active State, Investment in Human Capital, and Economic Growth: France 1825–1975." *American Sociological Review* 53:824–837.

Hagen, Everett E. 1962. *On the Theory of Social Change*. Homewood, IL: Dorsey Press.

Hamilton, Richard F. 1996. *The Social Misconstruction of Reality: Validity and Verification in the Scholarly Community*. New Haven: Yale University Press.

Hamilton, Richard F., and James D. Wright. 1986. *The State of the Masses*. New York: Aldine.

Harbison, Frederick. 1973. *Human Resources as the Wealth of Nations*. New York: Oxford University Press.

Harrison, Bennett. 1994. *Lean and Mean: The Changing Landscape of Corporate Power in the Age of Flexibility*. New York: Basic Books.

Harrison, Lawrence E. 1985. *Underdevelopment Is a State of Mind: The Latin American Case*. Boston: University Press of America and Harvard University Center for International Affairs.

Harvey, David. 1982. *The Limits to Capital*. Chicago: University of Chicago Press.

———. 1989. *The Condition of Postmodernity*. Cambridge, MA: Blackwell.

Hayek, Frederick A. von. 1935. *Collectivist Economic Planning*. London: Routledge and Kegan Paul.

Henderson, Jeffrey. 1996. "Globalisation and Forms of Capitalism: Conceptualisations and the Search for Synergies." *Competition and Change* 1:403–410.

Hicks, Alexander. 1988. "National Collective Action and Economic Performance: A Review Article." *International Studies Quarterly* 32:131–153.

Hirst, Paul, and Grahame Thompson. 1996. *Globalization in Question*. Cambridge, MA: Polity Press.

Hopkins, Terance, and Immanuel Wallerstein. 1986. "Commodity Chains in the World Economy Prior to 1800." *Review* 10:157–170.

Hoselitz, Bert. 1957. "Economic Growth and Development: Non-Economic Factors in Economic Development." *American Economic Review* 47:28–41.

———. 1960. *Sociological Factors in Economic Development*. Glencoe, IL: The Free Press.

Huntington, Samuel. 1968. *Political Order in Changing Societies*. New Haven: Yale University Press.

Hymer, Stephen. 1970. "The Efficiency (Contradictions) of Multinational Corporations." *American Economic Review* 60:441–448.

———. 1972. "Multinational Corporations and Uneven Development" *Economics and World Order: From the 1970's to the 1990's*. New York: Macmillan.

Inkeles, Alex, and David Smith. 1974. *Becoming Modern: Individual Change in Six Developing Countries*. Cambridge, MA: Harvard University Press.

Jaffee, David. 1994/1995. "The Recalcitrant Human Factor: Social Control in Organization Theory and Management Practice." *Berkeley Journal of Sociology* 39:101–131.

Jaffee, David, and Randall Stokes. 1986. "Foreign Investment and Trade Dependence." *The Sociological Quarterly* 27:533–546.

Johnson, Chalmers. 1982. *MITI and the Japanese Miracle: The Growth of Industrial Policy, 1925–1975*. Stanford, CA: Stanford University Press.

Katz, Claudio J., Vincent A. Mahler, and Michael G. Franz. 1983. "The Impact of Taxes on Growth and Distribution in Developed Capitalist Countries: A Cross-National Study." *American Political Science Review* 77:871–886.

Katzenstein, Peter J. 1984. *Corporatism and Change: Austria, Switzerland and the Politics of Industry*. Ithaca, NY: Cornell University Press.

———. 1985. *Small States in World Markets: Industrial Policy in Europe*. Ithaca, NY: Cornell University Press.

Kenworthy, Lane. 1995. *In Search of National Economic Success: Balancing Competition and Cooperation*. Thousand Oaks, CA: Sage.

Kerr, Clark et al. 1964. *Industrialism and Industrial Man: The Problem of Labor and Management in Economic Growth*. New York: Oxford University Press.

Kester, W. Carl. 1996. "American and Japanese Corporate Governance: Convergence or Best Practice?" Pp. 107–137 in Suzanne Berger and Ronald Dore (eds.), *National Diversity and Global Capitalism*. Ithaca, NY: Cornell University Press.

Kohler, Heinz. 1989. *Comparative Economic Systems*. Glenview, IL: Scott, Foresman.

Kornai, Janos, 1986. *Contradictions and Dilemmas: Studies in the Socialist Economy and Society*. Boston: MIT Press.

Kornblum, William. 1988. *Sociology: A Changing World*. New York: Holt, Rinehart and Winston.

Krugman, Paul. 1994a. "The Myth of Asia's Miracle." *Foreign Affairs* (November–December):63–75.

———. 1994b. *Peddling Prosperity: Economic Sense and Nonsense in the Age of Diminished Expectations*. New York: W. W. Norton.

———. 1996. *Pop Internationalism*. Cambridge, MA: MIT Press.

Kunda, Gideon. 1992. *Engineering Culture: Control and Commitment in a High-Tech Corporation*. Philadelphia: Temple University Press.

Kuttner, Robert. 1997. *Everything for Sale*. New York: Knopf.

Laclau, Ernesto. 1977. *Politics and Ideology in Marxist Theory*. London: New Left Books.

Lairson, Thomas D., and David Skidmore. 1993. *International Political Economy: The Struggle for Power and Wealth*. New York: Harcourt Brace Publishers.

Lall, Sanyaja. 1975. ''Is 'Dependence' a Useful Concept in Analyzing Underdevelopment?'' *World Development* 3:798–820.

Lange, Oskar, and Fred Taylor. 1964. *On the Economic Theory of Socialism*. New York: McGraw-Hill.

Lehmann, J. P. 1982. *The Roots of Modern Japan*. London: Macmillan.

Lenin, V. I. 1948. *Imperialism: The Highest Stage of Capitalism*. London: Lawrence and Wishart.

———. 1964. *The Development of Capitalism in Russia*. Moscow: Progress Publishers.

Lerner, Daniel. 1958. *The Passing of Traditional Society*. Glencoe, IL: The Free Press.

Lewis, W. Arthur. 1954. ''Economic Development with Unlimited Supplies of Labor.'' *The Manchester School* 22.

Leys, Colin. 1982. ''Samuel Huntington and the End of Classical Modernization Theory.'' Pp. 332–349 in Hamza Alavi and Teodor Shanin (eds.), *Introduction to the Sociology of ''Developing Societies.''* New York: Monthly Review Press.

Lincoln, James R., and Arne L. Kalleberg. 1985. ''Work Organization and Workforce Commitment: A Study of Plants and Employees in the U.S. and Japan.'' *American Sociological Review* 50:738–760.

Lipset, S. M. 1963. *Political Man*. Garden City, NY: Doubleday.

Lowy, Michael. 1989. ''Weber Against Marx? The Polemic with Historical Materialism in the Protestant Ethic.'' *Science and Society* 53:71–83.

Loxley, John. 1986. *Debt and Disorder: External Financing for Development*. Boulder, CO: Westview Press.

Luke, Timothy, and Carl Boggs. 1982. ''Soviet Subimperialism and the Crisis of Bureaucratic Centralism.'' *Studies in Comparative Communism* 15:95–124.

Lukes, Steven. 1990. ''Socialism and Capitalism: Left and Right.'' *Social Research*: 571–578.

MacEwan, Arthur, and William K. Tabb. 1989a. ''The Economy in Crisis: National Power and International Stability.'' *Socialist Review* 89:67–91.

———. 1989b. *Essays on Instability and Change in the World Economy*. New York: Monthly Review Press.

Macpherson, C. B. 1973. *Democratic Theory: Essays in Retrieval*. Oxford: Clarendon.

Mandel, Ernst. 1976. *Late Capitalism*. London: New Left Books.

Mandle, Jay R. 1980. ''Basic Needs and Economic Systems.'' *Review of Social Economics* 38:179–189.

Martin, Andrew. 1979. ''The Dynamics of Change in a Keynesian Political Economy.'' Pp. 88–121 in Colin Crouch (ed.), *State and Economy in Contemporary Capitalism*. London: Croom Helm.

Massey, Doreen. 1985. *Spatial Divisions of Labor*. New York: Methuen.

McClelland, David. 1961. *The Achieving Society*. New York: Free Press.

McMichael, Philip. 1996. *Development and Social Change*. Thousand Oaks, CA: Pine Forge Press.

Miliband, Ralph. 1977. *Marxism and Politics*. Oxford: Oxford University Press.

Mills, C. Wright. 1956. *The Power Elite*. New York: Oxford University Press.

Moore, Barrington. 1967. *Social Origins of Dictatorship and Democracy: Lord and Peasant in the Making of the Modern World*. Boston: Beacon Press.

Morawez, David. 1977. *Twenty-five Years of Economic Development-1950–1975*. Baltimore: Johns Hopkins University Press.

Morishima, M. 1983. *Why Has Japan "Succeeded"?* Cambridge: Cambridge University Press.

Murrell, Peter. 1991. "Can Neoclassical Economics Underpin the Reform of Centrally Planned Economies?" *Journal of Economic Perspectives* 5(4):59–76.

Neff, Gina. 1996. "Microcredit, Microresults." *Left Business Observer* (October).

Nove, Alec. 1983. *The Economics of Feasible Socialism*. London: Allen and Unwin.

Nurkse, Ragner. 1962. *Problems of Capital Formation in Underdeveloped Areas*. New York: Oxford University Press.

O'Connor, James. 1973. *The Fiscal Crisis of the State*. New York: St. Martin's Press.

———. 1984. *Accumulation Crisis*. New York: Basil and Blackwell.

O'Donnell, Guillermo. 1973. *Modernization and Bureaucratic-Authoritarianism: Studies in South American Politics*. Berkeley: Institute of International Studies, University of California.

———. 1978. "Reflections on the Patterns of Change in the Bureaucratic Authoritarian State." *Latin American Research Review* 13:3–38.

———. 1979. "Tensions in the Bureaucratic Authoritarian State and the Question of Democracy." Pp. 285–318 in D. Collier (ed.), *The New Authoritarianism in Latin America*. Princeton, NJ: Princeton University Press.

Olson, Mancur. 1982. *The Rise and Decline of Nations: Economic Growth, Stagflation and Social Rigidities*. New Haven: Yale University Press.

Onimode, Bade. 1989. *The IMF, the World Bank, and African Debt: The Social and Political Impact*. London: Zed Books.

Ouchi, William G. 1981. *Theory Z: How American Businesses Can Meet the Japanese Challenge*. Reading, MA: Addison-Wesley.

Paige, Jeffery M. 1975. *Agrarian Revolution: Social Movements and Export Agriculture in the Underdeveloped World*. New York: Free Press.

Palma, Gabriel. 1978. "Dependency: A Formal Theory of Underdevelopment or a Methodology for the Analysis of Concrete Situations of Underdevelopment?" *World Development* 6:881–924.

Panitch, Leon. 1979. "The Development of Corporatism in Liberal Democracies." Pp. 119–146 in P. Schmitter and G. Lehmbruch (eds.), *Trends Toward Corporatist Intermediation*. Beverly Hills, CA: Sage.

———. 1980. "Recent Theorisations of Corporatism: Reflections on a Growth Industry." *British Journal of Sociology* 31:161–187.

Parsons, Talcott. 1951. *The Social System*. Glencoe, IL: The Free Press.

Passé-Smith, John T. 1993. "The Persistence of the Gap: Taking Stock of Economic Growth in the Post-World War II Era." Pp. 15–30 in Mitchell A. Seligson and John T. Passé-Smith (eds.), *Development and Underdevelopment: The Political Economy of Inequality*. Boulder, CO: Lynne Rienner.

Patel, Pari, and Keith Pavitt. 1991. "Large Firms in the Production of the World's Technology: An Important Case of 'Non-Globalization'." *Journal of International Business Studies* 21(1):1–21.

Pauly, Louis W., and Simon Reich. 1997. "National Structures and Multinational Corporate Behavior: Enduring Differences in the Age of Globalization." *International Organization* 51(1):1–30.

Perrings, Charles. 1996. *Sustainable Development and Poverty Alleviation in Sub-
Saharan Africa*. New York: St. Martin's Press.

Perrow, Charles. 1986. *Complex Organizations: A Critical Perspective*. New York: Random House.

Petras, James. 1970. *Politics and Social Structure in Latin America*. New York: Monthly
Review Press.

———. 1981. *Class, State, and Power in the Third World*. Montclair, NJ: Allenheld,
Osmun.

Pierson, Christopher. 1995. *Socialism After Communism: The New Market Socialism*.
University Park: Pennsylvania State University Press.

Piore, Michael, and Charles Sabel. 1984. *The Second Industrial Divide*. New York: Basic
Books.

Porter, Michael. 1990. *The Comparative Advantage of Nations*. New York: Macmillan.

Portes, Alejandro. 1976. "On the Sociology of National Development: Theories and
Issues." *American Journal of Sociology* 82:55–85.

Portes, Alejandro, and John Walton. 1981. *Labor, Class, and the International System*.
New York: Academic Press.

Powell, Walter W. 1990. "Neither Market Now Hierarchy: Network Forms of Organization." Pp. 295–336 in Barry M. Shaw and Larry L. Cummings (eds.), *Research
in Organizational Behavior*. Greenwich, CT: JAI Press.

Prebisch, Raul. 1950. *The Economic Development of Latin America and Its Principal
Problems*. New York: United Nations.

Prosterman, Roy L., and Jeffrey M. Riedinger. 1987. *Land Reform and Democratic Development*. Baltimore: Johns Hopkins University Press.

Psacharopoulos, George. 1988. "Education and Development: A Review." *The World
Bank Research Observer* 3(1):99–116.

Pye, Lucian. 1968. "The Concept of Political Development." Pp. 83–91 in Jason L.
Finkle and Richard W. Gable (eds.), *Political Development and Social Change*.
New York: John Wiley and Sons.

Reich, Robert. 1991. *The Work of Nations: Preparing Ourselves for 21st Century Capitalism*. New York: Knopf.

Ricardo, David. 1933. *Principles of Political Economy and Taxation*. London: Dent
(1817).

Rifkin, Jeremy. 1995. *The End of Work*. New York: Putnam.

Ritzer, George. 1990. "Micro-Macro Linkage in Sociological Theory: Applying a Metatheoretical Tool." Pp. 347–370 in George Ritzer (ed.), *Frontiers of Social Theory:
The New Synthesis*. New York: Columbia University Press.

———. 1992. *Sociological Theory*. New York: McGraw-Hill.

Roe, Mark J. 1994. *Strong Managers, Weak Owners: The Political Roots of American
Corporate Finance*. Princeton, NJ: Princeton University Press.

Romer, Paul M. 1986. "Increasing Returns and Long-Run Growth." *Journal of Political
Economy* 94:1002–1037.

———. 1994. "The Origins of Endogeneous Growth." *Journal of Economic Perspectives* 89:3–22.

Romo, Frank D., and Michael Schwartz. 1995. "The Structural Embeddedness of Business Decisions: The Migration of Manufacturing Plants in New York State, 1960–1985." *American Sociological Review* 60:874–907.

Ross, Robert J., and Kent C. Trachte. 1990. *Global Capitalism: The New Leviathan.* Albany: State University of New York Press.

Rostow, W. W. 1956. "The Take-off into Self-Sustained Growth." *The Economic Journal* 66:25–48.

———. 1960. *The Stages of Economic Growth: A Non-Communist Manifesto.* Cambridge: Cambridge University Press.

Ruccio, David F., and Lawrence H. Simon. 1988. "Radical Theories of Development: Frank, the Models of Production School, and Amin." Pp. 121–173 in Charles K. Wilber (ed.), *The Political Economy of Development and Under-Development.* 4th ed. New York: Random House.

Rueschemeyer, Dietrich, Evelyn Huber Stephens, and John D. Stephens. 1992. *Capitalist Development and Democracy.* Chicago: University of Chicago Press.

Sachs, Jeffrey D. 1993. *Poland's Jump to the Market Economy.* Cambridge, MA: MIT Press.

Samater, Ibrahim M. 1984. "From 'Growth' to 'Basic Needs': The Evolution of Development Theory." *Monthly Review* 36:1–13.

Sayer, Andrew. 1995. *Radical Political Economy: A Critique.* New York: Blackwell Publishers.

Scharpf, F. W. 1991. *Crisis and Choice in European Social Democracy.* Ithaca, NY: Cornell University Press.

Schmidt, M. 1982. "Does Corporatism Matter? Economic Crisis, Politics and Rates of Unemployment in Capitalist Democracies in the 1970's." Pp. 237–258 in G. Lehmbruch and P. C. Schmitter (eds.), *Politics in the Making.* Beverly Hills, CA: Sage.

Schmitter, Phillipe. 1981. "Interest Intermediation and Regime Governability in Contemporary Western Europe and North America." Pp. 285–327 in S. Berger (ed.), *Organizing Interests in Western Europe.* New York: Cambridge University Press.

Schumpeter, Joseph. 1949. *Change and the Entrepreneur.* Cambridge, MA: Harvard University Press.

Scott, W. Richard. 1981. *Organizations: Rational, Natural and Open Systems.* Englewood Cliffs, NJ: Prentice-Hall.

Sender, John, and Sheila Smith. 1986. *The Development of Capitalism in Africa.* New York: Methuen.

Sethuraman, S. V. 1981. *The Urban Informal Sector: Developing Countries.* Geneva, Switzerland: International Labor Organization.

Sheridan, Kyoko. 1996. "The Planning Mind: The Spirit of Japan's Political Economy." *Competition and Change* 1:299–319.

Sidelsky, Robert. 1979. "The Decline of Keynesian Politics." Pp. 55–87 in Colin Crouch (ed.), *State and Economy in Contemporary Capitalism.* London: Croom Helm.

Simmons, John. 1979. "Education for Development, Reconsidered." *World Development* 11/12:1005–1016.

——— 1983. "Education for Development, Reconsidered." Pp. 262–275 in Michael P. Tedaro (ed.), *The Struggle for Economic Development.* New York: Longman.

Singer, Hans. 1979. "Dualism Revisited: A New Approach to Problems of Dual Societies in Developing Countries." *Journal of Development Studies* 7:55–67.

Singer, J. David. 1961. "The Level of Analysis Problem in International Relations."

Pp. 77–92 in Klaus Knorr and Sidney Verbow (eds.), *The International System: Theoretical Essays*. Princeton, NJ: Princeton University Press.

Smelser, Neil. 1963. *The Sociology of Economic Life*. Englewood Cliffs, NJ: Prentice-Hall.

Smelser, Neil J., and Talcott Parsons. 1956. *Economy Society*. Glencoe, IL: The Free Press.

Spencer, Martin E. 1987. "The Imperfect Empiricism of the Social Sciences." *Sociological Forum* 2:331–372.

Spengler, J. J. 1966. "Economic Development: Political Pre-Conditions and Political Consequences." Pp. 253–268 in Jason L. Finkle and Richard W. Gable (eds.), *Political Development and Social Change*. New York: John Wiley.

Stark, David. 1994. "Path Dependence and Privatization Strategies in East Central Europe." Pp. 169–198 in A. Douglas Kincaid and Alejandro Portes (eds.), *Comparative National Development: Society and Economy in the New Global Order*. Chapel Hill: University of North Carolina Press.

Stewart, Frances, and Paul Streeten. 1976. "New Strategies for Development: Poverty, Income Distribution and Growth." *Oxford Economic Papers* 28:381–405.

Stinchcombe, Arthur. 1961. "Agricultural Enterprise and Rural Class Relations." *American Journal of Sociology* 67:165–176.

Stokes, Randall G. 1975. "How Long Is the Long Run: Race and Industrialization." *International Review of Community Development* 33–34:123–136.

Streeten, Paul. 1977. "The Distinctive Features of a Basic Needs Approach to Development." *International Development Review* 19:8–16.

Sunken, Osvaldo, and Pedro Paz. 1970. *El Subdesarroll. Latinamericano y la Teoría del Desarollo*. Madrid: Siglo Veintiuno de España Editores.

Sztompka, Piotr. 1997. "Civilization Competence: A Prerequisite of Post-Communist Democracy." http://www.friends-partners.org/friends/audem/audem92/Sztompka. htmlopt-tables-unix.english-.

Taylor, Frederick W. 1939. *Scientific Management*. New York: Harper and Row.

Teece, David J. 1992. "Competition, Cooperation and Innovation." *Journal of Economic Behavior and Organization* 18:1–25.

Theodorson, George A. 1966. "Acceptance of Industrialization and its Attendant Consequences for the Social Patterns of Non-Western Societies." Pp. 297–304 in Jason L. Finkle and Richard W. Gable (eds.), *Political Development and Social Change*. New York: John Wiley.

Thurow, Lester. 1970. *Investment in Human Capital*. Belmont, CA: Wadsworth.

———. 1983. *Dangerous Currents: The State of Economics*. New York: Random House.

———. 1985. *The Zero-Sum Solution*. New York: Simon and Schuster.

———. 1992a. "Communitarian vs. Individualistic Capitalism." *The Responsive Community* 2(4):24–30.

———. 1992b. *Head to Head: The Coming Battle among Japan, Europe, and America*. New York: William Morrow.

———. 1996. *The Future of Capitalism*. New York: William Morrow.

Todaro, Michael P. 1989. *Economic Development in the Third World*. New York: Longman.

Tonnies, Ferdinand. 1963. *Community and Society*. Translated by C. P. Loomis. New York: Harper and Row.

Trotsky, Leon. 1959. *The Russian Revolution*. Garden City, NY: Doubleday.

United Nations, 1990. *Human Development Report, 1990.* New York: Oxford University Press.

United Nations. 1995. *Human Development Report, 1995.* New York: Oxford University Press.

Usui, Chikako, and Richard A. Colignon. 1996. "Corporate Restructuring: Converging World Pattern or Societally Specific Embeddedness? *The Sociological Quarterly* 37:551–578.

Valenzuela, J. Samuel, and Arturo Valenzuela. 1984. "Modernization and Dependency: Alternative Perspectives in the Study of Latin American Underdevelopment." Pp. 105–118 in Mitchell A. Seligson (ed.), *The Gap between Rich and Poor: Contending Perspectives on the Political Economy of Development.* Boulder, CO: Westview Press.

Vanneman, Reeve, and Lynn Weber Cannon. 1987. *The American Perception of Class.* Philadelphia: Temple University Press.

Verba, Sidney, and Norman Nie. 1972. *Democracy and Social Equality.* New York: Harper.

Vernon, Raymond. 1966. "International Investment and International Trade in the Product Cycle." *Quarterly Journal of Economics* 80:190–207.

Wade, Robert. 1988. "State Intervention in Outward-Looking Development: Neo-Classical Theory and Taiwanese Practice." In G. White (ed.), *Development States in East Asia.* London: Macmillan.

———. 1990. *Governing the Market: Economic Theory and the Role of Government in East Asian Industrialization.* Princeton, NJ: Princeton University Press.

———. 1996. "Globalization and Its Limits: Reports of the Death of the National Economy Are Greatly Exaggerated." Pp. 60–88 in Suzanne Berger and Ronald Dore (eds.), *National Diversity and Global Capitalism.* Ithaca, NY: Cornell University Press.

Wallerstein, Immanuel. 1974. "The Rise and Future Demise of the Capitalist World-System: Concepts for Comparative Analysis." *Comparative Studies in Society and History* 16:387–415.

———. 1979. *The Capitalist World Economy.* New York: Cambridge University Press.

———. 1984. "The Present State of the Debate on World Inequality." Pp. 119–132 in Mitchell A. Seligson (ed.), *The Gap between Rich and Poor: Contending Perspectives on the Political Economy of Development.* Boulder, CO: Westview Press.

Walton, John, and Charles Ragin. 1990. "Global and National Sources of Political Protest: Third World Responses to the Debt Crisis." *American Sociological Review* 55:876–890.

Warner, Andrew. 1995. "Was Mexico's Exchange Rate Overvalued in 1994?" Harvard Institute for International Development. Discussion Paper #525.

Warren, Bill. 1980. *Imperialism: Pioneer of Capitalism.* London: Verso.

Weaver, James, Kenneth P. Jameson, and Richard N. Blue. 1978. "Growth and Equity: Can They Be Happy Together?" *International Development Review* 20:20–27.

Weber, Max. 1930. *The Protestant Ethic and the Spirit of Capitalism.* London: Allen and Unwin.

———. 1947. *The Theory of Social and Economic Organization.* Translated by A. M. Henderson and Talcott Parsons. New York: Oxford University Press.

Weisskopf, Thomas E., Samuel Bowles, and David M. Gordon. 1985. "Two Views of

Capitalist Stagnation: Underconsumption and Challenges to Capitalist Control.'' *Science and Society* (Fall):259–286.

Wharton, Clifton. 1983. ''Risk, Uncertainty and the Subsistence Farmer.'' Pp. 234–238 in Michael P. Tedaro (ed.), *The Struggle for Economic Development*. New York: Longman.

Whitley, Richard. 1994. ''Dominant Forms of Economic Organisation in Market Economies.'' *Organisation Studies* 15:153–182.

Wiley, Norbert. 1988. ''The Micro-Macro Problem in Social Theory.'' *Sociological Theory* 6:254–261.

Williamson, Oliver. 1975. *Markets and Hierarchies: Analysis and Antitrust Implications*. New York: Free Press.

Wolf, Eric R., and Sidney W. Mintz. 1957. ''Haciendas and Plantations in Middle America and the Antilles.'' *Social and Economic Studies* 6:380–412.

World Bank. 1980. *World Development Report, 1980*. New York: Oxford University Press.

———. 1987. *World Development Report, 1987*. New York: Oxford University Press.

———. 1988. *World Development Report, 1988*. New York: Oxford University Press.

———. 1991. *World Development Report, 1991*. New York: Oxford University Press.

World Bank (International Bank for Reconstruction and Development). 1995. *Monitoring Environmental Progress: A Report on Work in Progress*. Washington, DC: World Bank.

World Commission on Environment and Development. 1987. *Our Common Future*. Oxford: Oxford University Press.

Wright, James D. 1976. *The Dissent of the Governed*. New York: Academic.

Young, Alwin. 1994. ''Lessons from the East Asian NICs: A Contrarian View.'' *European Economic Review* 38:964–973.

Zimbalist, Andrew, and Howard J. Sherman. 1984. *Comparing Economic Systems: A Political Economic Approach*. Orlando, FL: Academia.

Index

About the Author

DAVID JAFFEE is Associate Professor of Sociology at the State University of
New York at New Paltz.

ISBN 0-275-95658-X

EAN

9 780275 956585

HARDCOVER BAR CODE